Almost Everything You Need to Know About

Aussiedoodles

Diane Klumb

All photos courtesy of the Doodlesville Aussiedoodle family

Almost Everything You Need to Know About Aussiedoodles

Table of Contents

Acknowledgements

Writing an in-depth and balanced book on any breed requires a fair amount of input from what writers generally refer to as "subject matter experts", and there are no greater experts on both the temperament and trainability in any breed than the people who live with them every day... in other words, their *breeders and owners*. Thanks to all those who took the time to share their expertise.

And a special thanks to the members of the extended "Doodlesville family" for their generosity in providing the wonderful photos used throughout this book, and of course to Nancy at Doodlesville for patiently identifying dogs, putting me in touch with their owners and procuring releases where needed.

I'd also like to thank two more of my longtime favorite SMEs, Dr. Leigh Ann Clark and Dr. Allison Moss from the Clark Genetics Lab at Clemson University, for their time, patience and expertise. There may be two brighter canine geneticists out there somewhere, but I personally doubt it.

CHAPTER ONE:

AN AUSSIEDOODLE PRIMER
(... so what's this "new kid in town" really like?)

In the world of dogs, one would be hard-pressed to find a breed with so many upsides and so few downsides as this winsome addition to the Doodle clan.

A singularly charming dog, the Aussiedoodle's particular combination of attractive looks, compact size, odorless low-shedding coat, attentiveness and easy trainability makes the breed a great fit for many modern families, as well as a Service Dog on par with few others.

An American Success Story

In spite of his name, the Aussiedoodle appears to be a purely American-made breed, slipping quietly onto the hybrid scene in the US a few years after the Goldendoodle with very little fanfare. In fact, there was so LITTLE fanfare it seems no one's even quite sure exactly who first came up with the idea, or exactly when. The obscurity was short-lived.

Within a very few years, the popularity of this new American hybrid literally exploded, and the number of Aussiedoodles out there now exceeds that of many breeds that have been around for a hundred years or more.

Ads for puppies can be found everywhere, and a quick Google search for "Aussiedoodles" will turn up over 200,000 hits, with pages upon pages of breeders' websites displayed.

How did this happen so fast?

His many virtues notwithstanding, the Aussiedoodle's sudden rise in popularity is a bit of a puzzle.

Traditionally, when a breed has exploded like this, it's been Hollywood's fault. RinTinTin, Lassie and 101 Dalmatians all famously contributed to the public's demand for German Shepherds, Collies and Dalmatians each in its turn. But alas, the Aussiedoodle has yet to grace the Silver Screen.

And sometimes it's simply a result of print media hype. The Puggle (a delightful fellow in his own right) would probably still be a relative unknown had he not been the subject of innumerable articles in the national press a few years back. For a while there, Puggles were literally the public face of the new "hybrid craze" sweeping the country, and their 'stint in print' no doubt gave their popularity a gigantic boost. So... is the Aussiedoodle, an equally adorable and photogenic fellow by any measure, a Media Darling?

Not so much.

In fact, one would be hard-pressed to find a *SINGLE SOLITARY ARTICLE* on the Aussiedoodle in the archives of the New York Times...or any other major media outlet. Or even online, if it comes right down to it— it's pretty obvious that all the information on the internet about Aussiedoodles has been provided entirely by breeders and owners. And, unlike the Puggle or the Goldendoodle, he's never been featured in magazine ads, although he's equally photogenic.

In fact, at this point in time, he doesn't even show up on Wikipedia, which is pretty astonishing considering that there are well over *FOUR MILLION* articles up there, many of them on topics best described as Beyond Obscure.

No, we can pretty safely assume that the Aussiedoodle's sudden popularity is not the result of media hype.

Could it be his catchy name?

Highly unlikely. Unlike the Puggle (which practically everybody on the planet knows is a cross between a Pug and a Beagle) or the Whoodle (an absolutely delicious name that sounds like something straight out of Dr Suess but is really just a cross between a Wheaten Terrier and a Poodle) the Aussiedoodle doesn't HAVE a catchy name, nor even one where the 'recipe' for the breed is immediately obvious...in fact, when it comes to the Aussiedoodle's name, "totally confusing" is more like it, since he's not even from Australia!

While the 'Australian Labradoodle' (which actually IS from Down Under and now pretty much qualifies as a purebred dog) tries to separate itself in the eyes of the understandably baffled dog-buying public from the garden-variety 'hybrid Labradoodles' still being created the world over by breeding Labs to Poodles, many people logically assume that 'Aussiedoodle' is a nickname for the Australian Labradoodle, which it isn't. But that confusion is hardly the Aussiedoodle's fault.

Aussiedoodle is the proper 'portmanteau' for a hybrid cross between an Australian Shepherd (commonly called an Aussie) and a Poodle. Which is what they are.

Now, the fact that most of them are produced from the smaller, or miniature, Australian Shepherds, which were recently accepted as a separate breed into the AKC as the Miniature *American* Shepherd, will surely further the confusion in the future. This is obviously not his fault either... back when the very first Aussiedoodles started appearing in the US (somewhere around 2003 or thereabouts), there was only ONE Australian Shepherd breed, and both the big ones and the little ones were called Aussies.

So, given the rules for a portmanteau (as laid out by Lewis Carroll, anyway) Aussiedoodle it properly is and Aussiedoodle it shall likely stay, that unlike the Puggle or the Whoodle, it's pretty clear that the Aussiedoodle's NAME is *not* what's caught the public's fancy.

Which still leaves us pondering the Aussiedoodle's sudden rise in popularity over the last couple of years and no closer to an answer. How are people finding OUT about them?

Now, many Aussiedoodle websites explain with no small measure of certainty that this breed is popular with fans of the Australian Shepherd who'd rather not deal with the shedding. Although this sounds logical at first blush, a little casual research into search engine correlations doesn't support the theory at all.

In fact, they would appear to be two VERY different groups.

To begin with, people searching for "Australian Shepherds" or "Aussies" are most likely to come from what the media likes to call the 'red' states, mostly the big square ones.

They would also appear to search for information on repairing the transmissions on pickup trucks, .357 Magnums, gun control legislation and Stetson hats. This pretty logically fits with the Aussie's reputation as a working stock dog.

On the other hand, it would appear that people doing Google searches for "Aussiedoodles" are most likely to come from 'blue' states, and are more likely to search for information on things like the safety record of the Ford Focus, the NCAA playoffs, home restoration, and (somewhat surprisingly) home-made sauerkraut recipes. Their interest in researching firearms appears to be pretty nonexistent.

And therein lies the answer to the Aussiedoodle's burgeoning popularity.
They're coming in the back door.

We know this because, with the exception of the sauerkraut part, the average potential Aussiedoodle owner profiles pretty closely with the potential owners of most hybrids both canine and automotive, *and with Doodles in particular.*

Even the sauerkraut thing is not all that surprising, as there are subtle correlation differences even between the various Doodles when people start narrowing it down to looking for an actual puppy— 'Goldendoodle puppy' searchers are more likely to be gardeners with an overriding interest in lawn care and perennials, and soccer is bigger than college basketball with them. (There's no doubt a whole book in here somewhere...)

But more to the point, what most likely happens is this:
A potential puppy buyer (who probably owned purebreds in the past), decides for a number of reasons — like better health and a desire for less dog hair around the house this time— to look at the Labradoodle and/or Goldendoodle breeds, and quite accidentally stumbles into the Aussiedoodle in the course of his research for one major reason:

The overwhelming majority of Aussiedoodle breeders are Doodle breeders
who picked them up as a second (smaller) breed.

This is a decidedly mixed blessing.

On the UPSIDE, sailing into the world of dogs on the coat tails of the ubiquitous Labradoodles and Goldendoodles (by simply having his name and pictures displayed on many of their websites) introduces the Aussiedoodle to a whole group of potential owners who'd never in a million years have found him otherwise... and for whom he may really be by far the best choice. We'll go into the reasons for that shortly.

On the DOWNSIDE, for a wealth of fairly complicated genetic reasons that we will also explain, producing consistently sound and healthy Aussiedoodles requires a LOT more animal husbandry experience, up-to-date genetic knowledge and financial resources than does the production of healthy Goldendoodles or Labradoodles, where hybrid vigor alone will erase most, if not all, of the major health issues plaguing their respective parent breeds.

What this means is that the potential owner is going to need to apply way more 'due diligence' in finding a good Aussiedoodle breeder than frankly would have been required had one decided upon a Goldendoodle or a Labradoodle, where even a novice breeder can usually produce pretty sound and healthy puppies if they stick to F1s.

Purely commercial and novice breeders (although the latter may be sincere and well-meaning) rarely have the extensive genetic knowledge needed to make the often complicated and multifactored breeding choices required to produce sound and healthy Aussiedoodles.

Nor do they usually have the experience to recognize and/or screen for problems that they may have inadvertently produced before selling those puppies to equally unwitting owners, who may not be prepared to cope with them. And since these problems invariably include congenital visual and hearing deficits, the affected puppies are literally born handicapped.

Several of these poor handicapped puppies have already ended up in Rescue.
And unless both breeders and buyers are educated in a big hurry
there will be many more in the future.

If this sounds like it was meant to scare you….it WAS! Pet owners who (because of ignorance, impatience or because they are enamored of a particular color or pattern) purchase puppies from substandard or inexperienced breeders allow those breeders to keep on producing more puppies, especially when demand is high. This will increase the incidence health problems until the breed is simply ruined, like so many purebreds before it.

On the other hand,
purchasing a puppy from a knowledgeable breeder
will help ensure a bright future for the entire Aussiedoodle breed.

And that's a very Good Thing, because this new breed is well-deserving.

Beyond the flashy "Zoot Suit" that often initially attracts people to them, the Aussiedoodle has a number of qualities unique in the Doodle world that make him far and away the best choice for a fair number of modern households, even if he's decked out in a less flashy "grey flannel suit", or one in basic black or serviceable brown.

Before we start discussing these qualities, though, let's get past the question that seems to pop up with tiresome regularity in the world of hybrids in general and Doodles in particular….to wit:

Is the Aussiedoodle actually a breed?

The short answer here is YES. In spite of what you may read by disgruntled purebred enthusiasts on the internet, the Aussiedoodle is NOT simply an "overpriced mutt". A mutt (also known as a mongrel) is defined by every dictionary in the world as "a dog of unknown parentage".

The Aussiedoodle is a **hybrid,** which is not the same thing at all. In fact, the majority of breeds recognized by AKC were originally created by combining two or more older breeds— including the Australian Shepherd, who wasn't registered *anywhere* prior to the 1950s.

A hybrid is defined by geneticists as the result of the deliberate crossing of two separate strains or homogeneous populations.

Although a hybrid may be the result of crossing two species, most are the result of crossing two separate 'strains' or 'races' *within* a particular species. What we call a 'breed' is really a strain, or race. In fact, both Merriam Webster and the American Kennel Club define the word almost identically:

Breed: A race of animals selected and maintained by humans, with a characterized appearance and a common gene pool.

So using that definition, let's see if the Aussiedoodle actually qualifies as a breed here:

Was the Aussiedoodle selected and maintained by humans?
YES. (There is no evidence that Aussiedoodles exist in the wild.)

Does the Aussiedoodle have a characterized appearance?
YES. (Color notwithstanding, all Aussiedoodles bear a striking resemblance to one another.)

Does the Aussiedoodle have a common gene pool?
YES. (All Aussiedoodles are descended entirely from purebred Poodles and purebred Australian Shepherds….that's a common gene pool by anyone's definition.)

OK, so it's pretty obvious that (at least according to the AKC's definition, which is admittedly pretty funny) the Aussiedoodle qualifies as a breed. And being a breed is a lot like being pregnant—you either are or you are not, with no real middle ground. So what are breeders talking about when they breed multigenerational Aussiedoodles with the goal of turning the Aussiedoodle into a "real" breed? It's *terminology* again...

What the Aussiedoodle is NOT is a **purebred dog,** which is what the American Kennel Club registers, and therein lies most of the confusion. This is how the American Kennel Club, who specializes in 'em, defines "purebred dog":

Purebred dog :

A dog whose sire and dam belong to the same breed
and who are themselves of unmixed descent since recognition of the breed.

Ah, there's the rub. In order to become a PUREBRED dog, Aussiedoodles would have to be bred only to other Aussiedoodles for many generations without any crosses back to the parent breeds until it "bred true". This is called a closed studbook. (In order to keep track of this, a studbook would have to be established so that it could be closed.)

But with each generation, more of the genetic diversity responsible for hybrid vigor would be lost, causing the autoimmune diseases that now plague its parent breeds to appear in Aussiedoodles in ever -increasing numbers. (It took less than 20 years after its studbook was closed for the incidence of autoimmune hypothyroidism in the once-healthy Australian Shepherd breed to reach **one in every eight** dogs.)

The truth is, anybody with a modicum of political and animal husbandry skills can create a new pure-bred dog that will "breed true" and be accepted by an all-breed registry in twenty years or less….hell, back around 1900, a lowly German dogcatcher named Louis Dobermann created his famous Pinscher in less than ten. But the real question is….why would anyone WANT to do this?

Purebred dog registrations are in freefall. Although the overall dog ownership numbers in the US are rising steadily, **American Kennel Club registrations have dropped by nearly half in the last 20 years.** Pet owners who've owned purebred dogs in the past are now purchasing hybrids and "designer breeds" in ever-increasing numbers, much to the consternation of the purebred dog world. And WHY are they doing this?

Because most purebred dogs are now plagued by genetic diseases
and autoimmune disorders. Including Louis Dobermann's famous Pinschers.

Since we now understand that most of these problems are caused by the lack of genetic diversity resulting from a closed studbook., arbitrarily closing studbooks to create NEW purebreds would seem to fit Albert Einstein's classic definition of insanity:
In case you're unfamiliar with it, here it is:

Insanity:
Doing the same thing over and over again and expecting different results.

Now, the traditional argument for choosing a purebred dog over a mongrel is because you know what to expect in terms of general size, coat, energy level and temperament, and can choose one that best fits your lifestyle and family situation. Is that ability lost with a hybrid? Not necessarily.

Depending upon which traits are dominant and which are recessive,
some hybrid crosses reproduce consistently in the first generation, while others do not.
(None reproduce consistently in the second generation.)

The Cockapoo is probably the best example here of a cross that does reproduce consistently in the first generation. Because of this, they are immediately recognizable and very popular...in fact, the Cockapoo actually boasts its very own entry in the Oxford Dictionary.! The name itself first appeared in print some 60 years ago, although the cross has probably been around much longer than that.
Yet in all that time, few if any breeders have ever 'bred deeper' than the first generation, **simply because they didn't need to,** since all F1 Cockapoos all look remarkably alike and share similar temperaments.
Is the Cockapoo a breed? You betcha. And he's managed to maintain the longevity and robust health that is a product of hybrid vigor for over half a century, which is what has kept his popularity high and his many fans loyal.

On the other hand, because of that dominant/recessive thing, many other F1 hybrids (Doxie-poos, Labradoodles and Yorkie-poos for example) tend to be all over the map, both looks and size-wise. From a 'characterized appearance' standpoint, it would take many generations of rigid selective breeding to turn any of these crosses into breeds, by which time all hybrid vigor would be lost. So unless one's goal is to ultimately see one of these "breeds" entered in Westminster, there's just no earthly reason to go there.

Luckily, the Aussiedoodle is also a cross that produces remarkable consistency in the first generation. That's why it qualifies as a breed.

This means is that if he does his homework, the educated pet owner can find a first-generation puppy that will reliably display the characteristics typical of the breed without having to sacrifice the longevity and robust health provided by hybrid vigor. Finding that knowledgeable breeder is still VERY important, because hybrid vigor is not a panacea for all ills, especially in this breed. What we call 'hybrid vigor' is really the layman's term for 'heterosis', which has a very specific definition.

Heterosis:

The average increase in performance traits (i.e. size, hardiness, disease-resistance and longevity) displayed by the offspring of a deliberate cross of two different strains when compared to the averages of the original parent strains.

Heterosis cannot erase deficiencies in quality or soundness that may exist in either of the parents, nor can it eliminate genetic mutations, which will be passed on to, and in the Aussiedoodle's case may actually be **expressed** in, those first-generation offspring.

So with that caveat in mind, let's take a look at what one can expect from a typical well-bred Aussiedoodle, which will allow you to answer the other all-important question…..

Is This the Right Breed for Me?

The first thing to know is that **there is no perfect breed**, just as there is no perfect dog. Some breeds may be absolutely perfect for some families while others may be...well...less so. The advantage of choosing a dog of a particular breed is that you can look at the breed's "profile" and decide if it's a good fit for your situation before you make what could be a very long-term commitment.

This profile consists of two parts– Breed Type and Breed Character. Let's look at them one by one.

Breed Type .... What does a "typical" Aussiedoodle look like?

Usually laid forth in a breed's standard, breed type is defined as "that unique set of physical characteristics that set one breed apart from all others." It's a physical description that goes beyond the four 4 legs and a tail shared by all dogs. Here's the unique set of physical characteristics (**or conformation**) of the typical Aussiedoodle, organized in the traditional order and terminology of a breed standard:

Size, Proportion and Substance.

An active, small-to-medium sized dog, Aussiedoodles rarely exceed 60 pounds, and those out of miniature Aussies and smaller Poodles generally end up in the 20-35 pound range. Although often divided into Standard, Medium, Mini and sometimes Toy sizes, there is a lot of overlap between these divisions, with Medium-to-Mini being the most common.

Average height is between 12-20 inches at the shoulder, with 14-16 inches probably average.

Whatever his size, the Aussiedoodle is a squarely built dog, rather high on leg and fairly light in substance, which is apparent when he is closely clipped. This refinement of bone causes him to weigh less for his height than the other Doodles.

Head.

Well-balanced and without exaggeration. The muzzle is refined without snipiness, and nearly equals the back skull in length. Lips are tight. Ears are of moderate length, set fairly high on the skull and ear leather is fine, making him less prone to ear infection than many Doodle breeds.. Eyes may be brown, blue or heterochromic, but should always be large and oval in shape. Expression is alert without sharpness..

(Note: Eyes that appear smaller than normal, especially on a predominantly white dog, should be examined by an ACVO-certified ophthalmologist for possible microphalmia and associated ocular dysgenesis, which can impair vision and/or lead to eventual blindness from cataracts, retinal dysplasia and glaucoma . One or both eyes may be affected.)

Neck, Topline, Body.

The neck displays a fairly pronounced arch, allowing for the high head carriage typical of the breed. The body is compact and the topline is level rather than sloping.

Forequarters.

As with most Doodles, the entire front assembly is clean and sound, with a sloping shoulder, a long, rather upright upper arm, long straight forelegs with little slope to the pasterns and forefeet that turn neither in nor out. Nails should be kept short.

Hindquarters.

Well-muscled with good angulation. Typically long from stifle to hock and short from hock to foot, allowing for both agility and speed.

Tail.

May be born with naturally bobbed tail. Long tails are docked or left natural. Natural tails are typically carried level with the back or slightly higher and heavily fringed.

Coat and Color.

The coat is very soft and silky, carries a slight to medium wave. It is generally odorless and low-shedding. Untrimmed, the coat will blanket the entire dog from muzzle to tip of tail and may reach 6-8 inches or more. It may be kept full-length, scissored into a "teddy bear cut", or clipped short.
Every color and pattern, or combination thereof, is possible, including piebald and merle. Colored patches on the head, especially surrounding the eyes and ears, are critical.

Gait.

Gait is free with good reach and drive. Capable of maintaining an endurance trot for extended periods, he is light on his feet, and quick and agile in his movements.

OK, so what does this brief physical description of a typical Aussiedoodle tell us? LOTS.

This is a compact dog of a moderate size, suitable for most modern households. His coat sheds little if at all, but will require regular maintenance one way or the other. In other words, *this is not a wash-and-wear breed,* and keeping him groomed will require an expenditure of time or money or both. Although there is a lot of consistency in coat texture, there is clearly a lot of variation in color.

And as you might have guessed from reading the section on eyes, all colors are NOT equally desirable in this breed; some colors and patterns are particularly prone to hearing and vision impairment. (Puppies displaying these colors and patterns should ideally be screened prior to sale.)

His light frame and lower weight makes the Aussie less prone to orthopedic problems than a heavier-boned dog, and less clumsy indoors than many breeds of similar height. The "agile" part provides a clue that this is not a dog inclined to keep all his feet on the floor. This is not just a SMALLER Doodle, it is a lighter, more refined and perhaps somewhat more graceful one. He is not inclined towards drooling or ear infections.

Breed Character

As with his physiology, in character the Aussiedoodle is very much his own dog as well, and not simply a 'scaled-down' version of a larger Doodle personality.

What makes the Aussiedoodle unique among the Doodles is that he is the only one of the bunch whose "other parent" is a herding dog.

This is important, because in times past, when most dogs had to "earn their keep", breeds were developed for specific functions. This was done by selecting for specific BEHAVIORAL traits as well as physical ones. Some breeds were developed to hunt, some to herd, some to fight bulls, some to guard, some to kill rats and some to pull carts and sleds. We now understand that these behavioral traits involve a collection of genes that control things like prey drive, territorial defensiveness, and aggression through the expression of various hormones and neurotransmitters in the brain.

The farmers, hunters and gamekeepers who developed these breeds didn't know that, of course. But early dog breeders were mostly also stockmen and they DID know that desirable traits of all sorts were clearly inherited and could be cemented through selective breeding of those animals who displayed them, which is what they did, in essence creating the "designer breeds" of their day. And as most were destined to work and live outdoors, they selected for physical toughness and weatherproof coats as well.

Because these selected-for traits are now literally hard-wired into the dogs, the original function of a breed largely determines what we call its "breed character" as well as its "breed type." And in many cases, those very same traits that made a dog good at his job just get him into trouble now that dogs have mostly joined the ranks of the chronically unemployed.

Most breeds hard-wired to herd or hunt or guard or pull
now have nothing to herd or hunt or guard or pull around
except for their poor unwitting suburban owners.

And "employment retraining" in dogs has largely met with the same limited success that it has in humans for exactly the same reason—unfortunately, whether walking on two legs or four, not everyone is temperamentally suited for indoor jobs in the service sector.

This situation changed radically in the 1990s when a guy named Wally Cochran in Australia decided to cross the Labrador retriever with the Poodle to produce a seeing-eye dog that could be tolerated by people with allergies.
His experiment actually didn't turn out particularly well (and by all accounts Wally now regrets having done it) for the simple reason that the Lab and the Poodle do not produce offspring with any consistency at all in the first generation, especially in the area of a hypoallergenic coat. In fact, for a variety of reasons involving the most basic Mendelian genetics, they don't produce reliable consistency in succeeding generations either, and as a result of an ongoing herculean effort to cement a consistently non-shedding hypoallergenic coat where it doesn't want to be cemented, what is now called the Australian Labradoodle is actually mostly Poodle and displays little or no hybrid vigor at all.

But what Wally DID unwittingly stumble upon in his misguided quest for a hypoallergenic seeing-eye dog was critical to the future of the modern dog. Here it is:

The unique characteristics of the Poodle could "take the edge off" many of the physical and
behavioral traits that made repurposed working dogs difficult to live with,
and combining its DNA with many of them could produce
a variety of dogs well-suited to indoor employment in the "service sector".

In other words, Wally came up with the recipe for the Perfect 21st Century Dog.

In all fairness, Cockapoo breeders figured this out some half a century before Wally, did, but for some reason the idea of poodle crosses never gained real purchase in the rest of the dog world.

This may be one of those situations where a name is everything.

By his own admission, no one was interested in Wally's cross until he came up with the name "Labradoodle". For some inexplicable reason, apparently more people prefer to own a dog whose name ends in "doodle" than one whose name ends in "poo." Go figure.

Now, it's probably worth noting that longtime responsible breeders of Poodles are less than excited that their beloved breed has become what might best be described as the "universal donor" in the creation of this new crop of designer breeds, sort of like combat soldiers with Type O blood.

(Actually, that's a really good analogy because, from an immune system standpoint, many of our purebreds are in critical condition and a "transfusion" of new genetic material is all that's going to save them. Without it, their particular combination of genes, and the many unique and desirable qualities contained within them, will be ultimately lost, because let's face it, the public is just NOT going to keep buying puppies destined to die of autoimmune diseases and weird cancers by the time they're five or six years old.)

So let's address the question that's become the classic Poodle Breeder's Lament...to wit: "But if people want an intelligent hypoallergenic and non-shedding dog, why don't they just buy a POODLE?"

The truth is, in spite of his many virtues and although he brings much to the party in a hybrid cross, the purebred Poodle is in no better genetic shape than any other purebred, and in worse shape than many. The list of genetic and autoimmune diseases found in today's modern Poodle is staggering, which is why all this repeated backcrossing is a bad idea.

So what does the Australian Shepherd, as a herding dog, bring to the Aussiedoodle party in the area of breed character that sets him apart from the other better-known Poodle crosses?

Lots. As with breed type and physical characteristics, the best place to find clues to breed character is in a breed's standard.

Luckily, as a purebred, the Australian Shepherd does have a written standard that we can turn to for clues— in fact, he actually has THREE. For entirely political reasons he is served by three National Parent Clubs and three different registries– four if you count the National Stock Dog Registry. (Just for the record, we're quoting from the AKC standard here, for no reason other than it's handy.)

20

A quick perusal of its standard reveals that the Aussie is both "attentive" and "intelligent"— in fact both words are used repeatedly throughout the standard. (By comparison, the Golden Retriever standard does not use the word "attentive" AT ALL, probably because that's not their strongest suit.)

And although the word "intelligent" is also used in the Golden standard (not surprising for a breed that always ranks in the Top Five in any measure of doggy IQ) it is always accompanied by the word "friendly", which certainly describes the positively Clintonesque "never-met-a-stranger" attitude of the Golden *and which is entirely missing from the Aussie standard.*

In fact , the Australian Shepherd standard actually states that the breed "may be somewhat reserved in initial meetings'.

This means that the Australian Shepherd is really not a social butterfly like the Golden Retriever. However, his standard does mention "loyalty", which is a word conspicuously absent from the Golden's. And if loyalty in a dog is an important trait for you personally, the Aussiedoodle is going to be a better fit than the Goldendoodle, because as a rule they don't display any. (In fact, no matter what the breed, uber-gregarious dogs rarely display loyalty– the two are pretty much mutually exclusive.)

In addition to intelligent and attentive, other words that show up repeatedly in the Aussie standard are "alert", "agile" (at least four times!) and "active". **LOTS of good clues here, folks!**

Now let's look at the Poodle's standard, since he's of course contributing the other half of the behavioral DNA.
The Poodle standard uses the words "intelligent" "alert" "agile" and "active" a fair bit also, which is not surprising since he certainly displays all of these traits in spades.

However, there are also repeated references in his standard to "an air of dignity", a characteristic of the breed that might less euphemistically be described as aloofness by anyone other than a Standard Committee. Although always polite, the typical Poodle tends to be discriminating in his choice of friends and as a whole does not suffer fools gladly. He also ranks #2 out of 100 breeds in intelligence.

Another thing to check are the *'temperament faults'* listed in a breed's standard, because no standard bothers to list faults of ANY kind that do not actually exist in that breed.
These standards are, after all, written for the purpose of evaluating breeding stock, and what we refer to as "faults" and "disqualifications" are usually existing traits breeders wish to eliminate from the

gene pool in order to ensure the physical and mental soundness of their breed. This is why responsible breeders do not breed dogs displaying a lot of faults or ANY disqualifications.

And although many standards do not, *both the Poodle Standard and the Australian Shepherd Standard specifically list "shyness" as a fault.*

So that's something we want to watch for in Aussiedoodles, because it's coming in from both sides

OK, armed with all this, we can now make some pretty accurate predictions about the typical character of the Aussiedoodle, and how this will affect our ability to meet the breed's **essential needs.**
The three categories of needs that must be met before ANY dog can reach his full potential and live a happy, well-adjusted life are **physical, social, and intellectual,** in no particular order– all are equally essential to his well-being, and they vary greatly from breed to breed.

Virtually ALL behavioral problems in a dog are a direct result of
the owner's failure to meet one or more of his essential needs.

Let's go through the Aussiedoodle's needs one by one and see what's actually required to meet them, as this can vary greatly from breed to breed based on Breed Character.

Meeting the Aussiedoodle's Physical Needs

Both the standard for the Poodle and the standard for the Aussie use the words "active" and "agile" repeatedly. Since these appear to be "fixed" traits in both breeds, when you cross them odds are pretty good you are going to get active, agile offspring every time.

The Aussiedoodle is not a couch potato— he's an active, agile dog who requires exercise. In fact, right after water and food, exercise is one of the essential needs of ANY dog, and insufficient exercise probably causes more behavioral problems than anything else. In the world of dogs, there is no truer adage than "a tired dog is a well-behaved dog".
But it takes a lot more to tire some breeds out than others, and dog descended from active herding and hunting breeds (one of whose standards specifically states that the breed "has the stamina to work all day") is probably not going to tire easily. The good news is, his compact size and tremendous agility generally allow the Aussiedoodle to get the exercise needed in a smaller area than might be otherwise

required.

To keep him from being "hyper", which is really just another word for under-exercised, the typical Aussiedoodle probably needs at least a half-hour of serious exercise a day in addition to a daily walk. (Serious exercise means running, not walking— a dog can walk all day without getting one bit tired, because unlike us, they're actually built for it.)

And this exercise needs to be DIRECTED. A dog descended from a breed like the Aussie, who is both "attentive" and "loyal" to a fault, is unlikely to display the independence needed to self-exercise, so turning him out in a fenced yard probably won't do it, unless he has a companion to chase and romp with.

Luckily, if that companion is YOU, you can reduce the amount of exercise you'll need to expend in the process by teaching your puppy to retrieve early on. That way, he does most of the running and you only have to throw, which is a lot easier on your knees. Although herding breeds were not generally selected for retrieving finesse, the ancient water-retrieving DNA from the Aussiedoodle's Poodle ancestors will usually more than make up for any deficits in that department.

If you cannot honestly manage a couple of 15-minute retrieving sessions indoors or out on a daily basis (or don't have any kids to whom you can assign the task) you're going to be in a little trouble and you may want to consider a dog whose ancestors do not have the word "active" plastered all over their respective standards.

Meeting the Aussiedoodle's Social Needs

There are also clues written into standards about a dog's social needs as well… if you know what to look for and can read between the lines.

The key words here are "attentive" and "alert", which are traits he has inherited from both parents, as well as "loyal" and that "somewhat reserved in initial meetings" part from the Australian Shepherd, which we now know is often a euphemism for a dog who tends more toward shyness than the exuberant gregariousness of the Golden.

But assuming he is properly socialized from Day One (which is another reason why choosing a knowledgeable breeder is so important) the attentiveness and alertness that are hardwired into an Aussiedoodle, along with an innate eagerness to please, make him VERY easy to train, even for novices, and ideally suited for Service dog work, especially in the area of medical alerting, where size is far less important than 24/7 attunement with his environment and the people he cares about.

The typical Aussiedoodle has an essentially sensitive (or what behavioralists call "reactive") nature. As dogs of this type are also by nature pretty soft and very eager to please, they rarely need much in the way of correction.

Potential owners who are most comfortable with "positive-only" training will have a far easier time with an inherently softer Aussiedoodle than they will with a Doodle descended from the tougher (i.e. less reactive) and more independent sporting dogs like the Labradoodle or Goldendoodle.

But an Aussiedoodle cannot be allowed (or even inadvertently encouraged) to maintain a position of pack dominance within a household, because the responsibilities of the job will turn him into a neurotic mess. These dogs, more than many other breeds, really require calm, confident leadership in order to maintain their emotional equilibrium. Being forced into a leadership role will stress him out.

All that said, the same qualities that make him so easy to train also make the Aussiedoodle a poor candidate to be left alone all day, and those that are will invariably suffer from painful shyness when they do have to go out in the big world. Doggy day care at least a couple times a week is a really good idea for this breed.

(Note: Any puppy who seems excessively shy or "spooky" away from home should always be BAER tested and examined by a canine ophthalmologist to exclude the possibility of hearing and/or visual deficits as the cause.)

Both do exist in this breed, and it's important to know early on if your puppy is affected so you can adjust your training accordingly.

Meeting the Aussiedoodle's Intellectual Needs

By virtue of his ancestry, the Aussiedoodle is a highly intelligent and trainable breed, and by virtue of his soft and willing temperament, that training rarely requires professional-level skill. This may be one of the best breeds out there for the novice trainer.

HOWEVER, this is not a breed for people who really have no interest in training a dog beyond the basics of sit, stay, come and heel. (Those people would do better with a hound— easy-going, independent fellows who generally consider training a bore.)

Like all intelligent dogs, Aussiedoodles both require and thrive on training– they are eager learners with an unusually strong desire to please.

Aussiedoodles generally like classic Obedience and Rally, and they are great at Agility. Like all hybrids, as of 2011, Aussiedoodles may now compete in all AKC Companion Events and actually earn titles, which is pretty cool.

The downside, though, is because Aussiedoodles learn so quickly, it's also pretty easy to train them "by accident". Sometimes this is harmless and funny, and sometimes it's not.

One of the Least Funny is **actually training your puppy to be fearful** by rewarding him (with petting and soothing words) for fearful behavior in order to make him feel better, instead of cheerfully ignoring it. Being smart, he'll repeat the behavior next time just for the reward, and you'll have to undo the damage you created your veryownself. If you let it get out of hand, you're going to need professional help— this is one of those things that's a whole lot easier to avoid than it is to fix, because it can lead to fear-biting.

The most common example of this, for the record, is "fear of the vet". It is positively amazing how many people literally teach their dog to be afraid of the vet without being aware that they are doing it. And it is the poor vet who ends up getting bitten.

This is one of the ways that an Aussiedoodle differs from the "other doodles" descended from sporting dogs. Unlike a sporting breed, the Australian Shepherd is a herding dog, and herding dogs are bred to use their teeth to maintain control in the course of their "job". (Nipping at the heels of livestock is one of the ways they control them, and that tendency is hard-wired in.) Because of this, herding breeds are among the most likely to resort to fear-biting when stressed.

To avoid this, NEVER allow your Aussiedoodle to use his teeth for anything other than eating or chewing on a bone!

With socialization so critical in this breed, training classes are a better choice than in-home "personal trainers" which may be more convenient for the owner, but NOT best for the dog. Aussiedoodle puppies need to get out in the big scary world as much as possible. Going to class once a week is really the best way to do that, because he'll know what to expect when he gets in the car, which is in of itself a confidence-builder.

So there you are.

If your household is not overly chaotic and a medium-sized, low-shedding active dog who's fairly soft, very loyal and attentive (but not naturally bullet-proof or indiscriminately gregarious) and easy to train using "positive only" methods is appealing to you, the Aussiedoodle might just be the perfect choice!

CHAPTER TWO

A COAT OF MANY COLORS
(or...there's way more to this than meets the eye!)

Besides his compact size, attentive nature and easy trainability, one of the things that initially attracts people to the Aussiedoodle is his hypoallergenic non-shedding coat and its veritable rainbow of color and pattern options.

In fact, one would be hard-pressed to find any other breed capable of producing the incredible varieties of colors and patterns that one can find in a single litter of Aussiedoodles..

But here's the downside of all that flashy color, and its importance can NOT be overstated:

The exact same genes that produce those flashy patterns can cause puppies to be born both blind and deaf if combined incorrectly.

Unlike Goldendoodles or Labradoodles, breeding Aussiedoodles requires a working knowledge of color genetics. Even breeders only producing F1s need to know the basics, because at least two of the genes associated with deafness and eye defects are found in BOTH the Poodle and the Australian Shepherd breeds, and hybrid vigor will not prevent these problems in the puppies if the genes are incorrectly combined.

And *potential owners* need a working knowledge of color genetics as well....*before* they choose a puppy!

It's an old adage that **"breeders will produce what puppy buyers want to buy"**, because without a ready market for their puppies, breeders cannot continue breeding.

In this breed, some patterns come with a much higher risk of deafness and eye defects. If potential owners understand these risks and what causes them, there will be less demand for these patterns and breeders will avoid those pairings that produce them.

So THAT is why puppy buyers and pet owners also really need to know this stuff… when it comes right down to it, the future health and soundness of the Aussiedoodle breed is in your hands!!

The Aussiedoodle Coat

Now, the amazingly soft and silky, wavy Aussiedoodle coat is really an element of breed type and the breed's crowning glory no matter WHAT color it comes in, so let's begin by looking at it a in terms of QUALITY rather than color. And let's answer a couple of the biggest "coat questions" first.

Are Aussiedoodles really hypoallergenic?

The short answer here is YES. That's assuming one actually knows the actual definition of "hypoallergenic", which a lot of people apparently do not. In the event you fit in that category, do not despair— here's help from The Heritage American Dictionary:

Hypoallergenic: Having a decreased tendency to provoke an allergic response.

Note the phrase "decreased tendency" there. This is not to be confused with:

Non-allergenic: Not producing an allergic response.

There are NO non-allergenic dogs. (Not on this planet anyway.) Most allergic responses to dogs are triggered by the *Can f 1* and *Can f 2* proteins, and these proteins are produced in the dog's SKIN, not on his hair. (These proteins are also produced in the dog's saliva and to a lesser degree in his urine, so dogs that drool and pee in the house a lot are also poor choices for people with allergies, although that doesn't get as much press for some reason…go figure.)

These proteins produced in the epithelial tissue end up in the dog's DANDER, or shed epithelial cells, which then stick to the hair, which spreads it around.

Research has shown that some breeds carry a lot more of these allergy-triggering proteins on their hair than do others, and the differences are actually connected to **seborrhoeac levels rather than hair length**. (Seborrhoeac dogs produce more *sebum*, the oily substance produced by the *sebaceous gland* at the base of the hair follicle, which both lubricates and waterproofs the hair.)

Seborrhoeac breeds like Labs carry the highest levels of Can f proteins because the epithelial turnover time on these dogs is only 3-4 days compared to the average 21 day cycle. Less oily breeds produce less dander. The Poodle is one of the least oily (it's why he has no "doggy" odor) and the Australian Shepherd is probably less than average. Since the F1 Aussiedoodle gets one gene controlling seborrhoeac levels from each parent, he's pretty consistently hypoallergenic.

Although hair length does not affect the amount of Can f proteins produced, hair length does affect the amount that gets spread around the house, because *long-haired dogs shed each hair less often* than do short-haired ones.

Which leads us to the next-most-popular question:

Do Aussiedoodles shed?

The short (and honest) answer here is YES. The truth is ALL dogs shed, except for the totally hairless ones, and they still have SKIN, so even baldness won't help people with severe dog allergies. .But for everyone else, the Aussiedoodle is a pretty low-shedding breed, and is not going to leave a lot of hair around the house, which is about as good as it gets. Here's why:

Every mammalian hair cycles through three phases– **anagen** (growth), **telegen** (resting), and **exogen** (shedding). Hair length is determined by how long a particular hair is genetically programmed to stay in the "anagen" phase— a longer anagen phase translates to a longer hair.

There are basically only three major genes responsible for most of the different coat variations found in dogs, and ALL of them affect shedding to some degree. One determines if the dog is curly or wavy, **and the other two determine how long each hair spends attached to the dog before ultimately ending up on the couch or the floor— in other words, how long the hair stays in anagen.**

The first gene is **FGF5, on chromosome 32,** and the "wild-type" version of this gene produces short hair, like that found on the wolf, one of the canine breeds Mother Nature came up with on her own.

A recessive mutated form (or allele) of this gene produces what we call "long-haired" dogs, like the Australian Shepherd, which has long hair on the bottom half, medium length hair on the top half, and short hair on the face and the front of the legs. The lower-case l (for "long") is used by geneticists to denote this allele, and its dominant shorthaired "wild-type version" by the upper-case L.

The second gene is **RSPO2, on chromosome 13**. A variant on this gene causes hair pretty much all over the dog to stay in anagen longer, and is responsible for furnishings on the face and feet. Because it is dominant, dogs only need one copy of the allelic variant (denoted as F) to have furnishings. The "smooth-muzzled" ancestral gene variant is denoted by f.

The third gene, **KRT71, on chromosome 27** regulates the amount of curl in the coat, which really only affects shedding insofar as the curlier the dog, the more likely the hair is to get caught in the neighboring hair when shed, rather than falling on the floor. Wavy/curly dogs are said to "shed into their coats", and will mat easily if not brushed frequently to remove the shed hairs. (There is yet another gene that allows for the *expression* of the wave or curl that's clearly a player here also, but it has not yet been identified. Straight-coated Aussies obviously carry it while curly-coated Poodles do not.)

Aussiedoodle Coat Genetics

F1 breeding	Parent A ll cc FF long, curly, with furnishings	
Parent B ll CC ff long, wavy, no furnishings	ll Cc Ff long, wavy, with furnishings	ll Cc Ff long, wavy, with furnishings
	ll Cc Ff long, wavy, with furnishings	ll Cc Ff long, wavy, with furnishings

This first chart shows what happens genetically in the typical "F1" Aussiedoodle cross.

You'll notice that both of the parent breeds involved here are homozygous, or "fixed", for coat type, and in addition, both are fixed for the longhaired ll phenotype, which is important—hybrids produced by crossing ll Poodles to LL (shorthaired) breeds like Labradors end up with tremendous variations in coat.

But because both parents are ll, of our F1 Aussiedoodles will be soft and silky, wavy, and low-to-non-shedding.

Also, because they are all Ff, their coats will take a while to really fluff out, especially on the muzzle and legs. This is typical of Ff dogs, who are often pretty "scruffy-coated" adolescents.

Now, when you breed two F1 Aussiedoodles together (an "F2" breeding) consistency is lost and all sorts of coats are produced, including some that look like the original parent breeds.

The chart to the right clearly shows why, like all hybrids, Aussiedoodles cannot produce consistent coats in the second generation.

In this breeding, because both F1 parents are heterozygotes for both curl (Cc) and facial furnishings (Ff), 25% of the resulting pups will be cc, with curly poodle coats, while another 25% will be ff, and display the smooth faces and feet of the Australian shepherd. (Some of these smooth-faced pups could also be curly (cc), as there are obviously more possibilities than can be pictured here.)

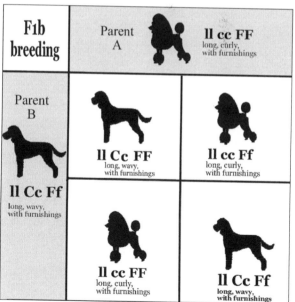

Some breeders try to avoid this by backcrossing F1 Aussiedoodle bitches to Poodle sires, or vice versa, in what plant and livestock geneticists refer to as an "F1b" cross. (The "b" stands for "backcross".)

But as shown here, although you don't end up with any smooth-faced "ancestral" Aussie coats, a full 50% the litter end up with frizzy Poodle coats rather than the wavy Aussiedoodle coats.

Even *worse,* it significantly raises the odds of producing pups with the same genetic and autoimmune disorders plaguing purebred Poodles, because some puppies will also end up homozygous for the Poodle DLA haplotypes associated with them.

And 50% of the pups from this breeding (the Ff dogs) can STILL produce smooth-faced offspring. Without gene testing, recessive genes are impossible to eliminate, which makes repeated backcrossing hardly worth the loss of hybrid vigor.

However, breeders who want to keep Aussiedoodles for breeding without risk of producing "ancestral" coats (and without the loss of hybrid vigor from Poodle backcrosses) can now simply gene-test their F2 puppies and choose the CC FF dogs for breeding.

gene-tested breeding	Parent A tested F2 homozygote **ll CC FF** long, wavy, with furnishings	
Parent B tested F2 homozygote **ll CC FF** long, wavy, with furnishings	**ll CC FF** long, wavy, with furnishings	**ll CC FF** long, wavy, with furnishings
	ll CC FF long, wavy, with furnishings	**ll CC FF** long, wavy, with furnishings

As you can see from the chart to the left, all the resulting puppies will have the "ideal" wavy Aussiedoodle coats! How cool is THAT?

And these CC FF dogs can also be bred to F1s (Cc Ff by definition) without sacrificing coat, which will further lessen the decrease in hybrid vigor.

These coat tests are both inexpensive and non-invasive and are available from several labs in the US and Canada.

So as we can clearly see, "coat-gene testing" now allows breeders to produce dogs that "breed true" in only TWO generations, with minimal loss of hybrid vigor.

(F2 and even F3 animals will maintain more hybrid vigor than those produced by backcrossing, where it is lost pretty rapidly.)

Since these coat-gene tests have only become commercially available in the last few years, many Aussiedoodle breeders are unaware that they even exist, but hopefully that will change in the near future, and more breeders will make use of them.

And those breeders worried about losing genetic diversity and resulting hybrid vigor in "multigen" breedings now have the ability to monitor that as well. At least one lab is now running tests for genetic diversity at the DLA locus, which is largely responsible for immune function in the dog. Although more expensive (currently $160 per dog) it effectively takes the guesswork out of that part also, as they can choose dogs for breeding who do not share the same DLA haplotypes.

Why breed "multigenerational" dogs at all?

Now, some breeders believe that it's best only to produce F1 puppies out of Poodles and Australian Shepherds. And *without* gene-testing, they do have a point, because most hybrid vigor will be rapidly lost through the repeated F1b Poodle backcrosses most "multigen" breeders have had to rely on.

However, it's also pretty clear that *with* gene-testing, one can successfully breed healthy and robust multi-generational dogs that will also "breed true" in just a couple of generations without significant loss of hybrid vigor, although it's a lot more expensive and complicated. (And we haven't even begun to discuss the other gene-testing that may be required in multigenerational dogs!) So why would anyone WANT to?

There are a couple of reasons, all equally valid. Mostly, it depends on why one breeds dogs in the first place.

Commercial breeders produce puppies solely for profit, which is probably the poorest reason. Trying to make one's entire living breeding dogs is dicey at best, because too many things can go wrong. Dog breeding is really "animal husbandry", which is a nice name for livestock farming, and any farmer will tell you that the best way to make a small fortune farming is to start with a large fortune!

Unless they are well-capitalized (that's the "starting with a large fortune" part) trying to pay the mortgage and put food on the table solely through puppy sales invariably requires cutting corners, and in this breed especially, it's usually the puppies (and the puppy buyers) who pay the price for that.

Hobby breeders, on the other hand, are like hobby farmers— they do not rely upon it as their sole source of income. They do it because they enjoy it, and if they turn a profit, great. If they don't, they keep on breeding anyway. And hobby breeders the world around generally fall into one of two groups.

The first group loves dogs, but REALLY loves puppies. They love whelping them, nurturing them and raising them. They love the smell of puppy breath. They tend to provide lots of support to their puppy buyers, and are very knowledgeable about health care and nutrition, early socialization and training. Although the best of these breeders learn enough about basic genetics to produce healthy puppies in their breed, genetic research is certainly not their passion and in the world of hybrids they are usually content to produce healthy F1 hybrid puppies indefinitely.

The second group also loves dogs, but their real passion is the genetics end of breeding rather than the puppy-raising end. They learn what they need to in order to whelp, raise, and socialize puppies well, but puppy breath does not provide their primary gratification in breeding. For them, the intellectual challenge of producing dogs that both fit their personal "vision" and will breed true is the motivation.

(In the AKC purebred world, these people are invariably the "show breeders" because dog shows are the traditional venue for measuring one's success in this quest, and many hybrid breeders of this type were successful AKC show breeders who turned to hybrids because of insurmountable health issues in their breeds.)

As a rule, these breeders are rarely content to simply replace their retired breeding dogs with new breeding dogs of the parent breeds as the "puppy-lovers" do. They want to keep *moving forward*, so they keep their best young hybrids and attempt to get them to "breed true"— i.e. to produce puppies who are at least as good as themselves and hopefully better examples of the breeder's vision. And because it is their primary tool and critical to their success, this group is invariably most knowledgeable about canine genetics, a subject that admittedly makes most people's eyes glaze over.

In the world of Aussiedoodles, there are good breeders in both categories.
Unfortunately, there are also some flat-out awful ones in both categories as well.

And in this breed, insufficient understanding of color genetics by EITHER category of breeder can result in puppies that are born blind, deaf or both. In order to understand why, we need to know a little about canine color genetics, so here we go. (A pot of strong coffee may help.)

Aussiedoodle Color Genetics 101

For many years, virtually everything breeders and canine geneticists knew about color genetics in dogs came from only one source —-a book called **the Inheritance of Coat Color in Dogs**, written back in 1957 by Clarence C. Little ScD.
And unfortunately, although he was undoubtedly brilliant, Dr. Little was also a pretty terrible writer, which is why so few breeders understand color genetics to this day. (I don't know how the geneticists have fared, but very few breeders over the years have been able to slog through that wretched book without slipping into a coma after the first chapter. It is stunningly dull.)

A geneticist at Bar Harbor's famous Jackson Laboratory, Dr. Little theorized that there were at least 10 genes that determined most canine coat colors and patterns, and that each one had its own particular location, or **locus**, on various chromosomes across the canine genome. To simplify things, he assigned each "color locus" a letter– A, B, C, D, E, G, M, P, S and T. (These are still used today.)
He also determined that each of these genes had one or more variations, called **alleles,** that had arisen over time, and each of which altered the gene's expression in different ways.

When molecular geneticists gained the technology to actually examine canine genes some fifty years later, they discovered that a lot of Little's theories were indeed correct, although he did miss a couple of loci (the K and H loci were recently identified and added) and his theories about several alleles on the C and S loci haven't panned out. But given what he had to work with, he did remarkably well.

Using data from thousands of breedings, Little also determined that a particular set of variations was "fixed" through years of selective breeding in some breeds, causing every dog of that breed to carry the exact same alleles and display the exact same color or pattern (Golden Retrievers and Basenjis are examples) while other breeds were variable at many loci, allowing for wide variation in color and pattern.

Our little Aussiedoodle, it turns out, is descended from two breeds with LOTS of variations on those color genes!

For example, it has been established that there are some 254 different color genotypes possible in the Australian Shepherd, and that only includes the colors and patterns allowed in the show ring.

(The allowable variations from a genetics standpoint are ***B/B or B/b*** **blacks** and ***b/b*** **reds** (genetically brown-nosed browns) as well as ***M/m*** **merles** in either base color, all **S/S self-colored** or with **S/*si* or *si/si* Irish pattern white trim** and ***at/at*** **copper points**. Several more color and pattern variations, (including sable, harlequin, piebald and pattern white with or without ticking) exist in the breed but are disallowed by the standard and discouraged from use in breeding.

And although the AKC Poodle standard only allows **S/S self-colors,** those include black, brown, café au lait, cream, silver, and all shades of red/apricot and white Many Poodles also carry the dominant gene for silvering, which is allowed in their standard. And though *not allowed in the AKC standard,* several patterns (including tan points, part-colors, sable and merle) also exist in the breed.

Given that ancestry, it's pretty apparent that when it comes to color genes, the Aussiedoodle is not "fixed" for anything…in fact, he appears to be variable at every single color locus and carries pretty much every color and pattern variation known in dogs!

Of course, every dog does not carry every variation, but since each dog carries **two alleles** (one you see and one you don't) **at each of at least 12 different loci,** breeding any two Aussiedoodles together can result in a veritable rainbow of colors and patterns— it's a little like the Powerball Lottery.

Now, most of these colors and patterns are pretty "benign"—aside from affecting the pigment on the coat and or skin, they don't seem to do much else that could affect the dog's quality of life.

However, mutations in three different "pattern genes" are associated with deafness, eye defects and even neurological problems in any breed in which they appear, and one is actually *lethal* if two copies are inherited. **These patterns are merle, piebald and harlequin and all are found in the Australian Shepherd.** The gene mutations responsible for all three of them have recently been identified and for some breeds gene tests are now commercially available.

And geneticists now understand a little more about the *chemistry* behind coat color as well, which goes a long way toward explaining how the color of a dog's coat can actually be connected to something as seemingly *unconnected* as whether or not he can hear normally or is born deaf.

The many colors we "see" on a dog's coat are the result of two different forms of "pigment granules" in the hair shaft called **melanin.** Most people probably know that the amount of melanin in the skin determines how dark or light the skin is, but not that it also determines hair color and eye color.

 The two most common forms of melanin are **eumelanin**, a dark brown/black polymer, and **phaeo-melanin**, a lighter yellow/red. **Both are produced in skin cells called melanocytes.**

We now know that the "color genes" described by Little are actually genes that affect the production of both eumelanin and pheomelanin in the hair and sometimes the skin, and at least one "pattern gene" affects the distribution of the melanocytes themselves.

For example, we now know that the E locus is the home of the MCR1 (*Melanocortin Receptor 1)* gene. If a dog inherits two copies of a particular recessive mutation at this locus, eumelanin will be produced in the skin *but not the hair*, which will be comprised entirely of yellow/red phaeomelanin granules instead.

These dogs will have dark noses but their coats will be some shade of red or yellow without a single black or brown hair anywhere. Goldens and Irish setters are both fixed for this mutation, although the coat color may range from pale cream to deep red due to the actions of other modifying genes.

It is also the genotype of most (but not all) cream, apricot and red poodles, and so can show up in Aussiedoodles.   Because it does not allow any dark pigment granules to be produced, the e/e coat can "mask" the presence of the "merle" gene, which can be dicey if one is breeding multigen Aussiedoodles. To understand why, we need to understand a little bit about merle.

Merle and the SILV gene

To begin with, merle is not a color at all. It is a COAT PATTERN caused by the insertion of a unique mutation called a *transposon* in the *SILV* gene at the M locus. (Another mutation in this gene causes black mice to appear silver, which explains its name.)

This mutation appears to degrade the structure of the pigment-producing melanocytes in random areas, causing dilution of the pigment granules in both the fur and the stroma of the iris in those areas and resulting in patches of lighter and darker fur, and sometimes one or two blue eyes, depending on where a "dilute patch" happens to land. This pattern is called merle and is designated with a capital M. (Lower-case m is used to designate the ancestral "non-merle" gene.)

Although not always visible, merling can occur on any color dog because the action of the gene simply reduces (in random areas) the production of whatever pigment granules are already genetically destined to be there.

Because it is a dominant mutation, only one copy of the merle mutation will cause enough dilution to produce the random patches of lighter and darker fur– these dogs are called "single" or **heterozygous merles, designated as   Mm.** Merle is an old mutation, and it is caused by the same mutation in all breeds in which it appears.

Although the incidence of deafness in these Mm dogs appears to be slightly higher overall than in solid-colored "non-merle" breeds (but lower than several non-merle "parti-colored" breeds), no other serious defects are associated with dogs carrying a single copy the merle gene.

TWO COPIES of the merle gene, on the other hand, have long been associated with all sorts of problems, primarily involving hearing and vision.

In Australian Shepherds, most "double" or **homozygous merles** often have predominantly white coats, with various amounts of merle spotting. Genetically, they are **MM.** Often called "lethal whites" (a term borrowed from horses) the MM phenotype is not generally lethal, but when actually screened, it appears very few MM Australian Shepherds have normal hearing and/or vision.

Whether this is caused entirely by greater degradation of the melanocytes from a "double-dose" of the merle mutation, or by the combination of merle with other modifying genes (such as piebald and harlequin) in all cases *a lack of normal melanocyte development* is the underlying problem.

Breeders and geneticists have both observed that the likelihood of deafness and ocular defects in BOTH Mm *and* MM merle dogs increases with the amount of white on the dog, especially on the head.
In Aussies (from whom the Aussiedoodle inherits both the merle and piebald genes) some studies have shown **the incidence of unilateral and bilateral deafness in MM dogs, all of whom displayed excessive white, to be pretty close to 100%** , and eye defects are common.

The next gene we need to understand is the MITF gene, because mutations on this one are also major players in the "color genetics" game and can cause problems, with or without merle.

the MITF gene

To begin with, "MITF" stands for **microphthalmia transfer factor,** which tells you something about this gene right out the gate. ("Microphthalmia" is the medical term for a small, underdeveloped eye.) This gene is also responsible for what look like white spots on a dog's coat– in some cases, the dog may be totally white, with maybe only a patch or two of color.

However, it's important to know that genetically, there are at least three different kinds of white in dogs.

Some white breeds are actually genetically self-colored black or red dogs that appear white due to the action of several modifying genes affecting the *expression* of pigment in the hair.
These dogs generally have complete black or brown pigment on their noses and eye rims and the skin is pigmented to some degree. (White Shepherds and most white Poodles are of this type.)

On the other hand, "true white" is caused by the **complete absence of pigment development during embryogenesis**— in other words, the pigment simply fails to develop in those places while the pup is growing in the womb. (White Boxers and Bull Terriers are of this type.)

The third white is simply a combination of the two, where modifying genes cause the colored patches on a piebald dog to appear white, and blend in with the "true white" areas caused by failure of pigment development, causing an overall white appearance. (Bichons are often of this type.)

The first is caused by mutations on the MCR1 gene acting with other modifying genes, while the second and third involve mutations in the MITF gene. These last two can come with other problems.

This is because MITF is essential for the development and distribution of *melanocytes,* or pigment cells.

And the role of these so-called "pigment cells" reach far beyond pigmentation of the skin and coat of the dog— they also play a vital role in developing sight and hearing, as well as several brain and digestive functions. Here's what happens:

38

In the embryo, a fold develops down the back called the neural tube, which contains an active region called the **neural crest**. This region supplies the *melanocytes*, which are pigment-producing cells that migrate all over the body.

These cells migrate to pairs of specific sites on either side of the body as well as the backline. In mammals, research has identified three such sites on the head (near the eye, near the ear, and near the top of the head), and six sites along each side of the body, and several along the tail. These sites are particularly rich in melanocyte receptors.

A few melanocyte cells migrate to each of these sites, where they proliferate and migrate outwards, joining up to form larger patches, spreading down the legs and down the head until they meet up under the chin, and down the body until they meet up on the belly.

Once the melanocytes have finished migrating, they take up positions at the base of the hair follicles. There they synthesize **melanin**, and feed it into the growing hair. Normally, all follicles have melanocytes associated with them and all of the fur is pigmented to some degree. But if the gene process is disrupted and the melanocytes don't *reach* a particular follicle, there is no pigment at all in that hair.

Various mutations that affect melanocyte distribution during the development of the embryo determine which parts of the body have pigment cells and which parts have none.

The melanocytes also normally migrate to both the iris and retina of the eye, and to the inner ear, where they are critical for normal eye development and hearing.

MITF and Ocular Development

The stroma (front) of the **iris** in dogs is normally pigment-rich and appears brown, which protects the eye against UV damage.
If melanocytes don't reach the stroma, no pigment is produced and the eye will appear blue— for the exact same reason the sky does. (In solid merles, a random dilute patch in that area can affect the underlying structure of—and subsequently reduce the amount of pigment produced by— the melanocytes there, also causing the eye to appear blue.)

Heterochromia, where one eye is blue and the other is brown, is caused by a lack of pigment in the iris of one eye but not the other, and may occur in either situation.

A lack of functioning melanocytes in the **retina** is far more serious, because it prevents this structure from fully differentiating in the embryo, causing a malformation of the choroid fissure and resulting in drainage of vitreous humor fluid.

Without this fluid, the eye fails to enlarge and develop normally, resulting in **microphthalmia and ocular dysgenesis.** The acuity of the vision in these smaller eyes varies with the degree of deformity, which varies widely.

In some cases the third eyelid permanently covers the small eye, blocking vision. And in the most severe cases, no eye develops in the socket at all—this is called **anaphthalmia.**

Because of the lack of functioning melanocytes in the whole area, these eyes are also invariably blue, and often display abnormalities that can be observed with the naked eye.

One such defect is called **coloboma,** a condition in which the iris is not completely formed and pieces are missing. This can result in squinting in bright light as the iris is not able to function properly helping to reduce the amount of light let into the eye.

In some cases the pupil is not positioned properly in the center of the iris. This is referred to as an **eccentric pupil** or **dropped pupil.** One or both eyes may be affected.

A **starburst pupil** or **sunburst pupil** is where the pupil is not properly formed and looks as if it is sending out rays into the surrounding iris. These dogs also have a problem with bright light as the pupil is unable to contract as it should to protect the eye.

MITF and Hearing

Melanocytes also migrate to the cochlea and stria vascularis of the inner ear, where they play an essential role in hearing.

If these areas of the inner ear do not have functioning melanocytes
(which are the *melanin-producing cells*, not the pigment granules themselves)
the dog will be deaf. It's that simple.

When the strial melanocytes are absent or degraded, the stria degenerates, after which the hair cells die and the various cochlear structures collapse and the auditory nerve fibers start to degenerate. The nerve cells of the cochlea subsequently die and permanent deafness results. This occurs in the first few weeks after birth while the ear canal is still closed, and is irreversible.

And we now know a dog can have *pigmented hair* on the outer ear and still have *no pigment –producing cells* in the inner ear. In fact, a study published in 2012 involving close to 900 Australian Cattle dogs revealed that close to half of unilaterally deaf dogs with only one colored ear were actually *deaf in the col-*

ored ear rather than the white one! This indicates that an entirely different melanocyte migration path is involved for the inner ear. (Full and/or symmetrical pigmentation on the head is associated with a decreased risk of deafness, even if most of the rest of the dog —including the muzzle— is white.)

Is congenital deafness a *polygenic disease*, as has long been believed, or can it be caused entirely by disruption of MITF? Given what we now know, a pretty strong argument can be made for the latter, although other genes (like merle) may also cause deafness by affecting melanocyte function
.In English cocker spaniels deafness is absent in solid colored dogs but present in parti colors. **In bull terriers, deafness is 10 times more prevalent in whites than in colored dogs, which still have white trim.**
But yet all "true white" dogs are *not* deaf, although in some breeds up to 1 in 3 may be...and in at least one breed a whopping 75% of them are. What's with that?

According to LSU's Dr George Strain, in both dogs and cats with white-producing gene mutations, deafness appears to result from **strong expression of the mutation or mutations..** (The stronger the expression, the greater the disruption of normal MITF migration.) When it is strongly expressed, it suppresses melanocyte migration not only in the skin, but also to the iris and the stria of the inner ear. Weak expression of the gene is associated with a reduced likelihood of deafness. Dalmatians with blue eyes (who display strong piebald expression) are statistically *more* likely to be deaf, while Dalmatians with colored patches (weak piebald expression) are statistically *less* likely to be deaf. A fully colored head would indicate very weak expression. Variation in expression may be caused by the combination of several mutations on the MITF gene alone, or in combination with mutations on other genes (like merle).

MITF and the Brain

Melanocytes also migrate to the brain, to areas such as the substantia nigra (the part of the midbrain that regulates mood, produces dopamine, and controls voluntary movement), and the locus ceruleus (the part of the brain that deals with the stress response) as well as other areas. A lack of melanin in these areas is associated with a wide variety of effects, such as movement disorders (e.g. seizures and White Dog Shaker Syndrome in dogs and Parkinson's in people), and diverse effects on both behaviour and the individual's response to stress.

Because pigment cells are implicated in areas of the brain related to mood and the stress response, the connection between depigmentation and behaviour probably played an important role in animal domestication.

By selecting for "tameness", breeders selected for a different pigment cell migration in the developing nervous system, leading to calmer animals. A side effect of this selection for behavior was the change in pigment cell migration in the skin as well, leading to a "piebald" coat. (Piebald exists in many domesticated species, but is non-existent in the wild, where tameness provides no evolutionary advantage.) In fact, Russia's famous fox study showed that deliberate selection of wild animals simply for tame behavior over generations unexpectedly resulted in piebald foxes. *However, as we shall see, this may be one of those cases where if some is good, MORE is not necessarily better.*

MITF Mutations and White Patterning

Because the domestication of the dog by definition involved selection for tameness over the millennia, mutations that affect pigmentation and produce white spotting are seen in many breeds. And because these mutations arose long before dogs were formally divided into "breeds", many breeds should logically share the same mutations. And they do.

Back in the 1950s, Clarence Little theorized that all these white patterns were caused by various mutations on what he called **the S locus.** He decided that there were three separate mutations on this gene responsible for all the white patterns observed in dogs, including harlequin (which turned out to be totally wrong), each dominant over the one below it in the "epistatic order" shown at left, and any deviations from what should occur based on this "hierarchy" were caused by what he called plus or minus modifiers.

the S Locus

S - Self-colored (solid)

s^i - Irish pattern

s^p - Piebald

s^w - extreme piebald

Now, probably 99% of breeders today still assume this is the way white spotting is inherited, and you'll find this same stuff everywhere that color genetics is explained on the internet. In the world of canine color genetics, Little's "S locus theory" is accepted as Gospel.

**The problem is, although he guessed right on a lot of color genes,
it appears the "S locus" is maybe a little more complicated than was originally believed.**

Decades after Dr Little himself shuffled off to the Rainbow Bridge, a mutation responsible for what we call piebald (pr "parti-color) was finally identified on the MITF gene. But rather than the single-point mutation expected, it consists of a *short interspersed nucleotide element* (called a SINE for short), essentially a chunk of DNA inserted in the gene in exactly the same place in every piebald dog.

This SINE mutation is responsible for white spotting in dozens of different breeds. Unfortunately though, it does not behave the same way in every breed in which it appears.

In some breeds the SINE mutation (probably due to other modifying genes on MITF or elsewhere) appears to act in a completely "dose-dependent" manner.

Solid/ SINE

In other words, one copy causes white trim on the coat in the typical Irish pattern, while two copies causes what Little assumed was a third mutation for "Extreme piebald"— a mostly white dog with a spot or two.

So here we actually have this one "piebald" mutation responsible for both Irish and Extreme piebald patterns, with no "classic piebalds" anywhere to be found!

In these breeds (like the Boxer and Bull Terrier) when two dogs carrying a single copy of the piebald SINE are bred together, 25% of the litter will be solid ("self-colored"), 50% will have varying amounts of Irish markings, and another 25% will be mostly white.

Solid/ SINE

And, as with Dalmatians (a breed "fixed" for the SINE) an estimated 20-30% of these mostly white SINE/SINE puppies will be either unilaterally or bilaterally deaf...even though none of them carry the merle mutation. (That's up to *1 in 3* white puppies, folks.)

(In fact, to reduce the risk of producing deaf puppies, as of 2013 the British Kennel Club will no longer register any pups resulting from breedings between two "flashy" Boxers– at least one of the parents must be solid.)

Irish/Irish

But the same pattern produced by Solid/SINE also exists in some breeds that do not carry the SINE mutation at all. And when bred together, these dogs produce no solids, no classic piebalds, and no extreme piebalds– just more Irish pattern pups every time.

This "true" Irish pattern is a fixed trait in several breeds. These breeds (like the Basenji and the Bernese Mountain Dog) are not plagued by deafness or vision problems, likely because melanocyte migration to those areas of the head is not disrupted. Whether the causative mutation for this Irish pattern is also on the MITF gene is unknown at this point in time.

However, what we DO know is that it's pretty hard to tell which dogs are Solid/SINE and which are true Irish pattern just by looking at them!

Irish/Irish

This similarity has long presented problems for breeds that carry both mutations, because in those breeds, accidentally breeding two of these "pseudo-Irish" dogs together will statistically produce 25% extreme piebalds, and the risk of deafness in those pups is increased. And the Australian Shepherd is one of those breeds.

This is a SERIOUS problem for the Aussiedoodle, where deafness in extreme piebald puppies is already occurring, *even in F1 puppies.*

It is occurring in F1s because in Poodles, piebald is also caused by the SINE mutation. Depending on the other modifying gene mutations present, breeding parti-colored Poodles together may result in "color-headed whites" with patches of body color (where the risk of deafness is pretty low), OR it may result in piebald puppies with asymmetric color patches on a mostly white head, where the risk of deafness is high. This variation in parti-colored Poodles has not been well-studied for one reason:

The AKC Poodle standard allows solid colors only. Any parti-colored pattern (including merle), or any amount of white on a colored dog, is a disqualification.

Because the only white allowed is the solid white dog produced by the MCR1 gene unrelated to piebald and merle, deafness and ocular dysgenesis are virtually non-existent within the gene pool of well-bred AKC Poodles. It's admittedly draconian, but it's been effective.

Now, in addition to solids and merles with no white trim at all, Australian Shepherds may display Irish pattern, also with or without merle. They also may display classic piebald, color-headed whites and asymmetric "extreme piebald" with just a patch or two of color and a lot of white on the head. (This is not really surprising given that the breed was developed fairly recently in the US and is likely descended in large part from older herding breeds, where all of these patterns are found.)

Since the earliest days of the breed's development, however, *excessive white* has been a disqualification in the Australian Shepherd breed.

Because breeders have long observed that dogs who produced extreme piebald pups (called "pattern whites" in this breed) often displayed more white trim than those that didn't, all Aussie standards have strictly-defined limits on the amount of white a dog can display in order to qualify as "breeding quality", and where that white can be located—basically, only the Irish pattern of the Basenji is allowed. By eliminating dogs with excessive white from breeding, and strongly discouraging the breeding of merle to merle, responsible Aussie breeders have kept the problems associated with the piebald and merle genes pretty well under control over the years, even prior to the availability of gene tests.

In fact, they've been so successful that no Australian Shepherds tested to date have been found carrying the SINE mutation, leading some researchers to conclude the breed is "fixed" for the Irish pattern. (Of course, since solid colors are also allowed in the breed, this is clearly not the case!)

Now logically, this longtime diligence on the part of Poodle and Australian Shepherd breeders should put the Aussiedoodle in good shape. And it would…EXCEPT FOR ONE THING:

Although researchers are unlikely to run across these dogs (as their breeders rarely participate in Parent Club-funded genetic studies) many "backyard-bred" Aussies, like Poodles, still DO carry for piebald and pattern white. And because they were developed from breeds already found to be carrying the SINE, piebald and pattern white in Aussies is unlikely to be caused by another mutation.

And way too many novice Aussiedoodle breeders are purchasing inexpensive "pet-quality" Australian Shepherds displaying excessive white from backyard breeders for breeding, and THEN crossing these dogs with (also inexpensive!) pet-quality "parti-factored" Poodles with white trim, in order to produce "parti-colored" Aussiedoodles.

And as shown at right, this combination can end up producing the same 25% extreme piebalds, exactly as if one were breeding Boxers or Bull Terriers.

And if they were BAER testing (which most are not) they would likely find the same high incidence of deafness common to many extreme piebalds.

Now, some of these pups are "merle partis" and some have solid markings, but it really makes no difference, because as we have seen, the extreme piebald phenotype (characterized by a lot of white on the head) is associated with deafness even in the absence of merle.

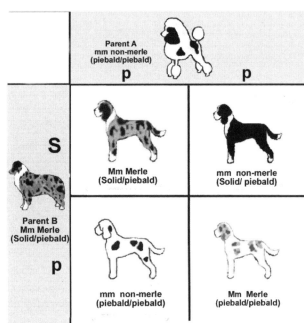

	Parent A mm non-merle (piebald/piebald) p	p
Parent B Mm Merle (Solid/piebald) S	Mm Merle (Solid/piebald)	mm non-merle (Solid/ piebald)
p	mm non-merle (piebald/piebald)	Mm Merle (piebald/piebald)

Some breeders are going a step farther, using parti-colored poodles in order to totally avoid solid-colored puppies.

This too can be dicey, because IF the parents happens to be carrying for extreme piebald as shown in the chart at right, fully HALF the puppies in the litter could be extreme piebalds, and at high risk for deafness.

These puppies should ideally be BAER tested prior to sale, and *both* parents should be BAER-tested prior to breeding. (Breeders of parti-colored Poodles rarely BAER-test—in fact, most people don't even know that the pattern is caused by the exact same SINE mutation associated with deafness in other breeds.)

Multigen breedings involving parti-colored Poodles should be undertaken only by experienced breeders.

And in order to produce more *merle* puppies in the litter, some breeders also deliberately breed merles to merles.

This is the WORST possible breeding choice.

Indeed, statistically three-quarters of the resulting puppies will be merles, which are often in highest demand, but roughly a quarter of them will also be homozygous (MM) merles.

In addition to the high risk of deafness, some of these poor puppies may be born blind or at the very least vision-impaired.

Anyone contemplating either doing such a breeding *or even buying a puppy from one* really needs to visit **www.amazingaussies.com,** home of a rescue organization dedicated to finding homes for abandoned white Australian Shepherds (most of whom are deaf or blind or both) to see the real-life results of this breeding combination.

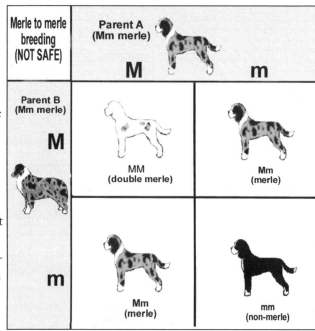

Merle to merle breeding (NOT SAFE)	Parent A (Mm merle)	
	M	m
Parent B (Mm merle) M	MM (double merle)	Mm (merle)
m	Mm (merle)	mm (non-merle)

Avoiding Potential Problems in Aussiedoodles

Although this all sounds pretty complicated and scary, avoiding problems with deafness and vision defects in Aussiedoodles is stunningly easy— breeders simply need to use *only* those Australian Shepherds and Poodles that conform to their respective AKC standards for breeding.

In fact, breeders who produce puppies out of correctly-marked Australian Shepherds and Poodles of any solid color (as shown below and in the photo at the beginning of the Chapter) have no real need to BAER test or CERF them, since the white these pups display is most likely caused by the gene for true Irish pattern and there is no evidence that this mutation is linked to either deafness or eye defects. And they can display all sorts of cool color variations.

If the Aussiedoodle is to move forward into the future healthy and problem-free, breeders really need to educate themselves *and prospective puppy-buyers* about the problems associated with merle and excessive white, rather than intentionally risking these problems just to satisfy market demand because puppy buyers think these white-headed puppies are "cute".

The wise and dedicated breeders who developed and nurtured their parent breeds over the years understood this, and deliberately selected away from piebald. And as more is discovered about these genes, it is pretty clear that Aussiedoodle breeders should *learn from them* rather than trying to "reinvent the wheel".

Now it is true that the UKC recently accepted parti-colored Poodles and many of them are winning in the UKC show ring. But this decision was made *prior* to the discovery that "parti-color" in the breed was caused by the same SINE mutation that causes piebald and deafness in so many others.

In a climate where the purebred dog fancy is under the gun for deliberately producing dogs with genetic defects simply because they like the "look" it produces, simply accepting parti-colors without a lot more study into the congenital defects associated with the various parti patterns may not have been a wise choice for UKC or the Poodle breed in the long run.

Parent A:
solid black, red, chocolate, silver, apricot, sable, phantom, or solid white

mm: non-merle (Solid/Solid)

Parent B
red or blue merle
with Irish trim

Mm: merle
(Irish/Irish)

	m	m
M	Mm	Mm
m	mm	mm

Any breeder inclined to dismiss the connection between white and deafness (as well as any buyer considering purchase of a mostly- white puppy who has not been BAER-tested) really needs to visit

www.deafdogatlas.com

This website contains literally *thousands* of photos of deaf dogs in dozens of breeds, along with their owners' stories. You can click on the interactive map and probably find some near you.

The first thing you'll notice is that nearly all of them are white. And although some are double merles, many are simply EXTREME PIEBALDS in breeds where merle does not exist.

Many of these dogs have been remarkably successful in spite of their handicaps— some are certified therapy dogs, some have Agility titles, and many more are well-loved family pets.

But in the overwhelming majority of cases, *the owners did not know the dog was deaf* when they bought him as a puppy or adopted him from a Rescue organization, nor did most know that deafness can be linked to lack of pigmentation until it was explained to them by their veterinarian. (And many of these dogs ended up in Rescue because their original owners could not cope with a "special needs" dog. Many deaf dogs end up euthanized for lack of a home.)

Can these breeders really not KNOW, or they just dishonest?

Because many white breeds have been "hiding" their deafness problems for years, many probably don't know. Puppies born with partial or total deafness (and vision problems) compensate well in a litter— because they've never been able to hear or see well, they quickly learn to respond to vibrations and air currents (such as a door opening) that other puppies probably wouldn't notice, and they "key" off the other puppies, following them when they are called by the breeder. So unless the breeder is aware of the possibility of these puppies turning up, odds are they won't notice anything different about them.

Once the puppy is in his new home, however, he's going to be at a disadvantage (especially if he is the only dog in the house) and odds are the new owner will notice something is a little off. Even then, it's amazing how many people do not immediately consider deafness or poor vision as a possibility!

The ONLY reliable test for hearing in a dog is a BAER test,
because it's the only test a smart and resourceful puppy cannot "cheat" on.

Painless and non-invasive (it's also used to test hearing on human babies) the BAER test measures electrical impulses much like an EKG. (More information on BAER testing is included in the Health chapter, and information on where to have it done is in the Resources section.)

Now, aside from the perils of doubling up on the merle and piebald genes, there are a few other colors that appear in Aussiedoodles that present **NO** problems at all when they appear in F1 puppies, but may present problems when doing multigenerational breedings. *(This is why in the Aussiedoodle, multigenerational breedings should really be left to those breeders with a lot of background in color genetics and a willingness to spend a lot of money on color-gene testing, as well as BAER and CERF testing.)*

Sable, which is really a pattern and not a color, exists in both the Australian Shepherd and Poodle breeds although neither breed allows it in their standard— Poodles because they have taken a draconian approach and allow for *no* patterns and Aussies because it can "muddy" or totally mask merle.

Sable puppies generally start out quite dark and lighten with maturity, as the darker pigment granules sort of "work their way" toward the end of the hair shaft, finally disappearing completely. (Sometimes, the merle pattern will become obvious at this point.) But any way you slice it, what color sable puppies ultimately end up is often hard to predict, although fawn is most common, and some "apricot" poodles are actually sable.

The other color that will mask merle is the e/e red, which may be any shade from cream through apricot to red, depending on other modifying genes. This mutation is common in Poodles.

There are no known health issues associated with either sable or e/e reds and yellows– they are attractive puppies and add to the wonderful rainbow of colors in the breed.

The ONLY danger here lies in multigenerational breedings, where both may mask merle (as shown at right) causing the appearance of double merle puppies, some of whom will be hearing and vision -impaired.

For this reason, any red/gold/apricot or sable Aussiedoodles should *really* be color-tested for merle prior to breeding.

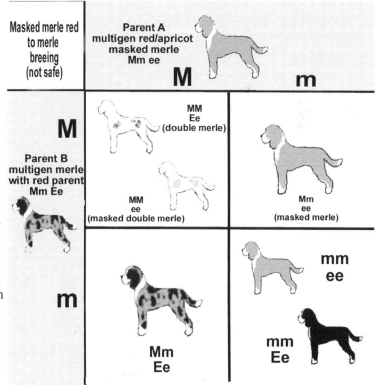

Harlequin

Another pattern that may appear in Aussiedoodles is harlequin. Harlequin looks a lot like piebald, but the patches tend to be irregular and have a "torn" appearance around the edges. The patches may be black or merle, and in Aussies and collies they often appear as fairly large individual patches of various shades of the base color.

Australian Shepherds have long recognized the harlequin pattern in their breed, although it is disqualified because it usually causes what appear to be lacey white "ribbons" on the body coat, and white has always been disallowed on the body in Australian Shepherds in order to reduce the number of "pattern whites" (extreme piebald).

And additionally, parti-colored Poodles in Europe have long been called harlequins. Genetically, some of the odder-looking parti-colored Poodles patterns actually may be caused by the harlequin gene, especially in lines that also produce merles, but at this point it really is not known.

The gene mutation responsible for harlequin in Great Danes was recently identified by the Clark lab at Clemson University, and other breeds in which it occurs are now being studied. However, it appears that, unlike merle, the causative mutation for harlequin may actually be unique to each breed in which it occurs.

Genetically, harlequin coat patterning results from the interaction of the harlequin mutation and the merle mutation Harlequin is essentially a dominant modifier of merle that removes the dilute pigment, leaving the background white. Harlequin Danes are all Mm Hh— without merle, the harlequin pattern cannot display itself.

But here is what breeders NEED TO KNOW:

Although a single copy of harlequin is not associated with any known genetic defects in Danes (where it has been well-studied) other than pigment-related deafness, the harlequin mutation is *dominant* and it only takes one copy (Hh) to produce the pattern in a merle dog. And HH is not viable.

In the homozygous state, the harlequin mutation is "embryonic lethal", which means all HH puppies will die in the womb before they are born.

In Aussiedoodles at least, harlequins should only be bred to *non-merle solids* who are not themselves carrying a copy of the harlequin gene. Because it also removes a lot of pigment, combining the harlequin mutation with white-producing mutations on the MITF gene is simply asking for trouble.

OK, we've covered a lot of information here, and because coat and color genetics are complicated, it's pretty easy to feel a little confused and overwhelmed by it all.

So let's summarize it, and see what the "take home" message is for the average puppy buyer:

- Aussiedoodles are typically *hypoallergenic,* but not *non-allergenic.*

- Because they shed very little, Aussiedoodles will require a fair amount of brushing.

- All dogs shed some, unless they are totally bald.

- Even totally bald dogs can provoke an allergic response.

- There's a LOT more to color and pattern in Aussiedoodles than just what's cutest.

- The more white on a parti-colored puppy's head, the higher his risk of deafness.

- Blue eyed white puppies are statistically most likely to have hearing and vision defects.

- Mostly white and blue-eyed puppies should be BAER-tested and CERFed prior to sale.

- Nobody should deliberately breed merle to merle because it is simply unethical.

- Aussiedoodles are NOT a good choice for "low-budget" commercial or novice breeders.

- Because his color and pattern can affect his quality of life, it is important to find an Aussiedoodle breeder who understands color genetics.

- Solid-colored Aussiedoodle puppies (of any color) with or without white trim are LEAST likely to suffer from hearing and visions defects. They are also very cute.

- Because so many Poodles carry the dominant "silvering" gene, most black Aussiedoodle puppies will actually end up silver as adults.

CHAPTER THREE:

Finding that Perfect Puppy
(or...gosh, where do I start?)

It is an unfortunate truth that puppy buyers as a whole put a lot more time (and a whole lot more research!) into choosing the RIGHT BREED than they put into choosing the RIGHT PUPPY.
Once they've done their research and decided that a particular breed fits the needs of their family, way too many otherwise intelligent people immediately go out and buy the first available puppy of that breed that they find on the internet as if they were all cranked out at the same factory like iPads, and all you had to worry about was price, color, availability and shipping costs.

This is a *really* big mistake.

As is true in any other breed, all Aussiedoodle puppies are NOT created equal, nor are all the breeders producing them. Your odds of getting the "right puppy"– ideally a healthy, happy, east-to-train fellow that's going to end up with the looks, coat and temperament you want – are really pretty dependent upon choosing the *right breeder*, since the breeder is really the "manufacturer" here, and the breeder's kennel name is really their "brand name". The breed itself is more general— deciding on an Aussiedoodle rather than a Goldendoodle is more like choosing a netbook over a full-sized laptop...there's still lots of quality differences within each category!

Unfortunately, given the current market situation, finding the right breeder can be daunting. *But not impossible* .

As is true in any breed, all Aussiedoodle puppies are NOT created equal, nor are all breeders– especially if you know what to look for. What's amazing is how many otherwise savvy consumers *don't*.

So let's look first at what you *definitely want to avoid*:

Pet Shops

Buying a dog from a pet shop is a poor choice on many levels. It does not allow you to see the parents or to get any sort of idea how the puppy was raised in the critical early weeks of his life, both of which are important factors that affect things like temperament and trainability.

It also keeps substandard breeders in business, because no matter what the nice kids in the pet shop tell you, responsible breeders do *not* sell their puppies through pet shops. Only the bottom-feeders of the dog-breeding world sell puppies wholesale. Because of that, you'll also want to avoid:

Virtual Pet Shops (aka Online Dog Brokers).

Buyers who want to avoid pet shops usually end up looking on the internet, where the odds are the first puppies they will find will be offered for sale in *virtual pet shops*, otherwise known as *dog brokers*.

The main difference between traditional brick-and-mortar pet shops
and their virtual counterparts is that in the latter case,
most people don't realize that they are buying from one.

And because these guys usually have cleverly-designed websites and pay top-dollar for website optimization, they pop up at the top of the results on an internet search for *almost any breed*. How to avoid them? Here are a couple of clues that should tip you off that you're really visiting an online pet store:

Clue # 1

The first clue is that they have a LOT of breeds available. With very few exceptions, responsible breeders rarely have more than a couple breeds at most, and more often only one.

This is because all breeds are different, and have different temperaments and different genetics (just look at the chapter on color!) and very few people can absorb all they need to know about a whole bunch of breeds to do a good job with them all.

But since these guys are not actually breeding these puppies themselves, they can offer *dozens* of breeds. And they often do.

Clue #2

The second clue is that they ONLY display "staged" photos of adorable puppies...there are never any parent dogs in evidence, and you never see pictures of their houses or lawns, even as natural background...usually the puppies are displayed on cutsie baby blankets with seasonal props.

 In fact, if you visit their sites repeatedly, you may notice that the same puppy photos often appear over and over, with different names attached – this month's "Freddy" may well be next month's "Phoebe". And some of these pictures are actually swiped from other websites, honest to God, which means you're actually getting a totally different puppy than the cutie you fell in love with.

Just like the brick-and-mortar pet shops, these guys are buying puppies wholesale from commercial breeders and selling them retail – *they're just less honest about it*. And unlike a neighborhood pet shop, they don't have any ties to the community – in fact, since the puppies are often drop-shipped from the breeder, it's often pretty hard to figure out just where on the planet they are located. (The largest one in the US is based in Florida but their puppies are dropped-shipped from all over the country.)

And because of a glitch in the law, there are no USDA inspections or even bare-minimum standards for the care and condition of their dogs, as are required for breeders who sell to pet shops.

These guys are the worst of the worst, and unfortunately they practically OWN the internet when it comes to online puppy sales. Steer clear of them. You want to deal only with a real breeder.

Sorting Out the "Real" Breeders

OK, so what you want to find is a BREEDER, which in simple legal terms means the person selling you the puppy is the same person who owns the parents and bred and raised the litter.

But because they come in all stripes, and all advertise in pretty much the same places, even after you actually locate a couple you're still not home free, because along with responsible breeders (which is what we are looking for) a lot of breeders who advertise puppies on the internet or in newspapers are what we might euphemistically call SUBSTANDARD BREEDERS.

 These substandard breeders may be actual puppy mills, or they may be smaller home-based breeders, but either way they represent the worst of dog-breeding.

Buying a puppy directly from a substandard breeding operation either in person or over the internet because you feel sorry for him (which some kindhearted people actually admit to doing) may SEEM like a kindness but in the long run it's entirely counterproductive – every puppy purchased for this reason ensures that another one will be produced right behind him.

Buying a puppy from a substandard breeder because **you didn't realize you were dealing with one** is really no better because the end result is the same, but unfortunately this happens a lot more often. And thanks to the internet, it's getting more frequent every year.

The scary truth is this: ANY dog breeder can make himself look good on the internet.

No matter how irresponsible or downright awful they may be, absolutely *no one* advertises themselves as an irresponsible breeder.

Absolutely no *one runs* an internet ad for puppies explaining that they're just cranking out puppies to make a quick buck, even if they really *are* just cranking out puppies to make a quick buck.

And absolutely *no one* runs an internet ad for puppies explaining that their puppies are whelped and raised in an unused chicken coop out back, even if they *are* whelped and raised in an unused chicken coop out back.

Nope, what substandard breeders invariably tell the buying public is this:
"We raise dogs as a family hobby."
"Our pups are raised underfoot with lots of love."
"Our pups get lots of socialization playing with our kids/grandkids."
"Our dogs and puppies are health-checked by our vet."
"Our puppies are de-wormed and are current on all vaccinations." ...and my personal favorite:
"Our puppies come pre-spoiled", which is ironically true in ways these breeders do not even under-stand...and about as intelligent as selling pre-spoiled groceries.

The problem with all this, of course, is that a whole lot of perfectly responsible breeders say a lot of the same things. (Of course, the big difference is they're probably telling the truth.) But by itself, this list does not guarantee or even indicate you're dealing with a responsible breeder, and if that's all they've got, it's a big red flag and you'd do better to look elsewhere.

Buying Local

The "buy local" movement is gaining purchase in the US, and whether one is looking at produce or puppies, it has much to commend it on several levels, not the least of which it is environmentally sound.

The absolutely best way to determine if a breeder's advertising is an honest representation of their breeding practices or a total load of horse manure is to simply GO THERE, meet the parent dogs and see where and how their puppies are raised. This gets a whole lot easier if the breeder lives within an hour or two of you.

(Do bear in mind that, though, that breeders are generally busy and do NOT run petting zoos!)

You can find out if you and the breeder "click", which is important if you consider your puppy's breeder to be your first resource when it comes to advice in the first year or so, which you should.

You can just drive over and pick your puppy up when he's ready to go home without worrying about the time and costs involved in getting him from one end of the country to another.

And, even best of all, if several or all the puppies in a litter end up in the same area, they can get together for play days and "Doodle Romps" and their owners can take turns pet sitting for each other when needed.

Unfortunately, finding a breeder nearby is a lot harder than it used to be back when people advertised puppies for sale in their local newspaper, and it's *amazing* how many people buy a puppy from another state only to find out later there's a great breeder right in their own city. This is one of the places where the internet has just *not* been an improvement, but we're stuck with it, so the internet it is.

Now, before you begin your internet search for a local breeder, you need to be VERY careful. And here's why:

If you Google " *your-state's-name-followed by any breed's name- puppies for sale*", or anything even remotely like that, I will guarantee you that most of the websites that pop up will actually be the above-mentioned dog brokers **masquerading as local breeders.**

These bandits have collectively purchased **thousands** of those domain names, in every breed and including every state and major metro area in the domain name itself. **(According to an investigation launched by HSUS, one Florida-based broker alone owns over 800 of these "local" domain names and ships a reported 20,000 puppies a year.)**

In a masterful marketing move, these commercial brokers swarmed in like a plague of locusts early on with a lot of capital and now practically own the internet when it comes to online puppy searches. Caveat Emptor.

Where to Look

Two places to find real local breeders on the internet are EBay Classifieds and Puppysites.com, both of which list breeders within a couple of hours driving time based on your zip code. Some of these breeders will be good and some will probably be awful, but at least you can drive over and check them out your veryownself. And at least they'll all be within driving distance.
Puppysites.com allows you to choose the breed first and then lists breeders by distance from you, while EBay Classifieds sorts entirely by city instead of breed, which means you'll have to plow through all the Bulldogs and Schnauzers and rescue Greyhounds and shelter dogs also listed in your area to find the Aussiedoodles.

If you can't find a local breeder you're comfortable with that way, you'll have to widen your search, and you'll probably end up buying a puppy sight-unseen from a breeder over the internet. And in spite of the perils, the internet can be a useful tool for finding a good breeder you are confident buying sight-unseen from… as long as you know what to look for.
So what SHOULD you look for?

Redefining "Responsible Breeder"

There's a lot of information on the internet defining what constitutes responsible dog breeding, but most of the time what you're really getting is someone's personal opinion, and usually that person is a longtime purebred dog show enthusiast. In other words, a "show breeder".

Serious show breeders (who may or may not also be responsible breeders) generally "breed for themselves", and to give them their due, very few are in it to make a profit—in fact, breeding good show dogs is right up there with compulsive gambling as far as a money-loser goes.
"Showing" dogs is really their hobby and the show breeder generally only breeds in order to produce another show dog – a dog which will do a lot of winning in the ring, finish to its championship and then be added to their breeding program.
A lot of them honestly believe that producing a litter of puppies for ANY other reason is irresponsible if not downright unethical, and are not shy about saying so.

Although many of them are also concerned with health and temperament, show breeders are primarily breeding for **conformation to the standard of their breed** – in other words, their breeding decisions are largely based on looks, which is really what the sport of breeding show dogs is all about. The ultimate goal in this sport (above and beyond winning) is to produce a dog that perfectly conforms to its written standard.

Of course, since breeding dogs is an inexact science at best, all puppies in a litter are statistically unlikely to be "show quality". Those puppies which do not closely match the written standard of their breed (which can include such minutia as the actual number of teeth in its mouth, a spot of white on its chest or the desired shade of brown in the iris of the eye) or do not have the "look at me" personality required of a successful show dog are sold as pets.

If the show breeder is responsible, these pups will be well-socialized and come from health-screened parents with sound temperaments and will be sold on spay/neuter contracts, where minor conformation flaws will probably not even be noticed. (The loss of a big chunk of this pet market to hybrids produced entirely as pets is the major reason show breeders loathe the new "designer breeds", by the way. Without a ready pet market for their non-show quality pups, show breeders cannot breed.)

It should be pretty obvious by now that if you're looking for an Aussiedoodle (or any other hybrid for that matter) a lot of the information provided by dog show enthusiasts on what constitutes responsible breeding just doesn't apply – hybrids do not have dog shows, or written standards to adhere to or argue over, or even National Parent Clubs with a written Code of Ethics for the breeder to belong to.

Unlike show dogs, hybrids are produced exclusively as companions and service animals, and conformation to a detailed physical standard is less important than a good temperament, trainability, soundness, health and longevity, all of which also are (or at least should be) important to show breeders but are frankly not that upon which they ultimately base their breeding decisions.

Decades out of Date

And a lot of the criteria for responsible breeding laid forth with such certainty by show breeders is frankly out of date even if you are looking for a purebred, because the sport is graying rapidly and so most of them are, well….*OLD*…and haven't exactly kept up with the technological advances of the modern world.

A spectacular example of this is found on one of the many "How to Identify a Responsible Breeder" websites out there, which states unequivocally *(*and I swear I am not making this up) that "only puppy mills accept Paypal", and so acceptance of Paypal should be considered a red flag.

Excuse me????

With the exception of Amazon, pretty much the whole WORLD takes Paypal, and how accepting only handwritten checks sent via snail mail could somehow make one a more responsible breeder simply defies the imagination.

(Actually, when it comes to payment, the only *real* red flag is the breeder who accepts "cash only", because odds are pretty good they've got some issues with the IRS and you've got little recourse if things go south… don't go there.)

So, with all that in mind and without further ado, here's what you need to look for to find a responsible breeder of Aussiedoodles on the internet:

Look for reviews…and get recommendations

One of the greatest advances of the twenty-first century surely came from Amazon. In fact, it's completely revolutionized the way America makes its collective purchasing decisions. You guessed it….it's the consumer review. And it's the best thing that's ever happened to puppy buyers.

Many breeders' websites now have testimonial letters from previous puppy buyers, with accompanying photos of said puppies all grown up in their new homes, which is pretty cool. But don't assume that's enough by itself, because the brokers also now have "testimonials" from buyers on their websites as well. Are they real? Hard to tell. But a responsible breeder will also provide you with names and contact information for people who own their puppies if you ask.

Some breeders also have forums for their puppy owners set up either on their own websites or on one of the big Doodle sites that anyone can read. Since logic tells us these would be pretty hard to fake unless one had a ridiculous amount of time on one's hands, they're probably worth checking out.

Bottom line is this: No matter what breeders say about themselves or their dogs, it's not going to be nearly as useful as what people who actually own the puppies they've bred have to say.

Now it goes without saying that breeders who've been at it the longest, and those who've produced a lot of puppies, are going to have more puppy owners out there than those who breed less frequently, so don't assume tons of references are automatically better than a few– this is one of those "quality-over-quantity" issues. But even breeders who do not produce enough puppies to maintain a forum for their puppy buyers should be able to give you recommendations.

Responsible Breeders are Knowledgeable

Let's face it, anybody can put two dogs together and produce puppies. But whether the puppies are destined for the show ring or service work or primarily as companions, breeding healthy, physically and mentally sound dogs requires a knowledge base.

This is ESPECIALLY true with Aussiedoodles, because unlike many hybrids, there are a lot of potential genetic problems in this breed that will not be magically erased by "hybrid vigor".

If breeders do not even know the potential for a problem exists, how can they assure buyers their puppies won't be affected? **When producing hybrids, a responsible breeder is knowledgeable about *the health issues in its parent breeds*, and current on research regarding them.**

There are also a wealth of books on canine structure and anatomy, genetics, behavior, health and reproduction available to the aspiring breeder to expand their knowledge base, and responsible breeders will avail themselves of them.
Even longtime breeders need to keep up, as what we knew "for a fact" 20 years ago may have recently been discovered to be totally wrong—molecular genetics has altered a lot of the dog world's knowledge base, and not only in the genetics of color.

One quick way to tell if a breeder is knowledgeable is by the terminology that they use. Dog-breeding, like medicine, engineering, law or any other discipline, has its own terminology, especially as regards canine anatomy, and knowledgeable breeders are familiar with it.

Just as you'd be hesitant to hire a contractor who called his hammer a "pounder", a puppy buyer should be hesitant about turning over his cash to a breeder who thinks a brood bitch is called a "dame" rather than a "dam", or that the physiology of a dog is its "confirmation" instead of its "conformation.", or who thinks a dog with substance has "good boning". Or above all (OK this one really drives me crazy) one who thinks that a dog's nose is attached to its "snout". **Dogs don't HAVE snouts, pigs do**. Dogs have "muzzles".

If a breeder is too lazy to learn basic canine structure and terminology, odds are they don't know much about genetics or health-screening or socialization, either.

Responsible breeders provide information on the parents.

The laws of genetics being what they are, the parents of any particular puppy, even a hybrid, offer the best clues about how it's likely to turn out. **Ideally, photos of the parents and information about**

.In most Aussiedoodles, the following screenings should ideally be performed prior to breeding. More information on this can be found in the Health Chapter and Resources section.

CERF exam.

Performed by a Board-certified canine ophthalmologist, this will exclude any genetic ocular diseases present *at the time of exam*. And although some hereditary eye diseases (like cataracts) may not show up until a dog is long past breeding age, **most of the hereditary ocular defects found in Aussiedoodles are there from birth.**

Because of this, a one-time CERF exam prior to breeding (actually at 8-10 weeks is best) can be performed to exclude any hereditary vision-impairing congenital eye defects (specifically colobomas and less commonly CEA) which may be passed to the offspring, and mostly white puppies should ideally be examined and cleared prior to sale.

Along with colobomas, cataracts are the most common *independently inherited* (meaning they are not connected to merle or piebald) eye problem in Australian Shepherds and the gene mutation responsible has recently been identified. **The mutation (on a gene called HDF4) is dominant.** This means dogs who inherit even *one copy* will likely develop cataracts at some point in their lives (some as early as a year and others not until age 9 or 10), and will pass the gene to half their offspring. **A gene test is now available for this mutation,** and hopefully Aussiedoodle breeders will begin to test their breeding stock, so puppy buyers won't have to worry about their pets going blind from hereditary cataracts.

BAER test

Congenital Hereditary Sensineural Deafness (also called Cochlear Nerve Deafness) is associated with the merle and piebald genes and definitely exists in the Aussiedoodle. (And hybrid vigor *will not* reduce the incidence.)

It is estimated that for every bilaterally deaf dog identified there are 2-3 unilaterally deaf dogs in the gene pool, most of whom are never identified, so breeding dogs should ideally be tested.

Some breeders automatically BAER test their parti-colored or mostly white puppies prior to sale, but they are frankly in the minority in this breed. *Buyers should really request this.* (Solid-colored Aussiedoodles, whether merle or not, are at lowest risk for either ocular or hearing problems and usually do not need to be screened prior to sale.)

The test is known as the *brainstem auditory evoked response* (BAER) It detects electrical activity in the cochlea and auditory pathways in the brain in much the same way that an EKG detects the electrical activity of the heart. The test takes about 5 minutes and is both painless and noninvasive. It can be performed on puppies as young as 5 weeks without anesthesia.

Cardiac exam.

Performed after a year of age, this will rule out congenital heart defects like SAS (subvalvular aortic stenosis) a hereditary disease which occurs in Poodles, one of the Aussiedoodle's parent breeds. Virtually all congenital heart defects can be ruled out by *auscultation,* which means a vet simply checks the heart with a stethoscope and signs a form certifying the heart is normal. It's the cheapest and least invasive of all health screenings one can perform prior to breeding. All puppies should be checked by auscultation prior to sale, with the results (in writing) given to the buyer.

Each test only needs to be performed once in a dog's life. And since the cost of totally health-screening a breeding dog is far less than the price of a single puppy, there's really no reason for a breeder NOT to do it. (And frankly, it's not like hybrid breeders have to plow their puppy-sale profits back into campaigning their breeding dogs to their championships as show breeders do.)

Temperament:

Since temperament is every bit as heritable as health, responsible breeders also provide information about the parents' temperaments and personalities. And any owner should be able to come up with something a little more informative than "Sadie is a real sweetheart and loves belly-rubs". Does Sadie love to retrieve? Does she like kids? Is she quiet or exuberant? Outgoing or cautious with strangers? Quick to learn? Willing to please? High or low energy? These are all heritable traits.

Responsible Aussiedoodle breeders do NOT deliberately breed merle to merle, nor do they use double merles for breeding.

Some Aussiedoodle breeders are using MM (double merles) for breeding, because when bred to a non-merle, they will produce 100% Mm merles. Although the resulting puppies do not generally have the severe defects associated with double merle, the litter that produced the MM parent certainly did. Where are the rest of the puppies from *that* litter?

Even worse, many of these breeding dogs (referred to by some breeders as "gold mines") have vision and hearing defects themselves, although they are rarely BEAR-tested or CERFed because frankly the breeder does not want to know.

Forcing a handicapped bitch to whelp and raise a litter (among other problems, a deaf bitch cannot hear her own puppies crying) just so the breeder can sell more merle puppies at top dollar is beyond unethical and borders on animal cruelty. No matter how much you want a merle puppy, do NOT help keep these unethical breeders in business by purchasing from them.

Responsible breeders have a sales contract.

Every breeder should provide one, and usually they are posted on their website. If it's not, ask for a copy prior to putting down a deposit. Sales contracts assure that both the breeder and the buyer understand and agree on what will be done in any contingency that may arise both prior to and after sale of the puppy. Read through these carefully before committing yourself to a puppy, because they are NOT all the same, and the devil is in the details

Deposits:

Most breeders accept deposits to hold a puppy, and some to hold a place in line on an upcoming litter. Some are refundable if they cannot provide a puppy meeting your requirements within a specified time, and some are flat-out non-refundable for any reason whatsoever.

Few if any breeders will refund a deposit if you've simply changed your mind, nor should they be expected to. Putting down deposits with several breeders and then expecting to have all but one refunded once you've made up your mind is a *really bad idea* – don't do it. Many breeders plan their breedings based on the number of deposits in hand, and even if they don't return the deposits they've probably turned away puppy buyers if they assume a litter is all spoken for.

Payment:

More and more breeders are now requiring that you pay in full prior to picking up your puppy, sometimes weeks in advance. (The *reason* they are now doing this is explained in the preceding paragraph.) If you choose to go this route, make sure the contract allows for a "back-out" clause in case things don't work out as planned.

More and more breeders now accept Paypal, which is safe and convenient for both buyer and seller; usually the seller is asked to pay the points for this convenience. Some breeders accept personal checks and others prefer certified checks– it is best to find out ahead of time.

But do beware of the breeder who ONLY accepts cash....that really IS a red flag.
(I mean...*really*...what are the possible reasons here for avoiding a paper trail? Trouble with the IRS? There's a warrant out for their arrest? Maybe they're in the Federal Witness Protection Program?) If something goes wrong, you'll have little recourse if you only paid cash.

Responsible breeders provide a health warranty.

Each one is different, so read them carefully.

Some breeders will guarantee only against "life-threatening" genetic defects, which sounds good, but should be considered carefully in this breed. What if you pay $1,200 for a puppy and then find out he's totally deaf? No vet would consider that life-threatening. A contract that covers only life-threatening defects is in reality not providing much of a warranty at all.

Some contracts require that you return the puppy prior to replacement or reimbursement for medical costs (like surgery) associated with a genetic defect. The breeder is really counting on the fact that you won't do this, and most states' Puppy Lemon Laws don't require it. (State consumer laws supersede individual contracts.) Currently, 19 states have enacted specific Puppy Lemon Laws; in others, buyers may be protected under the state's consumer protection laws, but there may be a filing fee required.

Responsible breeders take dogs back.

All responsible breeders are concerned with the welfare of puppies they've bred even after they have been sold, and will take them back and/or assist in rehoming them if the owner cannot keep them for any reason at any time in the dog's life. Some will reimburse the owner for part of the purchase price while others do not. (The breeder's policies in this regard should be clearly stated in writing.)

But beware *anyone* who is unwilling to offer a place in their home to any dog whose existence they've called into being, because *they are the people responsible for dogs ending up in shelters.* In fact, don't buy a puppy from them.

Responsible breeders only own as many dogs as they can take care of.

There is really no correct number here – it depends entirely upon the breeder's resources. But a responsible breeder keeps only as many dogs as they can appropriately house, health-screen, socialize, exercise, groom and provide professional routine veterinary care for.

With dogs the size of Aussiedoodles, this very likely means that if they have more than a couple dogs they'll have some kind of "kennel" setup, although most breeders do not post photos of their kennel on their website, which is really too bad.

Contrary to popular belief, kennels are NOT a bad thing. They allow dogs to get adequate fresh air and exercise, both of which are critical to their health and well-being, and they get to interact naturally with other dogs (i.e. without human intervention), which is critical to their well-being.

Kenneled dogs should be clean, well-groomed, well-socialized and friendly, and the kennel runs themselves should be safe, clean, well-shaded with plantings and surfaced with something like pea rock or pavers so they may be easily cleaned. And you should be able to see it, even if the breeder doesn't want you mucking around in there petting everybody and spreading germs, which is understandable.

Some Aussiedoodle breeders use "guardian homes" for some of their breeding dogs, which is generally a win/win situation. The best pups are placed in nearby pet homes. When they are old enough and have passed their health-screening they come back to the breeder's home to be bred and (in the case of females) whelp a litter or two, after which time they are spayed and spend the rest of their lives as pets in the same home they started out in. This system allows the breeder to maintain more genetic diversity in their line than they would under the traditional breeding system (where genetic diversity is often limited by the number of dogs a breeder can practically keep) and it's a terrific deal for the dogs themselves, who get more individual attention than they would at the breeder's home. In fact, in a society where most people are restricted by law or practicality in the number of dogs they are allowed to own, the "guardian home system" probably represents the future of dog breeding.

Responsible breeders ask YOU questions.

Responsible breeders will either ask you to fill out an application or will conduct a phone interview (or both) prior to accepting a deposit. They will ask lots of questions about your living situation, the hours that you work, and your family. Because they want their puppies to be successful in life, they want to find out in advance if one of their puppies is likely to be a good fit for your family situation, and will tell you flat-out if they don't think it is. An irresponsible breeder will ask no questions and take anyone's money.

Responsible breeders provide ongoing support.

Responsible breeders are there 24/7 to answer questions, no matter how dumb they may be, for the life of the dog. They provide *written instructions* for things like vaccination, worming, housebreaking, early training, grooming and all the other things you need to know to get off to a good start. And they are available for advice at any hour by phone in an emergency. Do not, under any circumstances, buy a puppy from a breeder who will not provide you with his/her personal phone number—odds are, there's a good reason **why**.

Responsible breeders want you to come and pick up your puppy.

This one is probably the most important of all, and a lot of people get it wrong. Because of the possibility of infectious diseases like distemper and parvo, most breeders cannot allow their home or kennel to be used as a petting zoo by everyone considering the possible purchase of a puppy. In fact, some breeders only allow those puppy buyers who actually have a deposit on a puppy to visit after the puppies have received their first vaccinations for this reason. But you should never buy a dog from a breeder who will not allow you on the premises to pick up your puppy. NEVER.

Before you plunk down a single red cent (and even if the breeder is half a continent away), *always* ask if you can come and pick up the puppy. If the breeder demurs and immediately offers to ship or meet you *anywhere* other than their home, they have not just raised a red flag… *they've hoisted the JOLLY ROGER,* and odds are pretty good you're dealing with a pirate.

Breeders may ask you to remove your shoes, or wash your hands, but they will *not* keep you from entering their homes, or seeing the whole litter, or the mother, or the area where the dogs live, even if it's from a "safe" distance.

Responsible breeders do not hand puppies over to their new owners
and collect payment for them in the Wal-Mart parking lot.
They just don't.

OK, now that you have enough information to sort out the many, many (many!) Aussiedoodle breeders out there and narrow it down to the good ones, you're down to finding one with whom you "click", and whose expectations match your own.

Some breeders really encourage their puppy buyers to stay in close contact, and buying a puppy from one of them immediately makes you " family". (These are most likely to be breeders of the "puppy-lover" variety and often maintain forums and e-lists for their buyers.) Others are there for you if you have a question or problem, and certainly welcome updates and photographs, but assume you already have enough friends and family.

Neither is intrinsically better than the other; it's really a matter of personal preference.

Choosing the Right Puppy

Choosing a good breeder makes choosing the right puppy in a litter a whole lot easier, because you will have what amounts to professional help, but there's a lot you can do to help the breeder in this regard.

Dispelling the "pick of the litter" myth.

If one phrase should disappear from the world of dogs, that phrase should be "pick of the litter." Unless one is looking for a show dog, THERE IS NO SUCH THING. (Even then it's pretty dicey – many a Westminster Winner over the years was "third-pick puppy" in his litter!)

Since puppies are in essence fraternal rather than identical twins, every puppy in a given litter is going to be a little different, in both looks and personality. As with human siblings, one puppy is invariably going to be the liveliest, one the smartest, one the most assertive, and one the most easy-going.

A good breeder will spend time interviewing each new owner either in person or by phone and will try to match each puppy with the family into which he best fits.

For example, the most assertive puppy is probably not the best choice for a family with very young children. The "genius puppy" in a litter is probably not the best choice for an owner who is not all that interested in doing a lot of training – remember, in general, the higher the puppy's IQ, the more challenging training him will be. The liveliest puppy is not the best choice for the more sedentary owner.

A good breeder has spent a lot of time with the puppies by the time they are 7 weeks old, which is really when neurological development is pretty much complete in the canine and its innate personality is revealed. What the owner sees in an hour's visit may not be reality at all – for example, the "live-wire" puppy may simply be tired at that point from running around all morning and give a pretty good impression of Mr. Mellow, which will change once he gets home and has a chance to recharge his little batteries.

Choosing a puppy based on photographs is not a great idea either.

The most PHOTOGENIC puppy in a litter—the guy who mugs for the camera and is so cute you could just scoop him up right off your screen – is almost guaranteed to be the most challenging, while the one who looks a little like he's facing a firing squad is likely to be the easiest to live with. No one EVER believes me on this, by the way, but 40 years of taking puppy pictures has convinced me that I'm right. So if you want to live with the Mick Jagger of Aussiedoodles, go for it.

Color and gender are two other areas where people put more emphasis than they should when choosing a puppy.

No doubt about it, Aussiedoodles are a "color breed" and many buyers are attracted to them because of some of the flashy colors and patterns they can display.

But if you end up with a higher-energy puppy than you intended, or one whose personality is not a good match for your household, the particular pattern or color he displays is not going to matter much.

If a puppy you reserved based on color appears to be the wrong puppy for you based on temperament or energy level as they develop, a good breeder will advise you of this and may suggest a switch.

And if you really want an all-white dog, you'd frankly do better to choose a breed where the white coat is caused by something other than a double-dose of the piebald or merle genes and isn't associated with deafness and ocular disorders.

In the world of dogs, the majority of people who make a mistake that they later come to regret when choosing a puppy chose that puppy based on his color and not his personality. Shelters are unfortunately full of these dogs, and the internet has made it worse, because light-colored dogs simply photograph better than dark ones, who may actually be much cuter in person.

The same is true of gender. Individual temperament is much more important, and in the Aussiedoodle breed, there just isn't enough difference between males and females to figure into the equation. This is not generally a high-testosterone breed, and neutering removes most of what may exist naturally.

In the end, it's really best to explain your family situation, previous dog-owning (or child-rearing) experience and what sort of dog appeals to you and then let the breeder, who interacts with the puppies 24/7, choose the right puppy for you.

For reasons no one has really ever figured out, most good breeders have an intuitive gift for choosing the right puppies for each family. (Puppy owners will often attest to this, which is why it's good to read the reviews.) Maybe it's just part of being a good breeder.

But whatever the reason, when choosing which puppy is right for your family, it's really in the new owner's best interest to trust a good breeder's judgment.

A note of caution: The breeder who demands puppy buyers choose their puppy at birth based entirely on photographs of what look essentially like little slugs on a baby blanket is either lacking in experience or is primarily producing puppies for profit. In either case you may want to proceed carefully or better yet, "just slip out the back, Jack".

What About Price...?

Currently, the price of an Aussiedoodle puppy ranges anywhere from around $400 to maybe $2,000.

Although there are certainly exceptions (many breeders charge more for the flashier colors and patterns), by and large the differences in price reflect the differences in experience levels, breeding expertise, customer support provided and marketing skills that exist among breeders.

In general, puppies on the lowest end of the scale are mostly produced by substandard breeders, who are unlikely to do a lot of health-screening on the parents or early neurological stimulation in the puppies, both of which are critical. Nor are their breeding dogs likely to be high-quality animals. (Hybrid vigor cannot improve faulty structure, which can lead to orthopedic problems in the pups down the road.)

The exceptions to this rule are the slick online brokers, who are essentially selling $400 puppies produced by substandard breeders for thousands of dollars because of their deceptive advertising practices.
And beware the breeder who generally sells their puppies cheap but charges extra for "rare" blue eyes. In this breed blue eyes are not particularly rare and in some cases may come with serious vision deficits. No one should buy a blue-eyed puppy with a mostly white head unless he has had a CERF and BAER exam prior to sale. If the breeder is unwilling to do this, or –even worse!— does not know what a CERF or BAER exam is, move on and look for a more knowledgeable one.

In the middle range are usually small home-based breeders who probably don't do a lot of screening for genetic disorders and may not be particularly knowledgeable about canine genetics.

On the plus side, as a general rule these puppies are raised in a clean environment (usually the kitchen and family room rather than an outbuilding that once held farm equipment or poultry) and get a lot of "casually administered early socialization", which is another way of saying they get picked up, cuddled, and played with quite a lot by the family, which is good.
In truth, most of America's pet dogs have traditionally been produced by pretty casual breeders, and in breeds where there are few genetic disorders, they often turn out fine. Unfortunately, this is not one of those breeds.

At the highest end are the breeders who put the most time, money and energy into their breeding program, and offer the greatest amount of support both prior to and after purchase.

Their breeding dogs are health-screened where needed and their puppies are put through the early neurological stimulation program in addition to extensive socialization and early training, all of which are critical in this breed.

These breeders may produce quite a lot of puppies in a year, or very few. Their dogs may be housedogs or they may have a kennel built for them. (Usually the ones who have more than 4 dogs and breed more litters will have a kennel for practical reasons, and that is perfectly fine.)

But either way, these breeders are the most knowledgeable, put the most time and money into their breeding programs, and for whom the whole project is primarily a labor of love.

Even if they charge more for each puppy, odds are they' re worth it. And odds are these breeders are also turning *less* of a profit than the ones who may charge less for a puppy but put very little back into their breeding programs.

In the Final Analysis....

When it comes to deciding how much you are willing to spend on the initial price of a puppy, it's always good to remember that the cost of the puppy is a mere drop in the bucket when compared to the lifetime cost of feeding, grooming and providing veterinary care for a dog.

And because of the genetic problems that may be inherited from the Australian Shepherd, responsibly -bred Aussiedoodles in particular are not inexpensive for breeders to produce when compared with other hybrids where such problems do not exist.

If you simply want a low-cost pet for the kids, get a guinea pig.

CHAPTER FOUR:

Being Prepared
(or...how to spend lots of money waiting for your puppy)

Now, odds are there may be some lag time between when you plunk down your deposit on a puppy that probably looks like one of the guys on the left and when you can actually bring him home.

This time can best be used for collecting the astonishing amount of equipment, supplies and assorted paraphernalia required for successful puppy management, getting your home ready for the new family addition, and learning what you need to know to make the transition as smooth as possible for everyone concerned.

Raising a Puppy the Way Nature Intended

At 8 weeks, a puppy of any breed is still pretty immature. It is important to understand that removing him from his mother and littermates at that age is *not* the natural course of events for a canine. In the wild, most wolf cubs commonly stay with their parents for up to a year and if resources permit, often for life. The same is true of foxes and coyotes – in most wild canids, packs are really extended families, and domestic dogs are still psychologically hard-wired for that lifestyle.

What we are doing when we "adopt" a puppy is taking an incredibly immature pack animal out of his natal pack and incorporating him into another *very different* pack – one that's comprised of members of another species altogether, and (unless there's another dog in the family) one where no one speaks his language nor shares the same social rules of the pack into which he was born. It's really a credit to the inherent adaptability of the dog that so many of them manage to do so well...just try to imagine for a moment how well the process would work in reverse!

Raising a puppy successfully is a lot easier
if we work *with* his psychological hard-wiring instead of *against* it.

In order to do that, we need to understand what Mother Nature intended, and the best way to do that is to look at how wolf cubs develop and are raised in the wild, and try to adapt that to our own situation, because that's also how *our* puppies are also hard-wired.

Wolf cubs are born in a den, and stay there for the first few weeks of life with their mother. She rarely leaves them during this time, and her food is provided by the litter's sire (usually the alpha male) who delivers it to her door, bless his heart. At 4 weeks or so, the cubs first toddle outside the den into the spring sunshine, where they are greeted enthusiastically by the entire pack. At this point, the litter is beginning to be weaned, and the other pack members provide regurgitated solid food for them.

When the cubs are around 8 weeks old (not coincidentally when neurological development in the canine is completed), the pack moves them from the den to a carefully chosen *rendezvous site* within the pack's territory where they will stay until they are 7-8 months old, at which time they are nearly full-grown and are ready to become full-fledged members of the pack.

During this time, they are usually left in the care of a babysitter (most often a young wolf from the pack of either gender) during the day, and alone when necessary. Their days are spent playing with "toys" and learning the skills they'll need to become useful functioning pack members. Food is still delivered to them, and they sleep with the pack at night. These rendezvous sites are chosen carefully by the pack, with the physical needs (like access to shallow water) and safety of the cubs given highest priority. They are taken on short outings as they grow, but are still largely confined to the rendezvous area until they are mature.

Because this method has worked so well for untold millennia, it simply makes sense to stick to it when raising our own puppies, who share over 99% of their DNA with their wolf ancestors, including those that determine neurological and psychological development.

This method also requires THE RIGHT STUFF in order to work.
Luckily, most of it can be purchased online, and a lot of it is available on Amazon.

This really beats the heck out of driving across town only to find they don't have what you need.

(And to save hours searching online, you can just go to **www.dianeklumb.com**, where a lot of it is actually pictured and items can be purchased directly from the suppliers with a single mouse click. If you're not already an Amazon Prime member, signing up before you buy will save you a fortune in shipping. How easy is THAT?)

Setting up the Rendezvous Area

When we bring an 8-10 week old pup home, what we need to do is transition from the "den with mom" to the next naturally-occurring phase, which is moving him to a *rendezvous area*. We are also moving him into a new pack, which is going to be fairly stressful for the first week or two.

The territory of this new pack comprises your entire house and yard, and at his age, your pup should not have the run of it any more than a wolf cub would in the wild, and for exactly the same reason – safety. It is absolutely astonishing how much trouble a puppy can get himself into if he is granted full territorial privileges before he's ready for them.

So what the new owner needs to do before the puppy arrives is decide which area of the house is going to be the *rendezvous site*, and plan on confining him to that area, (usually with baby gates or an ex pen) when he is unattended.

As in the wild, this area should be the place where the older pack members congregate to relax when they are not working. This will vary from family to family and depends upon the layout of the house, but it is usually the kitchen/family room area. In some homes, if it is directly off the kitchen and not isolated but can be blocked off with a gate, a laundry area can work. It should also include a corner for the puppy's crate, which is where he will sleep during the day, and a door that leads directly to the area (whether that is the back yard, a terrace or the sidewalk) where he will eliminate, so he can learn to go directly to the door to signal when he needs to go outside.

Never, ever use a bathroom or laundry room with the door shut- for a young pack animal, that constitutes psychological torture, plain and simple.

Pet Gates...An Absolute Necessity!

Since it is entirely counterproductive to give a young puppy free access to the entire "pack territory", this rendezvous area will need to be cordoned off with baby gates—how many you will need depends entirely upon layout. It should also have flooring other than carpeting for purely practical reasons.

With mini Aussiedoodle puppies, an "exercise pen" can serve as an excellent rendezvous area (and in fact is what your puppy was probably raised in at the breeder's), but a standard-sized dog will outgrow one within a couple of months, so you might want to consider borrowing one or check out yard sales.

Even if you use an ex pen, you'll still need gates, and there are really only two caveats when selecting them. The first is to only select from those made with vertical bars or fine mesh, with no horizontal crossbars between the top and the bottom. These are the only gates that are climb-proof and *nothing* is more discouraging than installing a new gate only to watch your puppy immediately scamper over it like an oversized squirrel. The second concerns height – there's not much purpose in a gate under 30 inches, and for the agile Aussiedoodle, 36-40 inches is even better.

That said, the choice of materials (plastic, wood or metal) and color is really up to the homeowner, and you might as well get something that isn't going to look downright ugly. Wood gates should be sprayed with bitter apple right off though, or they'll soon look like they've been attacked by demented beavers.

Some gates have walk-through doors, which make sense, and some have little "dog doors" built right in, which make considerably less sense, although I'm certain there is some purpose there that escapes obvious notice. Exactly where to put the gates is a matter of traffic flow- it's a good idea to figure this out and live with it for a while *before* the puppy arrives, because you may well decide to move it. Better to figure that out before he gets there than confuse him by rearranging it later.

Puppy-proofing

Once you've decided where the gates are going to go, everything inside that becomes the rendezvous area and needs to be *puppy-proofed*. The best way to do this is to remove everything that can potentially be dangerous or disassembled that's within three feet of the floor – electrical cords (there is an unknown magnetic force that attracts puppies to outlets with electrical cords plugged into them), houseplants, knickknacks, books, magazines, antiques, sporting equipment, electronics and basically anything else of value that you do not wish to have damaged or turned into confetti or woodchips by industrious puppy teeth.

Anything that cannot be removed (like the woodwork!) should be sprayed with bitter apple *before* the puppy sinks his teeth into it rather than after. So you'll want to put a spray bottle of Bitter Apple on your growing list of Things You Absolutely Need.

Although it sounds weird, the best way to puppy-proof is to get down on your knees, lay your forearms flat on the floor, and look around. You now have the puppy's view of his new world, and it's amazing what you'll see that you may have missed standing up.

Food and Water

The rendezvous site should also contain the puppy's water and food dishes because this is where he is going to eat. As with pretty much everything else, there's a wide variety from which to choose, ranging from the most utilitarian to the most decorative. (As you've probably figured out by now, the days when dog ownership required a dog house, a feed pan, a water bowl and a nice butcher's bone are long gone....of course, those were also the days when a kid owned one pair of shoes, used a bicycle to get everywhere he needed to go and got an orange in his Christmas stocking. Right.)

Choosing the Right Bowls and Dishes

The main considerations in choosing dog dishes are that they be durable, easy to clean (ideally you should be able to pop them in the dishwasher) and not easily tipped over. The kind with sloped sides and a non-slip base are a good choice, and stainless steel is far and away the easiest to keep clean, the least toxic, and the most durable. Some owners prefer the "double diner" dishes because they tend to keep the dishes tidily in one place- if you go this route, make sure the dishes are easily removable from the platform for cleaning.

One of the newest additions to the world of dog dishes are those designed to slow down the rate at which the dog inhales his food and water. (In the wild this is not a problem, because the wild canine has to work quite a bit harder for both his food and water.) The food dishes have raised areas that the dog has to work around in order to scarf up his kibble, which slows him down a bit and lessens the chances of post-prandial barfing and general indigestion. The water bowls have a sort of "float" inside that keeps the dog from submerging his entire muzzle and filling both his mouth and facial furnishings with water, much of which invariable ends up dripping onto the floor.

In addition to making less of a mess, both these dishes are a good choice for breeds that are susceptible to bloat, and both of the Aussiedoodle's parent breeds fall into that category, at least the ones on the larger end of the size continuum. Unfortunately, most of them seem to be made of plastic instead of stainless steel, which means if they are left with an unattended puppy they'll end up as chew toys.

Dog Food Storage

Unless you plan to prepare fresh home-cooked meals for your Aussiedoodle every day (which really is the healthiest option even though you probably won't do it), you will need something in which to store his dry dog food (AKA kibble) to avoid creating a fast-food drive-thru for the local rodentia, which is what will happen if you leave it in the bag.

The best choice here is probably a tall plastic dog food storage bin with a tight flip-top lid and little castors so you can roll it out to fill it. It is *not* a good idea to keep this in the rendezvous area, however, because even a toy-breed puppy with motivation and a set of industrious little teeth can turn a plastic storage bin into a self-feeder in no time flat by gnawing a hole in the bottom corner – the laundry room or pantry is a better choice. If you absolutely need a chewproof one, you can also get stainless steel model, but it will cost you about a hundred dollars more.

A "step-on" stainless kitchen garbage can will *not* work, just for the record— any Aussiedoodle worth his salt will quickly figure out that stepping on the lever turns it into an all-you-can-eat buffet, whether it's used for kibble or actual garbage. The "touchless" ones with infrared sensors? Pure magic for the hungry puppy! (You may also want to keep this in mind when you're puppy-proofing your kitchen...the uber-intelligence of the Aussiedoodle does have its downsides…)

Yes, you DO need a crate!

No matter what PETA says, a crate is not a cage, it's a den. And when properly introduced, a crate is an invaluable asset to training. It will help speed the housetraining process considerably, as well as preventing property destruction when a young dog needs to be left unattended.

Some Aussiedoodles will outgrow the need for a crate when they reach maturity (rarely before a year and often closer to two), while others consider the crate to be their personal "den" and prefer to sleep in it their whole lives; the difference is largely temperamental. Either way, you're going to end up needing a crate large enough to hold a full-sized dog.

Crates come in a dizzying array of sizes, shapes and materials, and once again, the best place to start looking is Amazon, which pretty much carries every dog crate known to man. For Aussiedoodles, the wire crate is usually better than the plastic "airline crate", because these are social dogs and very alert to what's going on around them.

You can also buy really nice-looking wooden crates that look like furniture, but these are really only appropriate for dogs with no teeth or no imagination, because any other dog will turn them into a big pile of toothpicks in short order. (Been there, done that.)

However, for every problem it seems like someone comes up with a solution and one of the *coolest* additions to the world of crates is the new specially-designed wooden end table that slips right *over* the crate.
This allows you to incorporate the crate right into the furnishings of the family room where you can

even put a lamp on it, which beats having what unfortunately looks a lot like a circus tiger cage plunked unceremoniously in the corner of the room.

These are also available on Amazon; just make sure you buy the right sized-crate to fit it, because they are *not* adjustable. (Note: these tables are designed for the Midwest "i-crate" line of crates, not their Life Stages crate.)

Midwest crates, by the way, are an overall good value – many show breeders have been hauling the same Midwest crates around to dog shows for thirty years or more, which subjects them to a lot more abuse than anything the average pet owner can come up with.

The basic Midwest wire crate sizes are as follows:

Extra-Large: 48" x 33" wide x 33" high- good for the largest Doods and "sprawlers"

Large: 42" x 30" wide x 33" high- good for most standard-sized Aussiedoodles and large minis

Medium: 36" x 24"wide x 27" high- good for most minis

Other manufacturers' crates may vary by an inch or two either way. In general, it's best to err on the side of too big rather than too small, because a dog who feels cramped is going to put up more of a fuss in his crate.

It's also a good idea to buy a crate with 2 doors, one on the end and one on the side, which gives you a lot more flexibility when figuring out where to put it, especially if you're going to make it into an end table. (A puppy is likely to learn the "kennel up" command more quickly if he doesn't have to execute a maze to get in there.)

Now, the major problem with these crates is that during the first few months most baby Doods are going to do better sleeping in a crate in the bedroom with their new senior pack members, and all of them need to be crated in the car until they're old enough for a seat-belt harness.

These adult-sized wire crates are a real pain to carry around, especially if they've got a table wrapped around them. They are also too big to use successfully for housetraining – any puppy with more than three brain cells will soon figure out he can use half the crate for a bathroom and still have a comfy dry spot left to sleep in. Some crate models come with a removable divider panel to solve that problem, but that still won't make them any easier to schlep it into the bedroom every night, nor will it make it any easier to hoist into the backseat of a car. Wire dog crates were originally invented to go in the folded-down-flat backseats of station wagons and they still only really fit well in vans, since the backseats of many SUVs now no longer fold down totally flat for no apparent reason besides stupidity on the part of non-dog owning SUV designers.

The best way to get around this whole problem is to simply add a second, smaller plastic crate to your ever-growing list of supplies.

If your puppy was shipped via airline, you can use the crate he came in until he outgrows it, at which time he can probably move to his permanent crate at night and he'll be old enough to use a seat-belt harness in the car.

If you're driving to pick up the puppy from the breeder, you'll have to purchase or borrow one, because you'll definitely need it for the ride home. Try yard sales first, where they are usually cheap and usually almost brand-new. Or ask around—it's amazing how many people have a puppy crate stashed in their garage. Just make sure you wash it out with a bleach/water solution before using it- bleach kills every virus that can infect a dog.

If you can't find one to borrow or buy used, there are a lot of models available from Amazon; look for something in the 26-28" range, and don't bother with a top-of-line-model, because you'll only need it for a couple of months. The KennelCab Large is a good, inexpensive Doodle puppy crate. Just make sure you get the Large and not the Intermediate, which is too small for most Dood puppies much over 8 weeks of age.

Crate Pads and Dog Beds

Now that we've got the crate issues sorted out, it's time to look at dogs beds, and there are lots of options here as well. In fact, the world of dog beds has expanded to the point where it's almost impossible to figure out where to start!

The major factors to consider in choosing dog beds are washability, durability and good looks, since it's going to be part of your home décor for years to come unless it gets chewed up. Many gorgeous and very pricey dog beds score well in the "good-looks" area, but fall down badly in the first two, which are really more important.

Because dog beds can be expensive (Orvis carries a nice one that costs $350) this is one place where you really want to read the reviews.

When he's still a baby, it's pretty simple – the best choice in bedding for his "little" crate is a fluffy bath towel. You'll actually need two, so they can be laundered as needed. In spite of everyone's best efforts, puppies and accidents go hand in hand, and there's no sense in getting upset about it.

Some "experts" claim that if a puppy pees in his bed you'll never be able to reliably housetrain him, but this is sheer idiocy and causes a lot of undue worry on the new owner's part.

Hey, *think* about this for minute…little kids wet the bed with appalling regularity, yet most outgrow it and enjoy many years of a dry bed…at least until very old age sets in and we end up back where we started in the bladder-control department. It's much the same scenario with dogs. Where people come up with this stuff is a mystery.

When taking him for a ride in the car in his little crate, it's a good idea to take the extra towel along for the ride, because puppies also upchuck, although 99.99% of them outgrow that, too.

Helpful Hint: Put the extra towel in a small plastic bag in the car – that way, if he barfs on the first one you can just switch them around and tie the bag closed, which will keep the car smelling much fresher for the duration of the trip than it would if you didn't have the bag…many a perfectly good towel has ended up in a rest-stop trash can for this very reason.

When it comes to choosing a bed for his "real" crate, the most popular one among dog owners is probably **Midwest's Quiet Time Bolster Pet Bed,** which is available pretty much everywhere. (It currently ranks #26 in Amazon's Pet Products with 486 reviews at the time of writing.) Get two, so you can launder them frequently…they wash easily and dry fast, and can be laundered probably 100 times without falling apart. These beds are specifically sized for Midwest crates, which makes choosing the right size a whole lot easier.

Floor beds

Most dog owners also have a dog bed or two on the floor…in fact, some have one in every room, honest to God. Essentially "dog furniture", they will help keep the family Dood off yours. These beds are usually big squashy things and dogs universally love them.

The main thing to look for here is a bed with a *removable machine-washable cover*,
because most comfy plump Doodle-sized floor beds
simply won't fit in a standard washing machine.

And because they're pretty expensive, you want one that has a record of durability and a cover that won't fall apart after a couple launderings.

One of the best places to check here is **L.L. Bean.** They've been making tough dog beds for tough sporting dogs for many years, and as far as durability and quality for the price **goes**, they're hard to beat. (If your Dood is inclined to "de-stuff" the bolster on his crate bed, Bean also makes one of the most indestructible crate pads on the market—resistant to chewing and digging, they can literally be hosed off if need be.) Bean also sells replacement covers for many of its beds, which is brilliant. The denim covers are the most durable and least attractive to dog hair – you can choose a color that best blends with your décor and doesn't show dirt.

Grooming Stuff

Unless you are planning to have your dog groomed professionally on a weekly basis (which at $50-$100 per session is prohibitively expensive for most owners), you will need some basic grooming tools and supplies to keep him clean and mat-free between scheduled appointments.

In fact, having the *right* grooming supplies (and a basic knowledge on how to use them) will save you a lot of money in the long run in a couple of ways. You'll be able to stretch the time between grooming appointments without ending up with a matted dog that has to be shaved from nose to tail, which most Dood owners frankly hate. (The merle Aussiedoodles actually look pretty cute this way, but they don't really look like Doodles…more like Catahoula Leopard dogs.)

And you will often end up with a smaller grooming bill when you do take him in, because most groomers base their fees on the amount of time it takes to actually groom a dog, and that is often based on the condition of his coat and how well he is "trained to the table" as much as size.

A survey of professional groomers unfortunately reveals that Doodles in general are often deficient on both counts, which is why groomers often charge more for them than other coated breeds of the same size. Besides a lack of training, groomers most often cite the fact that Dood owners are invariably using the wrong grooming tools at home, resulting in a dog that looks good on the outside, but is often matted at the skin, which is why they end up shaved down.

Trying to figure out which tools you need, however, can be a little daunting, because there are literally hundreds of dog brushes and combs on the market, all designed for different coat types.

To make this a whole lot easier, what follows is a list of what you really need to have on hand when your Aussiedoodle puppy arrives, so you can get off to a positive start, as well as supplies and equipment you'll want to add later on. (Proper grooming techniques are covered farther along in the Grooming Chapter.)

Grooming table and grooming post

The single most important purchase after a pet gate and a crate is a grooming table with a grooming post and it's astonishing how many Doodle breeders never even mention this critical item to the new puppy owner. There's simply no way around it – with few exceptions, Doodles of all stripes are a high-maintenance group, and yours will require a fair amount of grooming over his lifetime. (Because of the textural difference, most professional groomers agree that the typical Doodle coat is actually higher-maintenance than that of the Poodle.)

This will be a whole lot cheaper and easier for everyone concerned if the dog is trained to enjoy being groomed on a table right from the time you first get him home, which is why you want to have it on hand right from the get-go. **In fact, it's probably close to impossible to keep your Dood free of mats without one.**

If you buy your grooming table before your puppy arrives, and you put him on it every single time you run a comb or brush through him from his first day at home, you will have a dog that is a piece of cake to groom. If you don't, you won't, and it will get worse and worse as he grows. It's that simple.

Unless you are a professional, a grooming table that can be folded flat and easily carried to whatever location you prefer is by far the best choice. (In nice weather, you may want to groom outside on a patio or deck, and move into the laundry room or basement in inclement weather.) The grooming post attaches easily to the table with a screw-on clamp and comes off for storage. The best place to check out the available options is once again Amazon, where you have the advantage of being able to read the reviews.

Virtually all Aussiedoodles will fit on a 36" grooming table. If yours is a mini, you can get by with one of the less expensive tables, which generally come with a 34" grooming post. (These start at under $70 including the post, which is a great price.) On the other hand, if you have a standard, you'll probably want to buy Midwest's 36" model, which is both sturdy and comes with a 44" grooming post. It costs around $130 on Amazon with the post included, and will probably outlast your dog.

The 36" grooming table is generally about 33" high, which puts the dog at just the right height for most people to groom without a lot of back strain. Those who are a lot taller or shorter than average, may want to consider a table with adjustable legs – the legs adjust from 24' to 36", so the owner can easily find a height that is comfortable. An adjustable table and post can be purchased for around $200, and may be well worth the extra cost if 33" is just not a workable height for you.

Comb and Small Scissors

A comb (the kind with rotating teeth that literally slide through the coat without pulling are best for puppies) and a 5-6 inch straight grooming scissors with rounded tips (for trimming hair around his eyes, pads, and under his tail, as well as cutting out things like gum that may get stuck in his coat and are impossible to brush out) are the other two grooming tools you really need to have on hand when the puppy arrives. The rest of the grooming supplies you'll need are listed in Chapter Eight.

Toys and Chew Bones

This may well be the longest treatise ever written on dog toys and dog chews, but **reading through it before you buy a single toy** can save you literally thousands of dollars and several trips to the vet's office, so it's probably well-worth the effort.

In order to satisfy his needs for both intellectual stimulation and chewing, your puppy will require lots of toys. In order to keep him safe, these need to be broken down into two categories – the kind he can play with under supervision, and the kind that can go into his crate with him when he's left alone. (The latter category is frankly pretty limited.)

Besides the more immediate and often life-threatening dangers of choking, every year hundreds of dogs end up having whole plastic, rubber and nylon "chew toys" as well as various parts of said chew toys surgically removed from their digestive tracts via extremely expensive gastric surgery because of intestinal blockage.
(In the last few years, the number of dogs – primarily those of the sporting breeds – who've had to have entire cell phones surgically removed from their guts has been on the increase as well…consider yourself warned.)

Along with hard chew toys, soft stuffed "plush" toys are immensely popular – virtually every Doodle puppy loves to play with them, "herd" them, and will usually retrieve them endlessly. He also loves to snuggle with them and have his picture taken while being so totally adorable.

On the other hand, this same puppy is entirely capable of totally eviscerating his favorite beloved stuffed toy (and ingesting both its stuffing and its squeaker) in ten minutes flat when no one is looking for no apparent reason and with apparently very little forethought. This puzzles owners no end – they simply cannot understand why a dog would systematically destroy (and very probably ingest) what was obviously a favorite toy.

The short answer is…..*they do it because they're dogs.*

Before buying a single dog toy, you need understand the hard-wired instincts driving a puppy's behavior, because once again you will be more successful working *with* a dog's DNA rather than *against* it.

In the wild, when a litter of wolf cubs is moved to its rendezvous area, the adults deliver whole small animals and birds as well as "leftovers" (like legs and antlers) from large kills as soon as the cubs have graduated beyond the regurgitated-food stage.

These items provide training, entertainment *and* nutrition all in the same package – Mother Nature is nothing if not efficient.

The bony leftovers and antlers satisfy the need to chew during teething while providing needed calcium and trace minerals for the growing cubs.

Small whole animals are dual-purpose as well – they are "hunted", captured and played with, tossed, used for games of tug-o-war, and then ultimately *eviscerated*, because in addition to protein, the internal organs provide vital nutrients like Vitamin A, various amino acids and cholesterol, all critical for optimum physical and brain development in the cubs. (Ironically, these highly nutritious organs are all classified by law as "byproducts" by the FDA and no one wants them in their dog food.)

Once the insides are eaten, the cubs will then ultimately consume around 85% of the rest, including hide, fur and feathers, all of which provides protein and fiber.

So what happens is when we, as senior pack members, present our own cub with toys (often modeled after human baby toys), his ancient canine DNA takes over. Consequently, he will gnaw industriously on his brightly-colored hard plastic teething toys shaped like car keys or baby pacifiers until he can break them into pieces he can ingest, even though they have zero nutritional value, and he will play with his latest plush "gingerbread man" or soccer ball until he gets bored, at which points his eviscerating instincts take over and he guts it, eats the polyester stuffing and the plastic squeaker, and then shreds the rest of it.

This happens because he is a baby *canid*, not a **baby *human*.**

As with humans, "playing" for immature canids is how they practice the skills they will need as an adult, and their "toys" often reflect that. (If this makes you wonder why anyone would design toys for an animal lacking opposable thumbs in the shape of *keys* you're not alone...chalk it up to a bad case of anthropomorphism.)

Unfortunately for his digestive system, however, a puppy's DNA does not allow him to distinguish between plastic and natural bone, real fur and acrylic, or even entrails and polyester fiberfill – it is the *behaviors themselves* that are hard-wired in.

This is the same reason that a dog will "bury" a bowl of food on a tile floor with imaginary dirt and leaves in an elaborate ritual and then smugly walk away, satisfied that it is well-hidden even though it's clearly still in plain sight.

Once we understand what Mother Nature had in mind and work with it, choosing both the right chew toys and soft toys gets a whole lot easier. Amazon reviews also help a lot, since virtually every bone and dog toy they sell has multiple reviews—one has an astonishing 959 reviews as of today. (That's not a typo, that's actually *959 reviews for a ten-dollar dog toy*...and I swear I am not making this up.)

Although the ultimate decisions are of course yours, the following rundown of the most popular will at least give you a place to start, so you don't have to spend the better part of the rest of your natural life reading dog toy reviews on Amazon.

(If you want to save some time, the best of these can also be found on **www.dianeklumb.com**.)

Chew Toys.

All puppies need something acceptable to chew on, especially when they are teething. With only one possible exception, none of them are totally without risk, but then, neither is driving a car – the key is to find a risk level you are personally comfortable with.

Chew toys can be divided into two basic categories- inedible (usually made of plastic and rubber) and edible (usually substances that used to be working parts of animals). Which you prefer is largely a matter of individual temperament and personal philosophy, because puppies will chew up and swallow pretty much anything. Those who don't like the idea of their dog constantly gnawing on and ultimately ingesting artificially-colored rubber and various plastic polymers will probably want to go the more "natural" route, while those who are not comfortable having parts of dead animals lying around their house will probably prefer the "artificial" options, which is what we'll start with.

Fake Stuff for Dogs to Chew On

In the artificial category, **Nylabone** products are probably among the best-known and the safest, if your puppy will chew on them – some will while others just ignore them completely. The larger bone-shaped and wishbone-shaped nylon Nylabones are good choices as long as someone's in the house. (The manufacturer specifically warns against leaving their products with an unattended dog.)

One thing worth knowing about classic Nylabones however is if swallowed in whole or in part *they do not show up on an x-ray*, which can be problematic. Nylabone's puppy keys and teething rings are certainly cute and fun for small puppies, but probably only for the first month or two for a full-sized Dood from a safety standpoint. (The good news is that at least the bright colors mean they'll show up on an x-ray if ingested.) *Most Nylabone products average 3-4 star ratings from Amazon customers.*

The ubiquitous **Kong** is another popular chew toy, and being made of rubber it also bounces, which makes it fun. Filled with peanut butter, it will usually keep a puppy entertained for quite a while, but again, should not be left with an unattended dog.
You might as well start right off with a big one so you never have to worry about it being accidentally swallowed. **Kong's Stuff-a-Ball** is one of the more durable and popular "treat toys" (as well as the hands-down quietest) and the **Kong Extreme Ball** rates a solid 5 stars, although it's not really a chew toy. *Kong products average 3.5 to 4.5 stars across the board.*

Real Stuff for Dogs to Chew On

In the "natural" department, let's start with what you DO NOT want to give your puppy, and those are chopped and compressed "bone-shaped things" of any sort. Although most big dogs can crunch them up, swallow the pieces and manage to get them all the way through their digestive tracts, they represent a real hazard for puppies and smaller dogs, who can pretty easily break off a chunk just large enough to choke on or to cause an intestinal obstruction.
For the record, the ubiquitous Greenie falls in this category—although the manufacturer clearly states they are only for *adult dogs* weighing over 15 pounds, it seems like everyone knows someone who's lost a small dog or a puppy to a Greenie.

Stay away from anything that uses the word "compressed" or looks like it's made from chopped-up stuff.

Real Bones

When it comes to bones, **Marrow and knuckle bones** are the time-honored natural chew toys for dogs, who've been happily gnawing on them for untold millennia, but they are not without inherent risk either; leaving a dog alone with even a huge one when no one is around is not recommended by anyone.

Cooked bones can splinter, presenting a risk of both choking and intestinal perforation, even though untold thousands of them are consumed by dogs around the world every single day without incident.

Raw bones, as their proponents are quick to point out, do not splinter as easily, but they do come with the inherent risk of food-borne pathogens like e-coli, campylobacter, and salmonella, to name just a few. Although dogs are indeed less susceptible to them than are people, most dogs *live* with people and can spread these pathogens via their saliva to their human pack members.

"Smoked bones" with bits of meat attached are a favorite of nearly all dogs, but they *are* strong-smelling and fairly messy, and many owners limit them to outdoors or crates for that reason. Both raw and cooked bones can cause stomach upset in some dogs, while others have no problem with them at all. Always monitor bone-chewing carefully and replace bones when they start to get small or chunks start to get chewed off. *Overall, most natural bones get an average rating of 3.5-4.5 stars from Amazon's dog-owning customers.*

Assorted Animal Parts

An alternative to actual bones are various other "natural parts", all of which puppies and indeed dogs of all ages adore, all of which are pretty nutritious and some of which you may find palatable enough to actually have around. The downside of all these "natural" chews, however, is that they're all pretty expensive.

This is really pretty hilarious if you consider that when they used to be routinely included in dog food as a cheap protein source, FDA required them to be labeled as "byproducts".

When dog owner decided they didn't want to feed their dogs food that contained "byproducts", those parts ended up dried, smoked, shrink-wrapped in plastic and sold individually at exorbitant prices to those same dog owners as "natural treats" for those same dogs. Go figure.

Anyhow, it's been a real windfall for the slaughterhouse industry, which just goes to prove once again that it's an ill wind that blows nobody good. Let's look at our options here, starting with ears:

Pig's ears (and the even less-appealing **pig snouts,** both of which big dogs merrily crunch up like large overpriced potato chips) *will* last awhile for puppies, and puppies adore them. On the other hand, they are, not surprisingly, greasy and "piggy-smelling" and have a tendency to stain everything they come in contact with.

Lamb's ears, which are dry, white, and odorless, are a cleaner choice and being less fatty are less likely to cause stomach upset. *In the customer review department, pig's ears and snouts probably average 3.5 stars while lamb's ears average 4-5 stars, with the 5 star ratings mostly from owners of puppies and small dogs, because they are very expensive potato chips for the big guys.*

Rawhide. Even though most dogs adore it, giving dogs rawhide in any shape is pretty controversial—although independent research has shown ingestion of rawhide is safe, large chunks of rawhide CAN be bitten off and swallowed, presenting the same choking hazard found in chopped compressed bones, so a lot of vets advise against it. (Of course, if you ask a vet, they'll tell you *nothing* is really safe for a dog to chew on, because the only time vets see a lot of this stuff is when they're surgically removing it from a dog's digestive tract.)

In spite of that, America's dog population probably consumes untold tons of rawhide chips, rolls and knotted bones on an annual basis. The key to rawhide chews for puppies if you choose to give it is to stick to big knotted rawhide bones and toss them as soon as the puppy starts to untie the ends into slimy strips he could ultimately swallow. Depending on the puppy, this can take anywhere from days to weeks, by which time it's probably pretty disgusting anyway. *Rawhide products rate 3.5-.4.5 stars*

Cow's hooves are another chew toy option for puppies. Once again, they all like them and will chew away merrily for hours without the hooves themselves getting slimy. Although they're not greasy like pig parts, they do have an odor and some people find them unappealing to have lying around the house, since they look a lot like, well…hooves. Totally unprocessed and pretty safe for young puppies, older dogs who are strong chewers can break chunks off if they work at it for awhile. *Cow's hooves have an Amazon customer rating of 3.5-4.5 stars.*

Bully sticks, also sold as "pizzle sticks" and "beef tendons", are universally loved by dogs, and are about as natural as you can get, since they are in reality simply raw bull or steer penises which are hung and dried without any cooking, processing or chemicals. (The other names are used in marketing because it turns out some dog owners are just not comfortable with the idea of their dog chewing on a penis, but they're really all the same thing.) They do have a fair amount of nutritional value, and because they are low in fat, they are unlikely to cause stomach upset.

Many owners feel bully sticks have a "calming" effect on their dogs, most likely related to the fact that they're high in taurine, an amino acid known to be protective against glutamate excitotoxicity in the brain – in fact, taurine is used to treat both seizures and head tremors in dogs. They're considered safer than rawhide from a choking standpoint, especially if you buy the thickest ones. In fact, if it weren't for the "yuck" factor, and the fact that they all smell pretty awful (even the so-called "odorless" ones), bully sticks would probably rate 5 stars based on safety, palatability and nutritional value. But what can you say about a product where one of the 5 star reviews actually starts out with "Gross, but worth it"? *Overall, 4 stars.*

OK, assuming you haven't fallen off your chair in a coma by now, you've probably figured out that a "5 star chew" would be 100% natural, nontoxic, nutritious *and* incapable of splintering or breaking off into chunks so you could leave it in his crate with him when no one's around, as well as odorless, not greasy, messy, or disgusting to look at or pick up, and hopefully not something you'll have a hard time explaining to Aunt Eleanor when she comes over at Christmas and asks what the dog is chewing on. "Sustainably harvested" seems like too much too ask, but what the heck, let's throw it in there anyway. Oh yeah, and dogs should actually *like* it.

Well, Mick, it might not happen often, but if you try sometimes, you just might find you get what you want...*and* what you need.

The absolute BEST puppy chew toy at any price is a good-sized chunk of antler.

Elk, whitetail, mulie or moose, doesn't matter, good quality antler meets all of the above criteria, *and is probably the only thing on God's green earth that's actually safe enough to leave with an unattended puppy.*

And unlike bones, rawhide and hooves, the majority of antler is harvested in the most sustainable manner one can possibly imagine, because no animals need be killed in the process.
In case you're not from Wisconsin, Minnesota, or one of those big square states out west and consequently didn't know this, antlers are not the same as the horns on a cow, who is stuck with the same set for life.
Although antler is also made of bone, bucks of all of the above species actually shed their antlers, or "racks", every year, and pretty much abandon them where they fall, after which they promptly begin to acquire a new and usually more impressive set. Sort of like iphones.

"Harvesting" these discarded racks consists mostly of wandering around the woods until you find a set, which is not as easy as it sounds. In fact, it is so difficult that some people are now training "shed dogs" to assist in the hunt. In order to get there before the local rodentia do, shed gathering (also known as "clinting" for no good reason) is done between December and February, and often requires tromping around in sub-zero weather on snowshoes, which is not everyone's idea of a fun time.

Because harvesting is so labor-intensive, antler dog chews are absurdly expensive, but when you factor in how long they last and how clean, odor-free and safe they are, they really are a great bargain.

In fact, one could make a strong argument for dispensing with the nylon and rawhide and pig parts and dried penises altogether and making antler pieces the *only* chewing option available for your puppy right from the get-go, in which case you'll want to buy a couple, because, like snowflakes, no two are identical and variety is good for puppies as well as people.

You do need to toss them when they finally are gnawed down to a size that could be swallowed whole, but it will take a long time, especially if the puppy is working on several at once.
Antler chews get 5 stars from Amazon's dog owning customers, with the exception of those who thought that for eighteen bucks they were getting a whole bag of them instead of just one.

Soft Toys

Unfortunately, there are no really "natural" alternatives in the soft toy department short of picking up actual roadkill, which is a little more natural than most of us are comfortable with.

There is an argument, however, for choosing stuffed toys that at least vaguely resemble what might actually be found in nature, though— in addition to being more "culturally respectful", dogs often innately prefer them. The best are animal- or bird-shaped, made of sturdy material, well-sewn, and have few appendages to be chewed off and swallowed. (Tags should be cut off with a scissors.)

But you do need to bear in mind that no matter how well-made, stuffed toys are not designed as chew toys by definition—they should always be used in an interactive manner to some degree, and under supervision.
When a puppy starts to seriously chew on or rip into a stuffed toy instead of playing with it, common sense should dictate that it's time to pick it up and replace it with a "real" chew toy like a bone or an antler – failure to do this teaches the puppy that destroying items made of cloth and stuffing is acceptable behavior, and it's *not*... unless of course you want your couch cushions to meet a similar end.

Toys that suffer small "accidental" tears caused by sharp puppy teeth should also be picked up immediately. (At the risk of pointing out the obvious, using a needle and thread to sew up a small hole before the first irresistible-to-puppies wisps of polyester stuffing appear will stop the process in its tracks and extend the life of the toy significantly. Your sewing skills really don't matter here, and it only takes a minute.)

That said, buying well-designed stuffed toys right from the get-go will actually lessen the chances that they will be destroyed.

In addition to durability, the best dog toys are designed with an understanding of the canine instinct to eviscerate small fuzzy animals.

And the manufacturer that literally owns this market is Kygen. They make several lines of plush toys designed with smaller stuffed squeaky toys that fit *inside* bigger stuffed toys, and they are nothing short of brilliant. The little toys may be easily removed, leaving the big one intact, by all but the dumbest of dogs after a little helpful instruction from the owner, who will then spend the rest of his life sticking them back in so that his dog can pull them out again. No matter, Aussiedoodle puppies adore them…in fact, puppies and dogs of nearly all breeds and ages adore them.

The undisputed winner here is surely **Kygen's Hide-a-Squirrel**. Essentially a fuzzy gray tree stump with three removable squeaky stuffed squirrels inside, it is Amazon's #1 best-selling dog toy and yes, Virginia, it is indeed the one boasting 676 reviews and counting. Even *more* astonishing is the fact that over 80% of reviewers gave it 5 stars, which is probably some sort of record. And because it speaks directly to their DNA, dogs just universally love it. It actually comes in 4 sizes, but since most people ultimately upgrade to the "ginormous" size (which boasts no less than *five* removable squirrels) you might just want to start there.

If an Aussiedoodle puppy could only have three personal possessions,
two good-sized chunks of antler and a Hide-a-Squirrel
would probably serve him well.

Since that's clearly not gonna happen, the next toy worth buying is **Kygen's Platypus**, another Amazon best-seller and part of its Egg Baby series.

Using the same principle as Hide-a-Squirrel, the squeaky eggs (which are remarkably sturdy) are gleefully removed from the Platypus by the puppy, then tossed around and played with until you put them back in, after which the whole process is repeated endlessly until the puppy gets tired, at which point you trade it for a chew bone so he'll go lay down and leave you in peace for awhile.

There are actually several toys in the Egg Baby series, and Harvey the Hedgehog is another good choice. *These are all 4 star toys.*

If you get tired of stuffing little toys back into big toys and want to add a couple of less-interactive ones, **Ethical's Skinneeez** line is pretty cool.

Because the bodies of these plush critters have no actual stuffing, the "eviscerating gene" doesn't automatically kick in, and the long skinny shape is extremely attractive to puppies, who'll immediately toss them around and shake them. (This is obviously another DNA-based thing...as anyone who's watched a dog destroy a stuffed animal knows, the "tossing and shaking" behavior naturally appears *after* the toy is gutted.)

There's a Skinneeez skunk, a squirrel, a fox and a raccoon among others, all fairly realistic – unfortunately this realism coupled with their flat shape may cause the uninitiated to mistake them for roadkill, but that's really their only downside. They're also all under ten bucks. *Skinneeez get 4 stars from Amazon's customers across the board, although apparently somebody's dog actually managed to swallow one whole and had to have it surgically removed, after which the owner posted warnings all over the internet. (This should not be a problem with the 24 inch model.)*

A couple more stuffed toys worth adding to the pile are all made by Coleman, the sporting goods company. All exhibit the "durability at a reasonable price" that's Coleman's stock in trade.

The **Coleman pheasant** is popular with dogs mostly because of its cool squawky squeaker, as is the **Coleman duck**, which actually quacks. (Even toy breeds are attracted to these "game birds", which is a little surprising.)

Their neoprene **Water Sport Duck** is great for teaching puppies to retrieve out of water in a lake or backyard pool.

Last but not least, **Coleman's Super-Sized Trophy Bear** is a sturdy and immensely popular "cuddle toy" for puppies of all ages with a good track record for longevity. *This last one is another dog toy with over a hundred Amazon reviews, and over two thirds of them are 5 stars. For some reason Coleman just got it right, and dogs instinctively love this bear. All of Coleman's stuffed dog toys are rated highly by customers, though – usually rating 4-5 stars across the board.*

Interactive Treat Toys

There is a last category of interactive toys which are fairly new to the market, and these are "treat toys". Unlike the interactive stuffed toys, the owner doesn't have to do much here— once it's filled, the dog simply interacts with the toy without a lot of input from anyone else. They are based on the premise that, unlike a grazing animal that just needs to put his head down, a canid is hard-wired to *work* for his food.

The fact that dogs think these toys are lots of fun and will often choose their food ball over a dish of food indicates the designers may be on to something. (Some trainers are now recommending these as the primary "dog dish", and many suggest their use to prevent or alleviate separation anxiety as well as food-bolting.)

Usually designed in the shape of a ball or cube with a hole for the food to fall out of when rolled, these will keep dogs entertained for anywhere from 10 minutes to an hour.

Two of the most popular are the **OurPets IQ Treat ball**, and **Kong's Wobbler**. Both are dishwasher -safe, which is good.

Kong's Stuff-a-Ball is one of the few made of rubber, which is harder to clean but quiet enough to allow you to watch TV in the same room.

The **Buster Food Cube** is another popular one, but its squarish shape makes it even louder than the hard plastic balls, especially on tile or hardwood floors. It's probably worth it to get a couple different shapes and switch them out just to keep things interesting. *Overall, this bunch rates 4-5 stars from Amazon customers.*

Obviously there are tons of dog toys out there, and while this will get you started, you'll no doubt keep adding to your Dood's collection as you go along. If you try to remember that he's a full-fledged card-carrying member of the genus *Canidae* and not a little person in a dog suit, and always read the customer reviews to check for safety and durability before you bring anything into the house, you'll do fine.

The most important thing to keep in mind, though, is that there is no amount of dog toys, no matter how "interactive", that can take the place of human attention.

Dog toys are all meant to be used by people as a fun way to interact with their dogs, NOT to entertain dogs left alone.

Because of the way they're hard-wired, any dog would rather play fetch with a plain old stick in the company of one of his human pack members than be left alone with a boxful of expensive dog toys.

Collars, leads and tags

The collar and tag is part of a dog's basic "wardrobe" – in fact, unless he's wearing a life jacket or a service dog jacket it's probably his *whole* wardrobe, and he should wear it at all times unless he's in the tub. Some experts advise against leaving a dog unattended in a crate with a collar on, but if you actually examine any modern crate you'll be hard-pressed to figure out how a dog can get his collar stuck anywhere in there, so this may just be outdated advice. Show dog owners never leave collars on their dogs, but that's really mostly about saving coat.

Puppy Collars

To start out, you'll want a **flat nylon puppy-sized collar with a matching 6-foot lead**. (Your breeder should be able to tell you which size is appropriate for your particular size of Dood.)
The choice between a traditional "buckle" collar and the kind with a plastic snap is entirely up to you, but bear in mind this is a temporary collar, because your puppy is going to outgrow it in short order. Just pick a bright color that complements his coat.

You'll also need a tag with his phone number on it, and these can (and should) be made up on the spot at any major pet supply store like Petsmart *before your puppy arrives*. (In fact, if you are picking up your puppy, which you should do if at all possible, you should bring it along and attach it to his collar before he leaves the breeder's property.)
Some people are paranoid about putting the dog's name on the tag as well, but if a puppy is lost, it's probably less traumatic for him if the person who finds him can actually call him by name. Even if he's microchipped, a simple phone number (your cell phone is probably best) is most likely to get him home the fastest.
.When shopping for collars you'll notice a dizzying array of "training" collars out there on the same

rack—martingales, slip collars (referred to as "choke" collars by people who don't like them), prong collars and head collars (the ubiquitous Gentle Leader is the best known), but if your puppy is reasonably tractable (as most Aussiedoodles are) and you actually take the time to train him to heel early he may never need any of them, and they'll all be the wrong size anyway.

Another handy item is one of those little plastic bag-holders that attaches to his lead—that way you'll never have to scrounge around in your pocket for a bag or Kleenex.

Check cord

In addition to the 6 foot nylon lead, what you will also absolutely need right out the gate is a 5/8 inch 20-foot, 5/8 inch **cotton web training lead**, also called a "check cord" or "drop lead", depending on the trainer's area of expertise.

This will allow your puppy some freedom to romp in areas that are open but not entirely fenced, like parks and beaches, as well as being a critical tool for teaching him to recall in your backyard. (Actually, with a check cord, you can practice the recall lots of different places, which is a very good idea.).

Check cords are infinitely safer than the ubiquitous "retractable" lead, which appeared like a nasty virus back in the 1980s and which too many pet owners now use and all experienced trainers wish would vanish from the earth.
Besides literally *teaching dogs to pull*, which is stupid, these leads are downright dangerous.

(The manufacturer of the FlexiLead actually suggests that to "reduce the risk of finger amputation" you remove your rings and wear sturdy gloves…it's right on their website.)

As if *that* isn't bad enough, if a retractable lead is accidentally dropped (which it will be sooner or later), it will immediately and loudly retract, and then the poor puppy will find himself being chased by a noisy chunk of plastic banging along right behind him no matter how fast he runs! Nine out of ten puppies will panic in this situation, for which you can hardly blame them, and the results can be lethal. Even if you can manage to get to the puppy and the damned leash before he gets hit by a car, the damage to his leash-training will be extensive, to say the least. For a hyper-reactive breed like the Aussiedoodle, it could take months to undo the trauma.

(By comparison, if you drop the check cord, you can casually scoop it back up, and odds are good the puppy won't even notice.)

To avoid these and other possible disasters, here's my advice:

- **DO NOT BUY A RETRACTABLE LEASH FOR YOUR PUPPY.**
- **DO NOT ACCEPT ONE AS A GIFT.**
- **DO NOT PUT ONE ON YOUR PUPPY UNLESS SOMEONE ACTUALLY HAS A GUN POINTED AT YOUR HEAD.**
- **DO NOT STAND ANYWHERE NEAR A DOG WHO'S ATTACHED TO ONE.**

Is everyone clear on that? The retractable leash is probably the *worst* thing that ever happened to dog training, and the second-worst idea to come out of Germany in the last hundred years.

Once your puppy gets bigger, you'll want to replace the 5/8 inch cotton web lead with a stronger nylon one (LL Bean makes the best ones), and you can buy them in lengths up to 50 feet. They are a great investment.

Books

If Amazon's *"Customers who bought this item also bought..."* is any sort of a guide, most people buy a handful of books on puppy-training and general dog ownership while they are killing time waiting for their puppy by ordering crates and dog beds and antlers and Hide-a-Squirrels. *But which ones should you buy?*

This can be extremely confusing, especially for the poor novice dog owner, as the various philosophies of dog training rival maybe only organized religion in both sheer number and intolerance for opposing opinions among their respective adherents. (For that reason alone, reading the reviews will only confuse you more.)

So let's make it easy:
If you are only going to buy one book on dog training, that book should **be *Mother Knows Best: the Natural Way to Train Your Dog* by Carl Lea Benjamin.**
Written back in 1985, it's been selling steadily ever since and it's now also available on Kindle.

What sets this book apart? Simply put, *Mother Knows Best* is to dog training what *The Art of French Cooking* is to cooking, and Carol Lea Benjamin is no less than the Julia Child of dog training— the person who first introduced dog owners to the idea of "natural training" nearly thirty years ago. **No one does it better.**

In addition to teaching you in clear and simple steps how to actually train your dog, Carol Benjamin teaches you to *enjoy* him. She makes natural training *fun* for both the dog and his owner, rather than an unnatural chore.

Mercifully lacking the endless autobiographical material and "case histories" that seem to plague nearly all training books, Ms Benjamin spends a little time explaining her philosophy and then jumps right into a practical "curriculum" for a typical 8 week old puppy. The section on Etiquette for Puppies includes a housebreaking schedule, broken down hour-by-hour.

It really is the only training book you will ever need, unless you want to add **How to Survive Your Puppy's Adolescence,** which you might as well break down and buy at the same time, since you'll need it in only a few short months, anyway. Not surprisingly, it's written by the same author.

Assuming you want to keep your Aussiedoodle as healthy as you possibly can (and who doesn't?) the other book worth buying right out the gate **is *Dr Pitcairn's New Guide to Natural Dog Care.***

Written by the world's foremost authority on natural and alternative veterinary medicine, this book offers some important insights into why modern dogs now suffer from so many chronic health issues and what you can do to avoid them. Newly revised, it now includes a chapter on environmental toxins and dogs that's a real eye-opener. Read it with an open mind and try to incorporate as much of it as you realistically can into your dog's care, even if you don't plan to make him home-cooked organic meals. The section on homeopathic and herbal remedies for minor problems will save you enough to pay for the book several times over…and you'll have avoided giving your dog a lot of unnecessary antibiotics to boot.

Another book worth buying, especially if you're thinking of cooking for your dog rather than feeding commercial dog food, is **Home-Prepared Dog & Cat Diets: the Healthful Alternative by Donald R Strombeck DVM PhD.**

The recipes are surprisingly EASY, inexpensive and backed by a lot of hard science. If you find the idea of home-cooked food for your dog appealing but are at all worried that it may result in nutritional deficiencies, this book is a must-have.
Dr Strombeck is Professor Emeritus at UC Davis School of Veterinary Medicine and is a recognized authority in canine nutrition. At 366 pages, it's packed with information; it's also *very* expensive, but you can usually buy a used copy on Amazon. It's worth knowing that much of the information in the book, including a lot of the recipes, can also be found online at http://dogcathomeprepareddiet.com.

If you're a compulsive reader, another book you might want to consider adding to your library is Stanley Coren's **How to Speak Dog**, which expands upon the guide to understanding dog language introduced in *Mother Knows Best*.

In the DVD department, **Cesar Millan's *People Training for Dogs*** is available on Amazon and worth owning. Like most of his books, this is not a "training manual" (by his own admission, Cesar Millan is not a dog "trainer" per se), but rather explains the psychology behind effective dog training.

Anyhow, this list should be enough to get you headed in the right direction, so you might as well pull out the plastic and start ordering so you'll have everything disinterred from its annoying packaging and assembled by the time you get your puppy.

And when the bills for all this stuff start coming in at the end of the month you'll immediately understand why the initial cost of the puppy really doesn't matter much.

CHAPTER FIVE:

Off to a Good Start
(or...surviving the first few days and nights and beyond)

The most important year of any dog's life is without doubt the first one. In fact, much of his future success in life depends upon what he learns not only in the first year, *but in the first 4 months.* Puppies start learning very early from their mothers. If you want a well-balanced and well-trained dog (and who doesn't?) you'll want to continue this learning process puppy right away, rather than waiting until he's old enough to go to training classes, by which time you'll already have problems to "fix".

Remember, Aussiedoodles are highly intelligent and if *you* do not train your puppy he will train *himself*, which rarely works out well for anybody. Virtually all the "problems" with which professional trainers have to deal really involve *retraining* the poor dog who was forced to train himself due to a lack of leadership on his owner's part when he was little and cute. Here's an example:

The dog who jumps on everyone was simply never taught how to appropriately greet a human when he was little, so he came up with his OWN greeting.

As with children and spouses, it's a lot easier and more effective to teach a dog what we DO want him to do than to only try to teach him what we DON'T, because in the latter case he won't have an appropriate alternative behavior with which to replace the unwanted one.

If you don't want a dog to jump up on his hind legs and lick your face to greet you when you walk into a room, exactly what *DO* you want him to do —-sit, lie down, roll over, stand on his head? I mean, think about it...he's got to do SOMETHING.

Dog training is not rocket science—- it's common sense. All you really have to remember is that no command should start with "don't" or "no" (as in "no jumping!") **because not doing something is not a *behavior*, and therefore can't really be rewarded**. And if it worked, we'd have "Don't Go" signs instead of "Stop" signs., wouldn't we?

Now, it takes a total of maybe 20 minutes to teach even the most dim-witted 8 week old puppy the *sit/stay command*. If a dog knows that command, once he even starts to think about jumping up, he can be given the sit-stay command and be *rewarded* with praise and a pat on the head instead of a knee in the chest and yelling… or even worse, his best-beloved person *ignoring* him while he gets more and more desperate to have his existence acknowledged.

> Whoever came up with the breathtakingly stupid idea
> that *ignoring* an unwanted behavior will cause it to disappear
> obviously never had children.

It's also kinder. The saddest cartoon ever is the one where two dogs meet and one says "My name is No No Bad Dog—what's yours?"

So the training begun by his mother should be continued seamlessly by you the minute you have your hands on your new puppy. Reading *Mother Knows Best* all the way through before you bring him home will give you all the confidence and tools you need to do it right. The clock starts ticking the minute you actually pick up your puppy, so let's start with that.

When is the best time to pick up your puppy?

Odds are you won't have a lot of leeway here—most breeders have a "pick-up weekend" based on what they feel is the optimal age for the pups to go their new homes. Usually with Aussiedoodles, this is between 8 and 9 weeks. So you need to find out when you're supposed to pick him up and clear your calendar well in advance.
But under NO circumstances should you buy a puppy from a breeder who will let them go before 7 weeks. Puppies taken from their litters before this time will often have problems getting along with

other dogs and in addition often lack "bite inhibition", which they learn from their mothers and siblings, especially important in Aussiedoodles with herding breeds behind them.

Is it Really Safe to Have a Puppy Shipped?

At the risk of alienating a lot of well-intentioned breeders, the short answer is NO. Convenient for breeder and buyer, yes. **But really safe? Not so much.**

For the better part of the last hundred years, buying a puppy meant looking for breeders pretty close to home, finding one you were comfortable with, and then driving over to pick up the puppy as soon as it was old enough to leave its mom and littermates. (*For a wealth of reasons, this "buying local" method is still by far the best.*) But the idea of flying a puppy across country was unheard of.

But in the internet world we now live in, buyers more often select a puppy online from a breeder halfway across the country whom they've never met, purchase the puppy without ever visiting the breeder's home and/or meeting the puppy or his parents, and then have the poor little guy shipped crosscountry when he turns eight weeks old as if he were a cappuccino maker. We're now all so used to online purchasing and having everything delivered that no one seems to think twice about this whole process, or whether or not it is actually in the best interest of the puppy himself. IT IS NOT.

For a multitude of reasons it is far better for a puppy to be picked up rather than shipped. The first, of course, is that it's far safer for the puppy.

Think about this for a minute— you're willing to trust your puppy's very LIFE to the same idiots who regularly lose your luggage???

It should not come as much of a surprise to learn that the airlines lose *puppies* as well as luggage. In fact, according to the US Dept of Transportation, between 2005 (when airlines were required to actually turn in reports for the first time *ever*) and 2011, US airlines killed, injured or lost 224 pets. Delta led the pack with 70, followed by Continental with 69, Alaska Airlines with 50, American Airlines with 45 and United with 24. Close to 90% of the deaths reported were dogs.
(And lest you think that these were perhaps all elderly animals or bulldogs (which is what the airlines would like us to believe) the 2000 Samoyed National Specialty Winner, a four year-old prime specimen of a dog, died in the cargo hold of a flight from Orlando to CA while his owners were in the cabin of the same plane.)
And as awful as that sounds, it's actually much WORSE than that….

Those figures only include dogs traveling as excess baggage when their owners are in the cabin. They DO NOT include "incidents" involving any of the thousands of unaccompanied puppies shipped each year as cargo from breeders to their new owners —like yours! — *because the airlines are not required to report those.*

How many of these puppies shipped "unaccompanied" are killed or injured? Because they do not need to be reported, no one knows the exact number, but according to the ASPCA, Air Transportation Association data puts the estimate at around *5,000 per year*, or roughly one in every 100 puppy shipped. This would include the 7 puppies that died of apparent overheating on a single American Airlines flight from Oklahoma to Chicago O'Hare in August 2010, as well as Maggie May, the Westie pup who was crushed to death in 2008 by a baggage cart on the tarmac at Atlanta's Hartsfield enroute to her new owner.

Although the airlines claim that the baggage holds are pressurized and air-conditioned, temperatures ranging from below freezing to 115 degrees have been recorded in the crates of shipped dogs, often because the plane was delayed on the tarmac. (When a Continental flight bound for Denver was delayed for 3 hours in Philadelphia, 3 Samoyeds in the cargo hold were found dead on arrival.)

What sorts of injuries are recorded? United was recently sued when a dog's eardrums were punctured during transport—the owner received $410.50 in compensation, based on the weight of the dog. And any dog that dies enroute to or at the vets' office rather than being found dead in its crate when they take it off the plane is listed as an "injury" rather than a death in the incident report.

So why do breeders assure puppy buyers that shipping puppies is perfectly safe,
when the numbers indicate pretty clearly that it is NOT?

That's easy....*you* didn't know any of this until right now, did you?

Odds are, neither does your breeder. Ask them exactly how many dogs died flying the friendly skies in the last five years— I guarantee they will not know. Hardly anyone does.

Because they make a lot of money shipping dogs, the airlines obviously don't advertise the risks, or the number of dogs and puppies lost each year, so most breeders remain blissfully ignorant until the awful day when one of their own puppies dies enroute.

The commercial breeders DO know, but for them, it's simply part of the cost of doing business online. Shipping puppies sold via the internet is the best thing that ever happened to puppy mills—instead of selling them wholesale to brokers, they can now sell them at retail directly to the consumer, who thinks he's buying from a responsible breeder. *They're making more money than ever.* What's the loss of a couple of puppies compared to that? They simply write them off as business losses.

In fact, puppy mills would be out of business in short order
if the airlines simply banned the shipping of puppies under the age of a year,
because it is absolutely critical to their continued existence.

Aside from the very real physical risks, there is also a lot less *psychological stress* if you pick up your puppy yourself directly from the breeder, because he will know he has "permission" to be with you – his care is simply being transferred from one higher-ranking pack member than himself to another, which happens in the wild all the time.

On the other hand, there's really no natural equivalent to a puppy being put in a crate and driven to an airport by one person, shifted around innumerable times, subjected to highly toxic lead-laden jet fumes and a noise level that requires ear protection for humans, and then ultimately taken out of the crate after all this by a person *he's never seen before* at the other end. He has nothing in his DNA to cope with the stress of that.

Besides being the most popular week to ship puppies, the eighth week also marks the beginning of the first "fear" period in canine development. Given the high reactivity of the Aussiedoodle, flying then can be a disaster.

The period between 8 to 12 weeks is when fear of loud noises develops,
and *anything associated with fear at this stage*
will be a fear stimulus throughout the dog's life.

If a puppy is subjected to shipping when he is going through the first fear period, the potential for long-lasting trauma is extremely high. Because no one has any idea exactly what may have frightened the puppy during shipping, there is no way to "undo" it with a program of desensitization. Some trainers believe that the fact so many puppies are now routinely shipped to their new homes explains a lot of the noise fears (hence the exploding popularity of "thunder shirts") and separation anxiety problems as well as the free-floating anxiety they now see in dogs.

If you think about these problems in terms of what a puppy may have experienced being shipped in the cargo hold on an airline during the first fear period, the theory has merit. How do you think your luggage gets so scuffed up???

The fact that many puppies apparently handle being shipped as well as they do is a credit to the adaptability of the canine psyche, but that's hardly an excuse for putting a puppy through the experience simply because it's more "convenient" for the new owner.

So if you want to keep your puppy safe, give him the best possible start in life and avoid creating any phobias you'll have to identify and figure out how to deal with later, **arrange to pick him up yourself** …your personal convenience is really *not* the most important factor here. Being responsible for a dog for the next 15 years is going to be pretty inconvenient at times, and this is as good a time as any to get used to it.

Does this limit you to breeders near your home? *Of course not.*

If you've selected a responsible breeder six states away, talked at length with the breeder via phone, seen photos and videos of the parents and litter in their environment (not just cute "posed" puppy shots!), and it's just too far to drive, *for heaven's sake just fly in and pick him up.* This is the twenty-first century, for Heaven's sake!

Flying in an underseat pet carrier is not stressful for a puppy at all because the cabin is pressurized, air-conditioned and he is never more than 3 inches from human feet— most will sleep the whole way, even on a cross-country flight, with no need for sedation.

In fact, for reasons unknown, puppies are less likely to get airsick than carsick, assuming they're inside the cabin. (If he gets squirmy mid-flight, he probably needs to relieve himself. Simply carry him to the loo right in his bag and spread out a piddle pad on the floor, which you'll of course have tucked into the pocket of the bag. When he's done, pop him back into the bag and go back to your seat. If you forgot the piddle pad use paper towels.)

If you use air miles or shop around for a deal, you can often pick up your puppy for less than the average cost of shipping, which is usually between $350 and $400. And some breeders will meet you at the airport so you can do it as a "turnaround".

Most airlines charge a fee of around $100 to bring the puppy into the cabin with you, which is irritating on principle but a great deal when you consider the alternatives.

On the other hand, if the breeder does not ENCOURAGE you to fly in

or drive to their home to pick up your new puppy,

but "prefers" to ship,

find yourself a new breeder, because that's the hallmark of a puppy mill.

Substandard breeders actually count on the fact that you will find it more "convenient" to have the puppy shipped, because that way, you won't see the God-awful conditions under which he was raised, or how many dogs they have or how many puppies they are cranking out.

Planning Your Pick-Up Trip

Whether you drive or fly, try to arrange it so that the puppy spends his first night away from his littermates in his new home rather than in a Holiday Inn somewhere along the way.

As everyone who remembers *Lady and the Tramp* is aware, the first night is going to set the tone for what follows, and what you'll have to do to keep a homesick puppy quiet in a hotel room probably won't make the next night any easier.

If you have a long drive it's best to stay at a hotel close to the breeder the night before. That way you can pick up the puppy early enough the next morning to make it home that evening, where his new setup will be waiting for him. (If you can't make the drive home in one day, it's really better to fly in and pick him up— less stress all the way around.)

In addition to a crate, you'll want to pack a "puppy pick-up bag" with the emergency supplies you will almost certainly need for the trip. This should include:

- His collar (with tag attached) and a leash
- A baggie of whatever food he's used to
- A bottle of water and a small bowl
- A big roll of paper towels
- Several plastic grocery bags
- Bonine (half a tab will help a lot if he's carsick)
- An antler to chew on
- A soft toy or towel you can rub on his littermates and/or mom

If you can manage the trip without an extraordinary number of small children and elderly relatives the whole thing will be easier, but two people are better than one— it's best to have a person sitting *next* to him on the ride home rather than sticking him in the back all by himself, where he's much more likely to put up a racket. You're also much more likely to know when he wakes up and has to go so you'll be able to pull into the nearest gas station or rest stop ASAP.

In that regard, if you have to stop to let the puppy out, do try to avoid the "official" dog-walking areas at a rest stop if you can – that's where all the dog germs are! It's far safer to find a less-used grassy area at a service plaza.

Housetraining

Once you've arrived at home, begin your housetraining routine immediately.

Take the puppy out of the car directly to the area of the yard (or sidewalk if your in the city) that you plan to use to for him to relieve himself, tell him to "hurry up". It's good to choose a not-too-stupid phrase and stick to it so your puppy will learn to relieve himself on command—and for Heaven's sake don't use "good boy!" or it will come back to haunt you!

Praise him lavishly when he goes, and then *walk him around a little to sniff and explore afterwards.*

And try to remember that unlike an adult, a puppy rarely empties his bladder all at once, and he's been in the car awhile, so let him squat a couple times so he doesn't have to finish emptying his bladder the first time he sets foot in the house, which is not an auspicious start.

Now, once you're pretty sure he's empty, bring him into the house and directly into his rendezvous area, where he can get a drink of water and a meal. A small meal is best if it's late, but no matter how late it is, you don't want to put him to bed hungry.

Give him time to explore and play a little inside, and as soon as he looks like he needs to go again, take his paw and ring the bell and then take him right out the door that you intend him to use directly to the area you want him to use (this will now be the second time he's been there), and praise lavishly again when he goes.

If he actually starts to relieve himself in the house, you missed the signals, because there always are some and you better figure out what they are—circling, sniffing the floor, whatever. (It varies from puppy to puppy.) But until you do, just say "Oops, outSIDE!" with sufficient volume to stop the flow, scoop him up quickly and take him out to the appointed area to finish (using his paw to quickly hit the bell on the way out), so you can praise him again.

Here's the magic key to housebreaking:

The more times the puppy does it right,
the faster he'll "get it" and let you know he has to go.
The more mistakes he's allowed to make because you're not paying attention
the longer it will take. It's that simple.

It's also good to keep in mind that the average age for a puppy to be really reliably housetrained is 6 months or so, although most Aussiedoodles are reliable way before then. ("Reliably housetrained", by the way, means the dog understands that he is not to eliminate inside, and will hold it until someone lets him out.)

Assuming you're feeding him at the same times each day, actually *writing down* the times when your puppy has a bowel movement and urinates for a couple of days can help a lot, because it allows you to be proactive.

Although this sounds a little OCD, it really *does* help—once you realize that your pup always has a bowel movement 20 minutes after he eats, you can get him outside at the right time; if you have no idea, you're going to have more accidents.

You'll also realize how many times in a single day a puppy pees, which is illuminating, to say the least. Use this information to make up a schedule. (If you're *really* OCD, you'll no doubt design a nifty spreadsheet, but a pen and paper will work just fine.)

Having a bell hanging from the door speeds housebreaking
because a puppy will learn to ring a bell way before he'll learn to bark at the door.

This will avoid puddles in front of the door, which indicates the puppy is learning faster than you are.

This is also a good time to reiterate that you'll get farther faster if you always let the puppy explore and play outside for a little bit *after* he has relieved himself in his designated area, as you did the first time.. If he is always brought inside immediately after he goes, he'll figure that out in a hurry, and it will take him longer and longer to relieve himself so as to stretch out his time outside.

Also, DO remember that young puppies do not generally completely empty their bladders all at once, which is why so many people complain that the puppy went outside and "did his business" and then came inside and promptly made another puddle on the floor. A puppy may have to squat twice or even three times before he's done, so it pays not to be in a huge hurry when he's outside.

Anyhow, continue this "playing-exploring-going outside" routine until it's time for the humans to cash it in and go to bed, remembering to cut off his water supply after 7PM.
(Giving him unlimited access to a big bowl of water 24/7 is not a great idea, by the way—young puppies will drink until they are tired, not until their thirst is satiated, and a puppy can drink a *lot* of water before he gets tired!)

Tuck the puppy in for the night in his little crate in your room (right next to the bed is best at first) with his blanket that smells like home, a stuffed toy for company and his antler chew in case he needs to relieve some stress by chewing a little, and try to get some sleep. He should settle in after some cursory whining, which you will respond to by cheerfully telling him to "go to sleep" rather than by letting him out.
If he's tired out and hasn't had water after 7 PM, he may sleep all night, or he may have to get up at 2 AM. If he does, take him outside (don't forget to ring the bell!), let him relieve himself but not play, and tuck him right back in his crate. (Note: *don't* turn on all the lights or he'll think it's morning and he'll want to play. Nightlights are good if you don't want to run into furniture on the way out.)

As soon as he makes any noise in the morning, take him directly outside, ringing the bell on the way. (If he walks well on a leash, there is an advantage to snapping it on and leading him quickly out the door, because he'll learn the route to the door with his feet. If he's not leash-trained, it's best to carry him, because he can't learn two things at once.) Have your slippers and robe next to the bed and your jacket and snow boots right by the door if need be. DO NOT STOP to go the bathroom yourself— you're a grown-up and should be able to hold it for a couple minutes, while your puppy surely cannot.

The week following should be more of the same, except he'll use his "big crate" for naps during the day, and assuming you don't let him "tank up" on water in the evening he should start making it through the night. This is the week when you want to be sure someone is home pretty much 24/7.

Crate-training

Although a necessary skill to learn (among other things, the desire to keep his bed dry will teach a puppy that he can actually hold it) being alone in a crate is not "natural" for a puppy, nor is it self-rewarding behavior, so you'll want to use treats for this.

Crate-training is best started when he's tired out from 10 or 15 minutes of running around outside and ready for a nap. Pop him into his crate, using a little treat as "bait" if you need to bribe him in there, give him an antler chew, close the door, and leave the room. If he falls asleep, leave him in there undisturbed until he wakes up, then take him immediately out to his exercise area.

If he's clearly not tired and barks and howls and you're sure his bladder is empty, *tell him "settle" (or whatever word you prefer,), and ignore him until he stops.* Immediately letting him out of his crate when he kicks up a fuss is a bad idea, because that rewards the behavior, and even the most dim-witted puppy will quickly learn that barking and whining is the way to avoid staying in his crate.

Once he's quiet for a while (even a minute or two will do it if that's all you can get between tantrums), you can praise him and let him out, because now you've rewarded him for *not* fussing. Run him around until he's really tired this time and try again.

Needless to say, crate-training is much easier if the puppy was already familiarized with the crate by the breeder. (Breeders who take the time to do this are worth their weight in gold. It also makes the ride home a lot easier.)

And NEVER leave a young puppy home alone in a crate so he is forced to eliminate in it, because you will lose ground in the housebreaking department. Until he's housetrained, an expen with a piddle pad or litter is the best choice if he needs to be left alone.

Giving Him Time to Recharge

It's not uncommon for the puppy to spend a lot of Day One or Day Two sleeping quite a bit and maybe seeming a little "off" – if he's eating OK and doesn't have diarrhea or a fever, odds are it's just a stress reaction and he needs the time to recharge his little batteries. (Not surprisingly, this is more common in puppies who've been shipped, which is a lot more stress than being picked up.)

On that note, you will want to take your puppy's temperature on his first full day home, so you have a baseline for what's "normal". (It'll probably be somewhere around 100.5—101.5, but like people, there is natural variance from dog to dog.) That way, if you need to take his temperature because he's throwing up or seems ill, you'll have something to compare it to. And it's often the first question the vet will ask if you call, so it's good to be prepared.

Once your puppy has settled in (which should take no more than a couple of days), you're ready to begin the training program laid out in Chapter 3 of *Mother Knows Best.* Hopefully, you will have read the whole book while waiting for your puppy, so you'll understand the basic philosophy of natural training. And do try to remember that for a puppy, praise is a better reward than food, and correction (which is critical to training a dog or a child) is not he same as "punishment", no matter what the dolphin trainers say. If you want to train a dolphin, get a dolphin.

One last caveat – although all your friends and relatives will be anxious to meet the new puppy, it's best to wait a few days until he's had time to decompress and recharge his batteries before introducing lots more new people into his life. Aussiedoodles (unlike their Goldendoodle cousins) are not among the most stress-tolerant dogs on the planet, so no matter how much the puppy enjoys the attention, being charming is a lot of work and innately stressful, and you'll want to make sure his immune system is up to the task.

Taking Him Out in the Big World

In order to have a well-socialized Aussiedoodle, it is absolutely *imperative* that he be exposed to new people, places and dogs within the first four months of his life. Without it, he can become shy of strangers and fearful of strange dogs and new places. Aussiedoodle breeders all agree that in this breed it is especially important, and failure to get these puppies out in the big world is the main cause of "shyness problems".

On the other hand, your veterinarian will no doubt warn you that it is unsafe to expose your puppy to new places, people and dogs before he has "completed his puppy vaccination schedule", which probably won't happen until he is 4-5 months old, when he gets his rabies shot. And that's *way* too late to start taking your puppy out in the big world for the first time.

This leaves the poor owner, who understands the critical need for socialization but certainly doesn't want his puppy to contract a potentially deadly infectious disease in order to get socialized, caught in the middle, not knowing what to do. Luckily, there is a simple solution here.

When you take your puppy to the vet for his puppy check-up,
simply ask to have a "serum antibody titer" run.

Vets can now buy in-house titer kits very reasonably, and these will tell you within minutes if your puppy is protected against Distemper and Parvo. The average price for having them run is about $30. (If your vet is not aware of this in-house option, a blood sample will need to be sent to an outside lab. Hemopet, which is the best lab to send it to, charges $45 for a parvo and distemper titer, and your vet will probably tack on a few dollars more for the blood draw.)

With MLV (modified live virus) vaccines like those in puppy shots, immunity begins about 5 days after vaccination, so if it's been at least a week since his last vaccination, the titer should accurately reflect his immunity level. If the results show your puppy has adequate immunity, he's good to go pretty much anywhere.

It's interesting to note that in England, puppies are generally vaccinated only twice rather than 3 times as is done here—once at 8 weeks and then again at 10 weeks, after which they are considered immunized and safe to go out and about in the world for socialization. (This abbreviated schedule is recommended by the RSPCA, in fact.) And they use the *exact same vaccines* used in the US!

Now, as your vet is legally bound to point out, your puppy still won't be protected against rabies, which is admittedly deadly to man and beast. But in all honesty a puppy's risk of exposure is just about nonexistent because the US has been free of canine rabies for years, and the only way dogs in the US now contract rabies is from direct contact with rabid skunks or raccoons. Statistically, your puppy is probably more likely to be eaten by an alligator (don't laugh- this is a real risk in some parts of the country!) than he is to contract rabies at Petsmart before he's had his first rabies vaccination.

Where to take your puppy?

A well-trained puppy, especially one as cute as an Aussiedoodle, can go *lots* of places as long as they're on a leash. They can go to soccer games, art fairs, and many outdoor markets. Most parks and downtown "pedestrian" areas are dog-friendly, and some outdoor cafes allow them. Petsmart welcomes leashed dogs, as do many other pet shops. In Florida, dogs are often seen riding in carts in Lowe's and wandering around the garden section.

And then, of course, there are dog parks. These large fenced areas give dogs a place to run and play and socialize with other dogs, and most well-socialized dogs love the experience. For many urban dogs, it's the only place they can safely burn off energy. Although some trainers don't recommend them for puppies, dog parks can be a great experience as long as the owner exercises some common sense. Most dog parks now have a "big dog" area and a "little dog" area, and when a standard-sized Aussiedoodle is a puppy, he should be taken to the latter, where there is less chance he'll be frightened by big rowdy dogs. (Smaller "min" Aussiedoodles will need to stay in the little dog section their whole lives.)

And of course you should be taking him for walks around the neighborhood on a leash from Day One even if you have a fenced-in back yard.

Dogs familiar with their own neighborhood who know their human and canine neighbors are much less likely to panic and get hopelessly lost if they find themselves accidentally loose, which will happen sooner or later no matter how careful you are.

The important thing is not *where* you take your puppy, but that you *do* take him lots of different places, because it's absolutely critical for his socialization. Dogs who are not exposed to what animal behavioralists call "novel stimuli" in the first 3-6 months of life will never be really comfortable away from home as adults, and this can be crippling for the dog and a pain in the butt for the owner.

So take him as many places as you can, and practice some basic on-leash obedience work in as many different places as you can, so he learns to be well-mannered everywhere he goes. And remember to bring clean-up bags!

The other thing you want to do with your puppy in the first 4 months is take him on lots of car rides. If the first and only car trips a puppy experiences in the first 8-11 week "fear" period are to and from the airport, the odds of his developing chronic "car anxiety" and carsickness go way up, because that is the only association he'll make with riding in the car.

Because of this, it's *really* important to take him for short little car trips to somewhere *fun* during this period so he will make positive associations *and* realize that he'll get to come back home again. If you live in Manhattan, take him for short cab rides in a carrier bag for as long as he'll fit in one.

Have Crate, Will Travel...

Dogs like vacations, too. A well-trained Aussiedoodle with a folding wire crate can be taken on most family vacations and is welcomed by many hotels, B&Bs, National and State parks, private campgrounds and more. To find out which ones, check online before you make your reservations— a

Google search for "pet-friendly travel" will bring up lots of helpful websites.

When vacationing with your dog, you might also want to consider vacation rental properties (which rent by the night or week) instead of hotels, as many are pet-friendly and come with fenced yards. And because they come with kitchens, you don't have to worry about the dog barking in a strange hotel room every time you go out for meals.

For lots of reasons, pet-friendly vacation rental properties are the best thing that ever happened to dog owners. VRBO is a great website to check in this regard – all listings with a paw print are pet-friendly. Even if they only accept pets under 20 pounds, you can often get around that by explaining that your dog is crate-trained and will be left in his crate any time he is left alone.

And if you are staying with family or friends, a well-behaved crate-trained dog is much more likely to be welcome than one who isn't.

And When He Just Can't Go Along...

However, no matter how well-behaved your Dood may be, there are bound to be some times he just can't go along.

For example, if you are flying and your dog doesn't fit under the seat in a soft-side carrier, it's really safer and less stressful for him to leave him home than to check him as baggage and hope he ends up in the same city you do. Even if you're driving, funerals are another event where even the best-trained Dood might not be welcome. Weddings can go either way, but destination weddings in exotic locations are usually not dog-friendly.

In those cases, you have three options—you can A) leave him with friends, B) hire a pet sitter, or C) take him to a boarding kennel. Each has its advantages and disadvantages.

If your puppy is young (like less than 4 months or so), you may want to consider leaving him with friends he knows, because a boarding kennel will be pretty traumatic and he'll be lonely staying home alone with a pet sitter, unless you can find someone to stay at your house full-time.
Geriatric dogs (who sleep a lot anyway), or dogs who live in a multiple-dog household, may prefer to be left at home with a sitter coming in a few times a day, especially if it's only for the weekend. Young energetic dogs will probably be safest (and have the most fun!) at a boarding kennel.

If you choose option C), be sure and do your homework first. Most boarding kennels now have websites, and you can see what their rates are and if you like the place before you even call. Some even have webcams so you can check on your dog.

It's still a good idea to physically visit the kennel before you commit to it, though. As with breeders, you want to steer clear of any place that does not encourage you to visit, or won't let you get past the office to see where the dogs are actually kenneled.

If you find a kennel you like and use it exclusively, you may find your dog is actually happy to go there—luckily, dogs often have a very different idea of what constitutes a "vacation" than people do, and social dogs like Doods can find a kennel situation, where there are lots of new dogs to run and play with, pretty exciting.

One of the things you want to find out is whether the kennel has secure "play areas" and scheduled exercise periods as well as individual runs. If it does not, your dog will be safe, but he'll be bored silly.

Also check to make sure the kennel accepts titers in lieu of annual vaccinations. Some do and some don't. Most will still require bordatella (kennel cough) vaccination, and all will require an up-to-date rabies certificate.

What to Expect in the First Year

It's important to remember that for a canine, most of their physical and psychological growth takes place in the first year. The old "dog years" rule does not apply to the first year, because a year old dog is not the equivalent of a seven year old– he's usually achieved his adult height, he's sexually mature, and he's mentally well into adolescence by 12 months.

And although Aussiedoodles do not grow with the blinding speed of their larger cousins (which is probably why there are few if any orthopedic problems reported in the breed) in the space of 12 short months, he will grow from a blind and helpless little slug weighing less than a pound to a physically and sexually mature animal that may weigh close to 60 pounds.

Even a small mini Aussiedoodle will go from 8 ounces to maybe 15 pounds...if you think about it, that means at a year he will weigh 30 times more than what he started at. Compared to human growth in the first year of life, that is still phenomenal.

This rapid mental and physical growth is biologically "expensive", and not surprisingly during this period his brain and his immune system may not always be able to keep up. This REALLY needs to be taken into consideration, in both training and *especially* in regards to vaccinations given and toxic anti-parasitics used in the first year.

Within a space of a few months your adorable puppy dashes headlong from roly-poly toddlerhood (that's usually when you pick him up) to gangly puberty and then without even stopping for breath charges into full-blown adolescence, at which point he appears to have forgotten everything he knew a few months earlier.

Virtually all of the critical phases of canine development take place within the first year.

These phases (which include the development of the fear response) are like so much else, hard-wired into his DNA and were necessary to survival in the wild, even if they seem less critical (and often counterproductive) in a domesticated suburban companion. Knowing what is occurring at various stages will help a lot in maintaining your sense of humor.

The Good News is, as long as you are consistent and firm in your training, and willing to correct and reinforce when needed as adolescence strikes, both you and your Dood will make it through just fine. It's also good to remember that if you can just get through the first two years, the next ten or twelve are pretty easy sledding.

CHAPTER SIX:

Feeding Your Aussiedoodle
(or...Ignorance is NOT always bliss)

Like a whole lot of other things, feeding the family dog is a LOT more complicated than it used to be. Even a decade ago, most people did no research at all before they bought dog food—they either fed the food the breeder recommended, or most often they just fed the same food they fed their previous dog.

Now, if those dogs lived a long and healthy life, this would appear to be a sensible approach, and it in fact it would be...except for one thing:

The INGREDIENTS in all dog foods have changed radically in the last few years, so they're not really "the same foods" at all.

As if this wasn't bad enough, what now happens all too often is that somewhere along the way, the new owner will no doubt run into someone who explains to them why the food that they have been feeding with great results is actually *poisoning* their poor dog, and why they should immediately switch to a "healthier", and often much more expensive brand.

The new owner, lacking confidence, will start feeding this new food (which probably won't be any better for their dog) because they figure this expert surely knows a lot more than they do.

These self-styled "dog food experts" also abound on the internet, and several maintain websites that "rank" various brands of dog food. Unfortunately, very few of them appear to have any related academic credentials, and although they certainly mean well, a lot of the information provided is inaccurate, and in some cases can actually endanger your dog's very life.

The two notable exceptions are Dr. Richard H. Pitcairn, who has a veterinary degree from UC Davis and PhDs in both immunology and microbiology from Washington State, and Donald R. Strombeck DVM PhD, a gastroenterologist and Professor Emeritus at UC Davis Vet School.
Both of them strongly advocate cooking for your own dog at home and both have written widely on the subject, including recipes that will provide the necessary nutritional balance.
Both of their books are on the book list in Chapter Four

So What's the Best Food to Feed?

This one's a no-brainer. Fresh food is best. And if you really want to feed your dog only fresh, high-quality food without having to worry about the quality or source of the ingredients, or contamination during manufacturing, or what god-awful chemicals might be in there, you unfortunately have very few options. The most economical is of course to cook it at home yourself.

Surprisingly, even for a large dog, this is much easier than one might expect and will cost no more, and often much less, than buying high-end commercial dog food. There are lots of books on the subject on Amazon, with lots of recipes. In fact, Dr Strombeck has a bunch of them right on his website **(www.dogcathomeprepareddiet.com)** if you don't want to buy a whole book. If time is a factor, you can easily cook up a week's worth in an hour or two and freeze it in 7 separate containers.

If you eat organically yourself and want the same for your dog,
cooking for your dog is the ONLY way to go,
because the word "organic" is used pretty loosely in the dog food world.

One of the most alarming trends in dog food is what's called *green-washing,* which is no more than a marketing trick to make the ingredients (which are often the exact same ingredients found in less-expensive foods, as you will see) simply sound more appealing by using words like "organic", "human-grade" and "natural", which is perfectly legal. This allows the manufacturers to charge more for them, although most are still loaded with creepy pesticide-laden genetically modified ingredients.

Genetically Modified dog food? You betcha!!

If you want to avoid GMO ingredients in dog food, you're going to have to work at it. Considering that around 80% of the corn, soybeans, canola and sugar beets produced in this country are now genetically modified, they are virtually impossible to avoid **unless you cook your own food**. (This is a relatively new situation, by the way—the first genetically modified crops started appearing in 1996 and have grown exponentially since then.) This is true of both human and pet food, by the way.

And because, unlike most other developed nations, at present *there are no Federal laws requiring labeling for GMO ingredients in either human or dog food in the US,* you'll have to take any dog food company who claims to use "only non-GMO ingredients" entirely at their word.

Even worse, a "grain free" dog food may not even be GMO-free, if the meat source has been fed GMO feeds. Although it was not supposed to happen, new research from a large 10 year study in Norway shows that the Bt toxin (an insecticide genetically engineered to be produced by the plant itself in many of Monsanto's GMO crops to make them insect-resistant) appears to travel right through the food chain. And a recent Canadian study found Bt toxin in the blood of 93% of pregnant women tested.

Can GMO products adversely affect a dog's health? *Very likely.*

That same Norwegian study published in 2012 showed that *in every species tested,* animals fed GMO corn got fatter, showed immune system changes and were less able to digest proteins due to changes in their digestive systems when compared to the control animals.
(It's worth knowing sweet potatoes, rice, oats, barley, potatoes and wheat are not, at present anyway, genetically modified. Monsanto's GMO wheat is expected to enter the market by 2013, though.)

And last but not least, if you cook for your dog yourself, you won't have to worry about whether or not your dog food has been recalled because of possibly deadly contamination by salmonella or e-Coli or aflatoxin or something, which happens a LOT more than people think.

These recalls due to food-borne pathogens have become at least as common in dog food as they have in the human food chain, and for the same reason– Agribusiness. Because of the way our food supply is now designed, when you eat a hamburger, you are no longer eating the meat of one cow— **the meat of up to a thousand cows can end up in a single pound of ground beef.** And because these cattle now spend months crowded together in feed lots knee deep in manure until the moment they are slaughtered, the possibility of bacterial contamination is astronomical.

Welcome to Dog Food Inc.
(or...the trouble with having an open mind is that your brains may fall out.)

What most people do not realize about American pet food is that it's a lot like American human food—in other words, it's Big Business. In 2010 alone, pet food sales in the US amounted to around 18 BILLION DOLLARS.

And although few people realize it, most of the dog food brands out there are in fact owned by only a small handful of the same multinational corporations we all know and love.

Some of these giants own their own dog food manufacturing facilities, while others subcontract production out to huge "contract manufacturers" you've probably never heard of, and some of whom have been shown by FDA to have appallingly low standards for basic hygiene.

Here's a rundown of who currently owns which well-known dog food brands, admittedly incomplete and subject to change at any given moment due to corporate mergers:

Mars, Inc. *Owns the Pedigree, Royal Canin, Kal Kan, Waltham and Nutro brands.*

Products in the US are manufactured in 16 Mars-owned plants around the country. It also contract manufactures the O' Roy brand for Walmart. Mars owns the Waltham Centre for Pet Nutrition in England, a state-of-the-art canine nutritional research facility, and is currently building one in the US. (And, yes, this is the same Mars that makes M&Ms. Mars also bought the Wm. Wrigley Jr. Co in 2008 for $23 billion in a cash deal. That's a lot of chewing gum.)

Nestle Purina Inc. *Owns the ProPlan, ProPlan Selects, Purina ONE, Purina ONE Beyond, Purina Dog Chow, Puppy Chow, Mighty Dog, Beneful and Alpo brands.*

In the US, Purina products are all produced in one of Purina's 13 company-owned and managed manufacturing plants. Purina does not contract manufacture for other companies. According to the company, all of their dog food ingredients are sourced entirely from the US, although they are not GMO-free. Ralston Purina, founded in 1894, merged with Swiss-based Nestle back in 2003, although the Nestle Purina Pet Care Division, including their (also state-of-the-art) canine nutritional research facility, is still based near St Louis, MO and is open for tours.

Proctor and Gamble Inc. *Owns the Iams and Eukanuba brands, and Natura's Innova, Evo, California Natural, Healthwise, Mother Nature, and Karma brands.*

Some products are manufactured at company-owned facilities (Natura products are produced at the P & G-owned Natura plant in Nebraska), while most are contracted out. P&G also makes many well-known cleaning products, and used to make Pringles but sold them to Kelloggs for $2.7 billion.

Colgate-Palmolive Inc. *Owns the Hill's Science Diet, Prescription Diet and Nature's Best brands, which are contract-manufactured.*

Longtime makers of toothpaste, dish soap and a gazillion other personal care products, they also now own the Tom's of Maine brand, which they purchased for $100 million back in 2006. **Bummer.**

Del Monte Inc. *Owns the Nature's Recipe, Milk-Bone and Kibbles N Bits brands. Del Monte also does contract manufacturing of various private label dog foods.*

Other than pet foods, canning industry giant Del Monte mostly produces canned fruits and vegetables now that they sold their Star-Kist Tuna brand to Dongwan Enterprises, a South Korean company, for $300 million.

Diamond Pet Foods Inc. *Owns the Diamond, Diamond Naturals, Chicken Soup for the Dog Lover's Soul, Kirkland, and Taste of the Wild brands, and does contract manufacturing for Dick Van Patton's Natural Balance, Wellness, 4Health Pet Food, Canidae and Solid Gold.*

Diamond only manufactures dry food and contracts out its canned foods, so some of these brands also offer products produced by other contract manufacturers. Foods produced by Diamond have been involved in several recalls in past years and at least one of its plants has been cited by FDA.

Simmons Pet Foods Inc – *A giant in the poultry processing industry, Simmons is the second-largest employer in the state of Arkansas after Tyson. Its pet food division is probably now the largest contract manufacturer and private label producer of dog food in the country and produces canned foods for most of the dog food industry, with the exception of Purina.*

Simmons bought contract manufacturer Menu Foods in 2010 for $239 million after Menu was caught up in the "tainted wheat gluten" scandal. As their website states:
"In a world obsessed with brand names, ours is conspicuously absent. You brand is our brand, and we wouldn't have it any other way." Now that's scary. What foods do they make? Who knows.

Other contract manufacturers of both canned and dry dog foods whose names you've likely also never heard but who manufacture foods for well-known brands include the following:

CJ Foods —*makes Blue Buffalo and Burns Pet Health canned foods*

Ohio Pet Foods —*makes Blue Buffalo and Life's Abundance dry foods*

Chenango Valley Pet Foods —*makes Drs Foster & Smith, Back to Basics*

Blue Sky - *makes Solid Gold.*

Crosswinds Industries —*makes Nature's Logic*

American Nutrition —*makes Natural Balance*

Ainsworth —*makes Dad's, VF, Rachel Ray's Nutrish*

For the record, Blue Sky is actually the contract manufacturing division of *Merrick Pet Care,* the dog food division of *Tejas Industries,* a family-owned Texas corporation whose holding include a nearby rendering plant that formerly operated under the name *Hereford Bi-products.* Merrick also manufactures and sells dog food under its own name.

The list of companies that produce their own dry foods in their own manufacturing facilities is far more limited, but includes the following ones, none of whom appear to have run afoul of the FDA in the quality-control department:

Nestle-Purina — *manufactures all its Purina-branded products and its new ProPlan Training Treats in its own plants, the only one of the "giants" to do so.*

Champion Pet Foods —*a Canadian company that owns and manufactures the Acana and Orijin brands at its own plant in Canada.*

Central Garden &Pet Company —*a California company that produces the Breeder's Choice Pinnacle and Avaderm brands at its company-owned Irwindale, CA plant.*

Fromm's — *a Wisconsin-based company that manufactures its Fromm's dry foods at its company-owned Mequon WI plant.*

In other words, with very few exceptions, dog food branding has become a deliberate shell game, and it's pretty hard for the average consumer to figure out where their dog food is actually made, or who actually owns the *company*, much less the factory.

So consumers believe they're buying from small companies that use only "carefully hand-selected wholesome ingredients", when they're NOT.

Instead, they're paying a premium price for the *illusion* that their dog food is made in a sunny kitchen full of cheerful elves mixing up vats of healthy meats and fresh colorful veggies from the local health food store, when odds are pretty good it's being churned out in ten-ton runs in a humongous totally mechanized factory (some of which are state-of-the-art and some of which are pretty awful) that may also manufacture much cheaper brands, using many of *the exact same raw ingredients*.
Here's why....

It is the *contract manufacturer* who purchases the ingredients, NOT the company whose brand name is on the bag.

For example, "chicken meal" is all purchased by the ton by the contract manufacturer from rendering plants and trucked in. It is frankly unlikely to be "carefully hand-selected", no matter what the pretty bags or company websites say. And every company they contract manufacture for is getting the same chicken meal. **Meat meals and poultry meals ALL come from rendering plants, no matter how dog food companies try to spin that unappetizing fact.**

The reason is simple: Although rendering lard can actually be done in one's kitchen (assuming you have a big pot, access to the fat of a freshly slaughtered hog and don't mind the smell), rendering whole animal *carcass*es into safe and usable meal requires millions of dollars in high-tech equipment if one does not wish to run afoul of the EPA. Even organic farmers don't render their own chicken meal—they can't. And no chicken meal is "carefully prepared from whole chicken breasts" like the kind you buy at Publix, no matter how much people *want* to believe that— it's the whole chicken carcass, sans the good meat, the feathers and the guts. (There's really no tooth fairy, either.)

The truth is, making dog food is a lot like making any other modern processed meat product like chicken nuggets, hamburger, sausage and hot dogs—decidedly unappetizing. (Think pink slime.) The bottom line is NOBODY should be eating this stuff—not us and not our animals— but unless one shops entirely organically or lives very close to the land, it's a fact of American life.

Another major problem with commercial dog food is that the labeling requirements are pretty loose. There are really no rules for terms like "all-natural", "organic", "holistic", or "human-grade", which represent the fastest-growing segment of the dog food market. Basically, you can call your dog food "Good Earth's Holistic All-Natural Organic Blend" even if it's made from recycled Twinkies and there's no law against it.

In fact, no dog food that meets the national nutritional guidelines can qualify as USDA 100% certified organic, because all of the vitamin and mineral supplements required to meet the guidelines are simply not available in organic form.

This makes all those websites that "rank" different brands of dog food pretty much useless, because they are all based on what the company itself says about their products and what's in them, *which is written by professional marketing guys who've probably never been to the plant and which may or may not be true.* In some cases, these ratings may be *worse* than useless.
Here's an appalling example:

One small company, which invariably receives "5 stars" on all the dog food rating websites, was recently sent a warning letter by the FDA. Why?

A random check of their products revealed that the meat in their "Lamb and Rice Dog Food" was really not lamb at all, but rather according to FDA analysis was *"bovine material"*. For their "Grain-free Duck Pet Food", ***"analytical sample results did not detect the presence of duck in the product."*** (Now the FDA did not specify what actually *was* in the food, just that it was *not* duck, which is a little scary if you think about it.)
And this is one of the most expensive dog foods on the market!

*It should also be noted that although the company was cited for "adulteration" by the FDA due to the discovery of meat other than what was listed on the label, these products **were not recalled**, presumably because they did not pose a danger to animals or humans. And their 5 star ratings are STILL up there on the "dog food rating" websites.*

Several other small companies boasting 5 star ratings from these websites have their dog food made by contract manufacturers who've received warning letters from FDA within the last two years citing them for salmonella contamination detected in their products, and/or detailing serious deficiencies in their manufacturing processes in areas ranging from temperature control and sanitation to failure of their raw ingredients to meet the nutritional specifications listed.

Although these letters are all duly archived deep in the bowels of the FDA's website and technically available to the public, odds are the average consumer will never be aware of their existence.

But the biggest danger in commercial dog food lies not in the admittedly unappetizing "sourcing" of ingredients or the possible long-term adverse effects on the immune system from genetically modified ingredients, but rather in the possibilities of *adulteration and contamination*, because these two can kill your dog within days.

Over the past 10 years alone, adulterated and contaminated dog food has actually *sickened and killed thousands of pets who ate the products before they were recalled.*

And in the case of e-Coli and salmonella, this contamination has the potential to do the same to people who come in contact with these dogs. (In April 2012, a rare form of salmonella linked to contaminated dog food produced at a Diamond plant in Gaston SC sickened over a dozen people in 14 states, including a 4 month old baby.)

In 2007, adulteration of imported wheat gluten (a fairly benign ingredient routinely used in many human and animal foods) with melamine caused kidney failure resulting in illness and death in thousands of pets across the country.

And because the manufacturing of so much dog food is outsourced, one single contract manufacturer who purchased this contaminated ingredient, Menu Foods, was responsible for the recall of *nearly 60 different brands,* including 5 of the 6 top-branded dog food companies in the US. (Heck, Newman's Own Organic was made at Menu!)

As with human food, because of the way commercial dog foods are sourced, manufactured, and packaged, contamination by food-borne pathogens (like salmonella or e-Coli) can occur at any point in the process, *even if the manufacturer has good quality control.*

The only real defense against this (in both the human and canine food chain) is to constantly test for adulteration and contamination at every point in the process, and if it is detected, to quickly identify the source of contamination and/or the ingredient containing it, immediately shut down the plant producing it, notify customers and remove all contaminated products from retail shelves ASAP if they've gotten that far.

Not surprisingly, this gets a whole lot easier if the company whose name is on the bag actually controls the entire process.

Companies that purchase their own ingredients, manufacture food in their own plants, and control the sale of it have the best chance of getting a product off retailer's shelves in a hurry if it's found to contain a potentially harmful pathogen.

As became appallingly obvious during the dog food recalls of 2007, companies that outsource the purchase of ingredients as well as the manufacturing and packaging of their foods simply cannot do that—in fact, it turned out that some of them did not even know what ingredients were really in their own dog food!

So… if you don't want to cook your own dog food, the safest option is probably to buy a brand from a company that purchases its own ingredients and manufactures its foods in its own facilities, and whose quality-control standards are such that they've not received any warning letters from the FDA concerning violations in the last few years at least. AND the company should allow the public to tour their manufacturing facilities.

Buying dog food from a company that won't let you to see where it's made is like buying a puppy from a breeder that won't allow you to visit— there's probably a good reason for it.

So how, exactly, do you determine if a company actually purchases its own ingredients and manufactures its own food? *The easiest way is to call the company and ASK them.* Every dog food company has a phone number on its website and its product labels. If you ask the questions, they'll pretty much have to answer them.

The most important question is: "*Do you own your own manufacturing plants? If not, what is the name and address of the company currently manufacturing your dog food?*"

There is not a single legitimate reason not to share this information with the consumer.

Another good question is: *"Are all of your ingredients sourced from the US?"*

If they say no, hem and haw, don't know, or flat-out won't tell you, for Heaven's sake *don't buy their food*. (And just for the record, virtually all US or Canadian-sourced corn, soy, sugar beet and canola products are now genetically modified.)

It's also important to note that although a company may manufacture all its own dry dog food, it may *not* manufacture its canned foods or dog treats, many of which are imported (usually from China), and they rarely volunteer that information

So What About Dog Treats?

For the most part, they're worse.
If the number of annual recalls is any indication (which it is), commercial dog treats in general seem to be much more susceptible to contamination than dry or even canned dog food.

In particular, given its symbiotic relationship with food-borne pathogens, the idea of drying poultry into jerky is really stupid, which is probably why no human culture has ever eaten it.
To keep your dog safe, don't buy dog jerky treats AT ALL, and don't try to make them yourself, either.

With few exceptions, most dog treats are imported or contract-manufactured in the US with ingredients imported from Asia, mostly because it's cheaper.

The whole "dog treat" business is sheer anthropomorphism anyhow. In general, dogs in the US have gotten a lot fatter as the treat market has grown, and overweight dogs are way more prone to health problems.
No matter what the "foodie" trainers say, it's far better for a dog's *health* if he works for praise rather than for constant food rewards… and he'll be a lot more reliable, too. (Drug and bomb-sniffing dogs have been traditionally rewarded with a quick Kong toss, so odds are your Aussiedoodle can learn to cheerfully execute a simple sit-stay without having to resort to bribing him with treats.)
Probably the *safest* thing to do in the treats department is to just buy your dog a box of little organic crackers made for people (wheat and rice are not, as of 2012, genetically modified, just for the record), or bake your own dog biscuits, which is really easy. A pocketful of Rice Chex cereal is a time-honored training treat for young puppies, and they are little enough so you don't have to wait forever for the puppy to chew them.

And if you need something really spectacular to reward your dog with (like after a grooming session), just buy some beef jerky *made for people*, for Heaven's sake.

Made entirely in the US, Jack Link's is hard to beat, and you can buy it at virtually any checkout counter in America, including the one at your local gas station. But even then, dehydrated meat should only be given to a dog in little teeny-weeny pieces because without the 80% water that comprises fresh meat, you're giving the dog a lot of extra protein.

And while we're on the subject of treats, giving a dog constant food rewards just for being cute or because you feel guilty is a bad idea on many levels—Lord only knows what the dog thinks he's being rewarded for, but odds are it won't improve his overall behavior. (Just for the record, that focused intense stare most people read as "begging" is actually *demanding* in dog language, and giving in to a dog's demands for food will not raise your status in his eyes.)

What about "Raw Feeding"?

In the world of dogs, probably nothing is more controversial than raw feeding. The whole concept of feeding Bones And Raw Food (get it?) began with a book by an Australian veterinarian named Ian Billinghurst back in 1993 called "Give Your Dog a Bone". His BARF Diet™ is now commercially produced and is sold on his website, **www.barfworld.com**. (I swear I am not making this up. Maybe "barf" is just not a slang term for "vomit" in Australia…but really… wouldn't you do a little research before you slapped a trademark on it????)

Although raw feeding proponents maintain such a huge presence on the internet it seems like practically EVERYONE is doing it, surveys show that actually only around 2% of dogs in the US are actually raw-fed. And here's why:

There's Simply No Hard Science ... yet.

Besides what might be called the Yuck Factor (many people are just not comfortable finding old dog-hair-covered chunks of raw chicken backs under the couch), the main problem with raw feeding is that virtually all of its health advantages are anecdotal.

To date there has never been a single controlled scientific study to either support or debunk the claims of raw food's nutritional superiority over cooked food.

Proponents of raw diets claim that enzymes critical to digestion of protein are destroyed by heating.

This is absolutely true. But dogs, like most protein-based animals, produce their *own* digestive enzymes for the digestion of protein, so this is really sort of a stupendously dumb argument.

In fact, one of the few digestive enzymes canines do *not* produce is amylase, which is needed for the digestion of raw plant matter. Dogs just can't get any useful amount of nutrients from raw grains and veggies, although they're great for people and whole raw carrots are good for cleaning a dog's teeth

As far as destruction of the protein itself goes, controlled laboratory studies have shown that the protein levels in fish is reduced by a whopping 1.5% after heating for 10 minutes at 266 degrees, which represents some seriously overcooked fish.
And an egg (one of the most complete animal-based proteins on the planet) contains 6 grams of protein cooked or raw. The *digestibility* of the protein in that egg, however, goes from 51% if consumed raw to a whopping 90% if cooked, which would appear to be an argument for cooking it.

The same is true of many vegetables and grains like corn (which for unknown reasons people suddenly believe is indigestible to dogs). Once cooked, the digestibility of corn, and the bioavailability of its nutrients, goes up to over 90%. Raw corn, like all other grains, is pretty indigestible, but you probably already know that. And Monsanto's double-stacked GMO corn (which is most corn available today) comes with its own problems and probably shouldn't be fed to anything, including livestock and farmed fish. Raccoons won't even touch that stuff.

In case you're curious, the digestibility of various foodstuffs is determined by measuring the nutrient levels of what goes into one end of the dog and comparing those numbers to the nutrient levels of what comes out the other end using *spectrophotometric analysis*. The difference is the percentage of digestibility. This is obviously not something the average dog owner can do at home.

But Isn't Raw Feeding More Natural?

As far as raw food being the "natural" diet for canines, that's pretty hard to argue with since the species has never managed to master the art of cooking, but it's also worth knowing that wolves in zoos, who are primarily fed commercial dog food supplemented with roadkill, live several years longer on average than the oldest recorded wolf in the wild. This may or may not actually have anything to do with nutrition, but it's a fact nonetheless, and at the very least it would indicate that cooked food doesn't automatically *shorten* their lives
All that said, anecdotal evidence indicates that a lot of dogs apparently thrive on a raw diet. The truth is, dogs apparently can thrive on *lots* of different diets—it's one of their strongest evolutionary advantages as a species, especially when compared to Pandas, who eat only bamboo.

131

But raw feeding (whether prepared at home or purchased commercially) has one HUGE disadvantage, and its importance cannot be understated, especially in the US:

Cooking kills most food-borne pathogens
that can pose a serious health risk to
PEOPLE.
(duhhh....!!!)

Although most healthy adult dogs appear less susceptible to them, food-borne pathogens like salmonella, E.coli, and campylobacter do sicken and kill thousands of people each year in the US alone. These three pathogens are ubiquitous in raw chicken—according to the CDC, probably three-quarters of the chicken sold in grocery stores is carrying one or another of them, and thanks to widespread antibiotic use in the poultry industry, many strains are now antibiotic-resistant. (In fact, new research indicates that some 85% of human urinary tract infections are caused by E.coli from chicken.)

No matter how carefully raw meat is handled prior to feeding, studies have shown that dogs fed a raw diet shed these pathogens in their saliva, urine and feces. As this presents a clear health hazard to humans who may come in contact with it, neither the FDA nor the USDA recommends feeding uncooked meat to household pets. Because they visit hospitals and nursing homes, where compromised immune systems abound, Delta Society, one of the nation's oldest and most-respected therapy dog associations, will no longer allow raw-fed dogs in its PetPartners Therapy program. Bottom line with Raw Feeding is this:

Raw Feeding may indeed be perfectly healthy for dogs,
and in fact it may even be BETTER for them, for all we know.
But it presents a serious and well-documented potential danger for the humans
they may come in even casual contact with—especially babies, children, the elderly, and those
with autoimmune disease or immune systems compromised by chemotherapy.

In a litigious society like ours (and where it seems like every third person you run into has either a compromised immune system or an autoimmune disease) that alone should give one pause.

Is there any Commercially Available "Fresh" Food?

So now that you know a whole lot more than you did about commercial dog food and how it's all made, you've probably realized that if you REALLY want your dog to have food made of "fresh, wholesome, natural ingredients", it's not likely to come out of a bag or a can no matter *what* the company's website says or what ridiculous price the company charges for it. **Does that mean you have absolutely NO fresh food alternatives other than to cook for your dog yourself?**

Until pretty recently, the answer to that was unfortunately YES, YOU DON'T, at least in the US, where the concept of refrigerated "fresh" food for dogs simply hadn't occurred to anyone— the whole multi-billion-dollar industry has been stuck in the "canning and extrusion" mode developed over 50 years ago. In Australia, however, refrigerated fresh pet food represents around 30% of the pet food market....who KNEW?

Apparently a group of guys from Secaucus, New Jersey did. And they started a company to introduce fresh, junk-free cooked dog food to the American market in 2007. Originally available in the NY/NJ area, their Freshpet line is now carried nationwide in refrigerator cases in selected pet stores, grocery stores and even some Wal-marts. (Their website, **www.Freshpet.com,** has an interactive store locator.) Price-wise, they are pretty comparable to any of the high-end brands.

Freshpet foods are not organic, but they are wheat, corn and soy-free and do not contain any genetically-modified grains or ingredients from rendering plants. (In fact, their ingredients list is pretty short and everything on it is totally pronounceable.) There are several formulas, including an entirely grain-free one. And as their products are refrigerated, they lack the over-processing necessary for canning or extended shelf-life in dry foods.

Their prodcuts come in casings (sort of like Jimmy Dean pork sausage) which you just slice and serve, or in little containers like you'd get at the deli. Some people mix it with kibble and some just feed it by itself, which is also OK because it's nutritionally balanced to stand alone. **And most important, Freshpet produces its own products in its own company-owned plant in Quakertown, Pennsylvania, which gives them total quality control.**

In addition to their basic foods, Freshpet has introduced a line of dog treats (including a line of turkey bacon strips that taste so good you could feed them to your family and they'd never know it was a dog treat!) and a doggy "cookie" dough you can bake at home in your own oven.

All in all, they currently represent the only really viable alternative (in the US at least) for those who want to feed their dog fresh food but don't have the time or inclination to cook it themselves. Hopefully more companies will follow their lead.

Actually feeding your Aussiedoodle.

Now that you have the facts about the production and marketing of commercial dog food, you should have sufficient confidence to decide whether to stay with the food he's on, to change to another brand you're more comfortable with, or to cook for your dog yourself.

Whatever you decide, this is something you'll want to do slowly by mixing the foods incrementally, or you will have "digestive upset" as sure as God made little green apples, and you'll have to clean up the results. And probably for the first couple weeks you'll want to stick with what he's used to eating, because there have been enough major changes in his short life already.

So the next step is actually getting your puppy to EAT. An awful lot of Aussiedoodles are reported to be sort of indifferent eaters, much to their owners' collective distress. This tendency is probably inherited to some degree from their notoriously picky Poodle ancestors, since the average Australian Shepherd would eat gravel if you put it in his bowl. Not surprisingly, in all Poodle hybrids the F1bs seem to be pickier as a rule than the F1s, and dogs with Mini or Toy Poodles behind them are generally pickier than those bred from Standards. But genetic tendencies aside, exactly how picky a dog ends up is largely owner-determined.

What typically happens is that the owner comes home with his new puppy and a bag of *the exact same food he's been eating since he started on solid food,* and the first time it's offered the puppy won't eat it. In fact, he looks at it like it's some sort of toxic waste you've put in his bowl to poison him.

There is no way to overstate this:
What you do in the next 48 hours will determine whether you have a picky eater for life,
or a dog who'll cheerfully and enthusiastically eat anything you put in his bowl.

Think about this carefully for a minute— besides his mother's milk, this particular food is *all your puppy has ever eaten.* In his limited experience, that's what food IS…he has absolutely no framework for "liking" it or "not liking" it.

Odds are, he's not eating because his system is stressed from changing homes, which means his level of stress hormones like cortisol are elevated. The first thing a dog's instincts tell him to do when this happens is to keep his tummy empty— it's hard-wired into his DNA from much earlier times, and is a logical part of the fight-or-flight response. Whether one ends up fighting or fleeing, it's easier to do it on an empty stomach. (In fact, man is probably the *only* animal that actually eats as a response to stress, or while traveling. And you can see how well *that's* worked out for us!)

If your puppy refuses a meal, simply pick up the dish after 10-15 minutes
and wait until his next scheduled mealtime,
at which point you simply offer him the exact same meal again.

And for Heaven's sake do not add anything to "tempt his palate", which is anthropomorphism at its worst. Dogs have spectacular olfactory capabilities compared to ours, but it is now known that they have significantly fewer taste buds. This should not come as a big surprise to dog owners…I mean, really—this is a species that collectively views a dirty cat litter box as an all-you-can-eat buffet. Gourmands they're not.

Once you start changing foods to get him to eat, you allow the puppy to initiate a game called "what do I feel like eating today?" and *it will never end*, because when it comes to this game, dogs play to win. It will also lead to other behavioral problems.

In the world of canines, the *alpha* controls the food,
which is what the "picky-eating" game is REALLY about.

In the wild, the pack's alphas eat what and when they want, and pack status is what is being tested here. Unless a dog is simply not hungry or is actually ill, picky eating is generally about *control*, not taste. This is also why keeping food down all the time so the dog can eat whenever he feels like it is not a good idea. A dog who is in charge of his own food will almost always expand the battle for dominance into other areas…growling over food and then possessions invariably comes next.

And while some dogs actually get a kick out of maintaining a high-ranking position in their "human" pack (although they will be a pain in the butt to live with), Aussiedoodles are going to be stressed-out if they find themselves in a higher position than that with which they are comfortable— it's sort of the "Peter Principle" for dogs. This breed really needs to know somebody is in charge in order to maintain emotional balance, and it is the owner's responsibility to reassure them of that..

Missing a meal is not going to hurt a healthy puppy – the canine is by definition a "stuff-or-starve" predator and in the wild, food for cubs does not appear on a rigid schedule. The reason we keep our puppy on a schedule is because it makes housebreaking much easier, not because it's critical to his metabolism

Clearly, if the puppy appears lethargic, is vomiting and/or has a fever, you need to call the vet...you do need to exercise some common sense here.

But odds are, if a puppy doesn't eat, it's because he's simply not hungry, and the next time you put the same food down, he *will* eat it, because he probably now is. (It's good to remember that humans are one of the few species that eats when not actually physically hungry...and look at the result of that!)

Switching Foods

The other big mistake you'll want to avoid is changing dog foods on a regular basis. Unless your dog food brand has been recalled or you've lost confidence in the company, you can really feed the same food forever, with the exception of maybe switching from puppy to adult formula. (Even then, it's best to stay with the same brand and just switch formulas.)

Although humans think it's the spice of life, variety is just not a big deal for dogs, and it upsets both their psyches and their stomachs. If your Dood is eating his food, is not too fat, has nice firm stools and his coat is thick and shiny.........don't switch foods just for variety's sake or you could regret it.

For some reason (probably because of all the experts on the internet!) as soon as a dog starts scratching, the owner assumes it's because he's "allergic" to something in his dog food and will immediately switch to another brand. This is usually a mistake.

Veterinary literature over the years has shown that 90% of dog allergies are caused by reactions to something *other than food.*

If your dog is scratching a lot, before you change dog foods you should probably run a flea comb through him nose to tail, because according to veterinary data, that's the #1 reason dogs scratch.

If there are no fleas and no flea dirt (a dog can scratch for hours after a flea bit him and jumped off or died, especially if he's allergic to flea saliva) then you need to next look at his environment for the possibility of a contact allergen—the stuff you are washing your floors or his bed with might be a good place to start!

Many a puppy has stopped scratching when his owner stopped using a chemical-laden Swiffer on the floor.

(Floor-cleaning products should be the first thing you look at if his underside is itchy or reddened.)

What else causes itchiness?
Generally speaking, pollen, mold, dust and environmental toxins, which include all the stuff we spray on our furniture, floors and in the air, as well as the neurotoxins we squirt on him to keep fleas at bay. Statistically, both inhalant and contact allergens are nine times more likely to cause a reaction in dogs than allergens in his food.

Recent vaccinations are also a possibility—we now know that all reactions to vaccines are not immediate anaphylactic ones, but may be more subtle and delayed.

So anyway don't keep switching foods – if your dog IS predisposed to allergies, constantly introducing new novel proteins can actually increase the odds of a food allergy developing, and you will have done more harm than good.

Although it is baffling to us, a dog who's a good eater will be absolutely thrilled when you put down his bowl, even if he's been eating the exact same food for 15 years. (It's one of the great things about dogs.)
Adding a dollop of yogurt or a handful of cut-up cooked chicken to plain old kibble will totally knock him out. And contrary to what the dog food companies would like us to believe, some fresh unprocessed food (also known as "table food") is good for everybody, including us.

Cooked (even canned) carrots or green beans or pumpkin or sweet potato are also good choices, and dogs can utilize all the good vitamins and phytonutrients in bright-colored vegetables if they're cooked.

How much should you feed?

This is probably the most important question of all.

The answer here is simple– if you want your dog to live a long and healthy life, you need to feed him enough to keep him lean, *and no more*. Most American dogs are NOT lean, by the way – in fact the obesity rate in dogs increased from 44% in 2002 to 51% in 2011, which is alarming on several levels.

An Important Study

In a groundbreaking study led by researchers at Nestlé Purina and including scientists at Cornell, the University of Illinois, Michigan State University and the University of Pennsylvania (published in the *Journal of the American Veterinary Medical Association* back in May 2002 if you want to read the whole thing)

For this study, 24 pairs of Labrador retriever siblings between 6 and 8 weeks of age -- matched by sex and weight-- were selected, with one of each pair assigned to eat 25 percent less of the same food than its sibling.

The dogs were a part of the study from the time they were weaned until they died, and their health was closely monitored throughout their lives. The study lasted 14 years. The median age of dogs in the reduced-diet group, the researchers found, was 13 years -- 1.8 years longer than the median age of dogs fed a normal diet. (That would be over 13 years longer for a person, just to put it in perspective.)

And they were healthier for their entire lives.

Leanness is especially critical in Aussiedoodles, because they are descended from two breeds predisposed to canine hip dysplasia (CHD). And how much you feed your dogs has a lot to do with whether or not a dog develops it— probably more than genetics alone.

.In the study, in the control group of "well-fed" dogs, 16 had CHD at 2 years of age, and 8 were normal.

However, of the 24 dogs in the "restricted diet" group, only 8 had CHD and 16 were normal!

The reduced diet was also found to reduce the risk of developing osteoarthritis, which generally is one of the most common sources of chronic pain in dogs.

Only six of the 24 dogs on the reduced diet developed osteoarthritis of the hip by age 10, while 19 of the 24 control group dogs did.

And for the dogs on reduced rations who did develop CHD, the odds of developing concurrent osteoarthritis decreased by 57%.

If that isn't a strong argument for keeping any dog lean, nothing is.

Roly-poly fat puppies are not healthy puppies, any more than roly-poly fat kids are healthy kids.

If your puppy is not lean (this means he should have a waist when viewed from above, a tuck-up when viewed from the side and although you shouldn't be able to see his ribs you should be able to feel them clearly enough to count them) he is headed for health problems no matter what his breeding.

But when it comes right down to it, the most important thing to remember about feeding your dog is not to obsess about it. Dogs are notoriously allelemenetic in their behaviors, and if *you* obsess about what your dog is eating, odds are so will he. And if you really think about it, dogs have managed to thrive on man's leftovers for millennia, which is also worth remembering.

CHAPTER SEVEN:

Aussiedoodle Health
(or...what you absolutely need to know)

Much has been written about the wonders of hybrid vigor, and indeed, recognition by the dog-buying public about the advantages it produces in health and longevity are in large part responsible for the soaring rise in popularity of many of the new "designer breeds". By simply combining two different breeds with multiple health issues, you produce puppies with none....How cool is THAT?

It's pretty cool. Too bad it's not true.

Because this model has actually worked well for breeds like the Puggle and the Goldendoodle, an awful lot of enthusiastic but inexperienced breeders assumed it would work for *all* hybrid crosses. Instead of having to spend all kinds of money health-screening and gene-testing, one could just combine *any two different breeds* and not have to worry about all that stuff any more. (This is why so many hybrids come from breeding stock that's had no health-screening done.) **Unfortunately, whether this works or not depends entirely on the disease in question.** For things like autoimmune disorders and cancers, hybrid vigor really does appear to help. For other diseases that may either be congenital (like deafness) or which may develop later in life (like heritable cataracts) hybrid vigor *will not reduce the risk at all.*

And there are at least FIVE serious and life-altering conditions in Aussiedoodles that are not affected in the least by hybrid vigor.

The genes for all five are found in the Australian Shepherd, which means these genes can be passed on to F1 Aussiedoodles. **They do NOT exist in Cockers, Goldens or Labradors,** which is why producing healthy Aussiedoodles is not as easy (or cheap!) as producing healthy puppies from any other popular Poodle cross.

And in some cases, *only one copy is needed to produce problems*, so the fact that the Poodle parent *isn't* carrying the gene doesn't help at all.

THE GOOD NEWS IS: These problems can now ALL be avoided through relatively inexpensive and non-invasive gene-testing of breeding dogs or by simply making informed breeding decisions.

THE BAD NEWS IS: Most of the people breeding Aussiedoodles *don't even know some of these health problems even exist,* which means they're probably not screening their breeding stock.

Before you decide to BUY an Aussiedoodle it's really good to know what the potential problems are so you can avoid getting a puppy who already has or may develop one of them.

Before you decide to BREED Aussiedoodles, knowing what the potential problems are will tell you where to spend your health-screening dollars most efficiently.

And if you already OWN an Aussiedoodle, knowing about a couple of them could save his life!

Understanding Disease and Heritability

There are basically five different kinds of diseases (or *disorders*) in dogs. Some are totally heritable, others are far less so, and some are not heritable at all. **This is important to know because in general, hybrid vigor has the greatest positive effect on traits with LOW rather than HIGH heritability.**

Some diseases can be avoided by wise decisions on the *owner's* part, while others are entirely dependent on choices the *breeder* made prior to the conception of the puppies, either knowingly or unknowingly. This latter group includes what are called *classical genetic disorders.*

Classical genetic disorders.

Although a whole lot of diseases are heritable to some degree and tend to "run in families", classical *genetic disorders* are actually rarer. Caused entirely by the action of a genetic mutation inherited from one or both parents, there are no environmental factors involved here at all– the presence of the mutation is enough to cause the disease no matter *what* you do. They are 100% heritable.

Despite media hype about some new "cancer" or "autism" gene, *genes do not cause diseases.*

Mother Nature is not a nihilist—genes are simply the recipes for specific proteins or enzymes needed for an organism to survive and reproduce.
It is when a particular gene *mutates* (usually through a random error in copying during meiosis which alters the "recipe" for that gene) and the mutated form of that gene is passed to the next generation that a genetic disease may result.

Now, the mutation may also be totally benign or even advantageous—gene mutations are responsible for evolution, after all, and without them we'd all still be swimming around in the ocean, breathing through our gills.
In the wild, mutations that provide some evolutionary advantage tend to be carried forward, because the animal displaying them usually exhibits "reproductive fitness", which really means he lives long enough to produce offspring, while those with none do not. (Color variations that allow an animal to blend in with his environment fall into this category– although they may occasionally occur, most pie-bald rabbits would probably not live long enough to reproduce in the wild.)

Of course, with domesticated animals, it is *humans* who decide if a gene variant that happens to pop up is beneficial or not, and whether or not the animal displaying it should reproduce.
Sometimes a particular genetic mutation might make an animal uniquely qualified for a job that some human decided dogs needed to do— like herding sheep, or in the case of the FGF4 gene that produces short-legged dwarfism, allowing the Dachshund to fit into holes to dispatch badgers, which is a bit of a problem for a longer-legged dog.
And sometimes, as is the case with a gene like merle, humans just decided it looked cool.

Now, if the mutated gene is ***dominant,*** inheriting one copy from either parent is all it takes for the dog to display the trait. (Those showing variable expression are considered "dominant with incomplete penetrance." Those showing weaker expression in the presence of a single allele and stronger expression in the presence of two are considered "incompletely dominant." or "co-dominant".)

A mutation that produces no change unless a copy is inherited from each parent is traditionally called a *recessive* gene. But there is often overlap here, too– it's now recognized that some "carriers" of a recessive disease can display subtler symptoms, so this whole dominant/recessive thing is not as cut-and-dried as we once believed.

Because of this, instead of using the term "carriers" at all, many geneticists now simply use the terms "heterozygote" for a dog carrying one copy of a genetic mutation and "homozygote" for a dog carrying two.

Here's a rundown of *classical genetic disorders* that can occur in the Aussiedoodle:

Hereditary Cataracts

Unfortunately, one dominant gene mutation that the Australian Shepherd can pass on is one identified recently on a gene called HSF4. **A single copy of this mutation is responsible for over 70% of the cataracts that occur in the breed.** (Some cataracts are not hereditary, and can be caused by environmental factors such as injury, but they are frankly the minority in the breed. Most are bilateral posterior hereditary cataracts, which are hereditary, irreversible, and can lead to total blindness.)

To date, two mutations have been identified on the HSF4 gene in dogs. One causes the recessive form of Hereditary Cataracts in Boston Terriers, Staffordshire Bull Terriers, and French Bulldogs. Because it is recessive, a dog must have two copies of this mutation to experience this form of cataracts. This mutation is responsible for early-onset hereditary cataracts, which typically occur between 12 months and 3 years of age in Staffordshires, and between 2-3 years in Boston Terriers.

A *different mutation on the same gene* was found to cause Hereditary Cataracts in Australian Shepherds. This mutation affects Aussies differently, in that the disease is *dominant*. This means that only one copy of the mutation is necessary to produce the disease, although every dog that has this mutation may not always develop HC.

However, current research suggests that even a single copy of the mutation *makes a dog 17 times more likely to develop posterior bilateral cataracts at some point in their lifetime,* and this number will likely increase. (Because the test is relatively new and age of onset is so variable, some young dogs found to be carrying the gene but who have not yet developed cataracts may do so later.)

The problem with Hereditary Cataracts in Australian Shepherds has *always* been the variable age of onset— it can occur in dogs as young as a year, or as old as 8 or 9. Even if breeders had CERF exams performed every year, the exam is "on the day" and many dogs already had many offspring by the time they finally developed cataracts themselves. So in reality, unless a dog developed cataracts early on, the annual CERF exam mostly provided a sense of false security.

This made the disease virtually impossible to eradicate, because a dog carrying two copies of the gene will pass it to 100% of his offspring, and a dog carrying a single copy of the HSF4 mutation will pass it to 50% of his offspring, and some of these offspring will develop cataracts early in life.

This whole frustrating situation, which has gone on for *decades* in the Australian Shepherd breed, ended with the development of a gene test for the HSF4 mutation.

Because there is no health database for the Aussiedoodle as there is for the Australian Shepherd, the incidence of Hereditary Cataracts in the breed is unknown, but unless all the Australian Shepherds who've contributed to the breed have been gene-tested (which they clearly have not) the HSF4 mutation is undoubtedly already swimming around in the Aussiedoodle gene pool, dooming a percentage of puppies to a life of what is now *totally unnecessary* blindness.

It's *unnecessary* because a simple $45 gene test (which involves no more than sending in a cheek swab and costs about the same as a single annual CERF exam) performed by breeders on the Australian Shepherd (or Aussie hybrid) parents once in their lifetime will ensure that no Aussiedoodle puppies are at risk for this form of cataracts...a bargain by any reckoning!

Hopefully, as more breeders become aware of this test they will begin to use it… and hopefully puppy buyers will encourage it and support those who do. (Information on ordering test kits for the HSF4 mutation can be found in the Resources section. Owners who are simply curious about their dog's risk can also order a test. Those carrying the gene should probably be examined annually —if needed, cataract surgery is most successful if cataracts are caught early, before complications like glaucoma develop.)

Ocular Dysgenesis

Here's another potentially devastating genetic disorder that is totally avoidable, and this one doesn't even need a gene-test….just common-sense breeding decisions.

Ocular Dysgenesis (also called Merle Ocular Dysgenesis) is a collection of vision-impairing congenital eye abnormalities entirely associated with mutations on the MITF and SILV genes, most often in combination. The condition may occur in double-piebald single merle dogs (and occasionally in white breeds that do not carry the merle gene at all) but is far and away most common and generally most severe in double merles displaying excessive white.

These abnormalities include microphthalmia, coloboma, eccentric, dropped and starburst pupils, lens luxation, congenital cataracts, retinal detachment, and lack of tapetum. Some abnormalities can be easily seen with the naked eye, and some require examination by a canine ophthalmologist for diagnosis.

microphthalmia in right eye

eccentric pupils

starburst and dropped pupils

iris colobomas

Sometimes there is minimal visual impairment, and sometimes the dog is functionally blind.

In the dog pictured at left, there is vision in the left eye (also blue but surrounded by pigment) despite an eccentric pupil while the right eye, which is small and displays a prominent third eyelid and eccentric pupil, likely has no functional vision at all.

The second dog (of a breed fixed for the piebald gene *but without merle*) displays coloboma and eccentric pupils and has functional, although probably not perfect, vision. Although the incidence of ocular dysgenesis is higher in blue-eyed double-piebald dogs, it is not limited to them— it also occurs in brown eyes (especially in double merles) but is harder to see.

Dogs with the iris defects pictured in the last four photos usually have functional vision, but because the pupils don't dilate and contract normally, they experience discomfort in bright light (they generally squint, which is a dead giveaway) and often do not see well in low-light situations at all.

Photos of anaphthalmia were not included because hopefully most breeders would notice a total lack of eyes in a puppy prior to sale, and they're frankly disturbing to look at.

Ocular dysgenesis is easy to avoid without gene-testing— breeders can simply refrain from producing homozygous (double) piebalds, especially in the presence of the merle gene, as described in the Color chapter. If a dog is born with it, however, whatever vision loss is there is irreversible. (And it is worth noting that in Australian Shepherds, *Iris Coloboma* is now believed to be inherited independently of merle and piebald, although the mode of inheritance has not been established.)

Multi-drug Sensitivity

This one is very scary, and the *scariest thing* about it is that very few breeders mention it on their websites and very few owners know it even exists. **Ignorance here can cost an Aussiedoodle his life!**

First discovered in Collies who had severe reactions to Ivermectin (Heartgard), a mutation on a gene called MDR1 has now been identified in many herding breeds. This gene encodes a protein, *P-glycoprotein,* which is responsible for pumping many drugs and other toxins out of the brain.

Dogs with this genetic mutation cannot pump some drugs out of the brain as a normal dog would, which results in abnormal neurological symptoms, including seizures and coma.. The result may be an illness requiring an extended hospital stay - or even death.

There is no "antidote", and treatment is mostly supportive — there's not much a vet can do except to try and keep the dog alive (i.e. breathing and hydrated) until the drug is finally cleared out, which can take days or weeks.

Around 50% of Australian Shepherds have been found to be carrying the MDR1 mutation.

When the causative gene was first identified, it was believed to be a recessive mutation, which meant a dog needed to inherit a copy from each parent in order to be affected. This would mean that F1 Aussiedoodles, at least, were at little no risk of being affected, so even those few breeders who were aware of the MDR1 mutation in Aussies did not bother to test, especially if they were only doing F1 crosses.

Unfortunately, as more cases have been examined, this has proven to be incorrect. According to researchers at Washington State University, who originally identified it and developed the gene test, *dogs carrying ONE copy of the MDR1 mutation have also been found to have increased sensitivity to these drugs*, although their reactions may not be as severe. (This would indicate the causative mutation is not recessive, but more likely incompletely dominant.) And the list of drugs to which they may react keeps getting longer all the time. What does this mean for the Aussiedoodle?

According to WSU, all dogs from breeds known to be affected by the MDR1 mutation, *as well as all crosses that include these breeds,* should be tested for their own safety.

With incidence in Australian Shepherds sitting at around 50% (and that includes miniature Aussies) the average Aussiedoodle, whether from an F1 or a multigenerational breeding, is clearly at high risk.

What drugs can cause a reaction in dogs with the MDR1 mutation? *Unfortunately, the list keeps growing.* According to information available from WSU at the time of writing, adverse reactions have been documented with use of the following drugs:

- **Several antiparasitic agents** (ivermectin, selemectin, milbemycin moxidectin and related drugs)

- **Loperamide** (a common antidiarrheal agent found in Imodium),
- **Erythromycin** (a commonly prescribed antibiotic)
- **Acepromazine** (a well-known tranquilizer and pre-anesthetic agent)
- **Butorphanol** (another common analgesic and pre-anesthetic agent)
- **Emodepcide** (a dewormer used primarily in other countries)
- **Several anticancer drugs** (vincristine, doxorubicin, others)

These are all drugs that are pretty commonly used in veterinary medicine, and unless your vet *knows* your dogs is sensitive to them, odds are he will be prescribed one of them at some point in his life. (The antidiarrheal agent is maybe the scariest in that regard.)

Luckily, testing for the MDR1 mutation is non-invasive, easy to do at home, and only has to be done once in a dog's life— a dog is either born with it or not; he cannot develop it later.
The cost for this one-time test currently $70, which is a whole lot less than you'll end up paying if your dog has a reaction to any one of the drugs involved. Instructions for ordering a test kit can be found at: **http://www.vetmed.wsu.edu/depts-VCPL/**.
Dogs found to be carrying the mutation should ideally wear a tag with that information on it, and it's also a good idea to print off your test results and the most current information from Washington State's website and take it to your vet's office to be included in your dog's file.

WAY too many vets still think that the only drug affected by MDR1 is Ivermectin, and that the only sensitive breed is the Collie.

The only Aussiedoodles who do not need to be tested are those whose Aussie or Aussie-hybrid parents were tested and shown not to carry the mutation. For everybody else....GET THE TEST, AND IF NEEDED, GET THE TAG.

Hereditary Congenital Sensineural Deafness

This one, which was discussed at length back in the Color Chapter, is also a classical genetic disorder— although deafness can be acquired later in life due to environmental factors such as a virus, **there is no indication that environment plays a part in HCSD at all—it's entirely due to genes.**

And although it is yet unknown whether or not there are other gene mutations involved besides those that affect melanocyte function (such as piebald and merle), it is pretty obvious at this point that the MITF and SILV mutations are the major players.

What is *also* known is that whether or not there are other genes involved, dogs carrying the SINE mutation on MITF who are deaf in either one or both ears produce significantly more deaf offspring than those with normal (bilateral) hearing.

So although there is no definitive gene test available for HCSD, its incidence can be significantly reduced by using only those "normal hearing" dogs carrying the piebald gene for breeding.

And this can only be ascertained by BAER– testing.

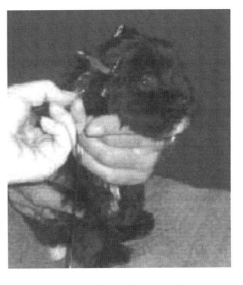

The photo at right shows a puppy (with little white trim but who has a piebald parent) being BAER-tested. Small electrodes are attached to the skin on specific parts of the skull, and ear buds are inserted in each ear. A computer screen will then record the brain's reaction to a series of clicks in each ear. A series of peaks at specific wave lengths record transmission of electrical impulses from the inner ear to the brain which indicate normal auditory processing.

The graph below is a printout of the results of a BAER test —this one was performed by Dr George Strain from LSU. The top line shows the results of testing on the left ear while the bottom line shows the results of the right. This dog has normal hearing.

In some breeds with HCSD (usually those fixed for the SINE) responsible breeders BAER test all puppies prior to sale, while in others (usually in breeds where the SINE is not fixed) only those deemed at risk by virtue of excessive white are BAER-tested.

In this way breeders can make appropriate placement choices for each pup—unilaterally deaf pups usually compensate well and make perfectly fine pets but should not be bred.

Bilaterally deaf pups need to be placed in homes with the time and resources to train them with hand-signals— in no case should they ever be sold to an unsuspecting owner without telling them!!!

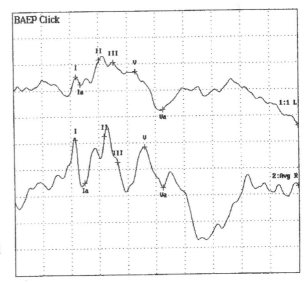

Cobalamin (Vitamin B12) Malabsorption Syndrome

Another genetic disease found in the Australian Shepherd, *Cobalamin Malabsorption Syndrome* is a serious and potentially life-threatening metabolic disease in puppies and young dogs. In affected dogs, the lining of the lower intestine will not absorb vitamin B_{12}.

Signs of CMS usually start around 6-12 weeks of age, but may not be noted until the dog is up to a year old. (Because age of onset is variable, the puppy may be perfectly fine until he's been in his new home for a number of weeks or even months.)

The disease can cause a wide range of vague clinical problems, including lack of appetite, lethargy, failure to thrive, wasting, vomiting, seizures, or simply general ill-health. The most serious complications include abnormalities of the blood and nervous system that are lethal if untreated.

Unfortunately, it is common for CMS to be misdiagnosed because of the varied clinical signs and because most vets don't know that it exists in Australian Shepherds, much less the Aussiedoodle.
The signs of CMS can mimic those of liver shunts, early-onset epilepsy and some immunodeficiency diseases. Failure to diagnose and treat CMS promptly can lead to the needless death of puppies.

Veterinarians presented with dogs exhibiting any of these signs may find led low counts of red and white blood cells, platelet and neutrophils; excess blood ammonia; and protein in the urine in standard diagnostic tests. *If these are found, vets should contact the University of Pennsylvania and request gene testing for CMS.*
Treatment of affected dogs consists of subcutaneous vitamin B_{12} injections every 2-4 weeks for life. Response is rapid and results will be seen in a matter of days. (Serious cases may require more intensive B_{12} therapy and supportive care for up to 10 days.)

CMS is caused by a mutation of a gene called *Amnionless* (Amn) and is currently believed to only affect dogs that inherit two copies of the mutation. Because the gene test is relatively new, and it is so often misdiagnosed, the incidence of carriers in the Australian Shepherd has not yet been established. And although it has been identified in several breeds to date, it is unknown at this time whether or not the mutation exists in Poodles. If it is not (and if two copies are in fact needed) then only multi-generational Aussiedoodles out of untested parents would be at risk of developing the disease.

If a puppy is diagnosed with CMS, it is critical that the breeder contact the owners of his littermates so that in those also affected, B12 supplementation may be begun *before* symptoms develop.

Pathogenic disorders.

Also called *infectious diseases*, these are caused by invading pathogens, most commonly viruses and bacteria. Lyme disease, Leptospirosis, Parvo and Distemper would all be examples of pathogenic diseases—the first two are caused by invading bacteria, while the last two are viral.

A dog's resistance to these "bugs" (many of which are pretty ubiquitous in the environment) is largely dependent on the ability of his immune system to identify them and mount an appropriate response after exposure.

On the surface, the heritability of infectious diseases is pretty much 0%, because whether or not you get one is entirely dependent on environmental exposure. In other words, no matter what his genetic makeup, if a dog never crosses paths with the distemper virus, he simply cannot contract the disease we call Distemper.

On the other hand, the immune system has a LOT to do with how well the body deals with foreign pathogens when they do cross paths.

This is because although the two terms are often used interchangeably, *infection* and *disease* are two different things from an immunological standpoint. Infection, which is the invasion by and multiplication of a foreign pathogen upon exposure, may or may not progress to disease, depending upon the body's ability to halt that multiplication before it gets out of hand and causes damage to the host.

This ability to halt the proliferation of foreign pathogens is what we generally refer to as *disease resistance.*

Innumerable studies in both plants and animals in recent years have demonstrated that diversity in the immune-regulating genes of both the Major Histocompatability Complex (the DLA complex in dogs) and the various cytokine loci confer resistance to everything from potato blight to HIV.

In fact, this theory of *heterozygote advantage*, which won a Nobel Prize for Doherty and Zinkernagel back in 1996, has become a cornerstone of modern immunology.

Not surprisingly then, resistance to infectious disease is one area where F1 hybrids have a huge advantage, because hybridization produces genetic diversity in the offspring.

Environmental disorders.

This bunch, which has gotten a fair amount of press in recent years, are not influenced by genetics much at all, because diseases caused by exposure to environmental toxins both natural and manmade are pretty dose-dependent. In other words, *no matter what your genetics,* exposure above one level will cause sickness, while exposure above another level will result in certain death. (Lead and mercury poisoning famously fall into this category, as well as exposure to radiation and most chemical herbicides and pesticides.)

This occurs because the immune system is primarily designed to recognize live pathogens—it has little or no ability to mount an immune defense against toxins or inorganic "toxicants". **Essentially, we're talking about poisons here.**

And because the body's ability to excrete poisons is limited (especially in Aussiedoodles carrying the MDR1 mutation!), the effects of most are cumulative – in other words, exposure to small amounts over a long period of time can have the same effect on the body in the end as a lot of exposure all at once. In general, the less exposure to toxins an organism is exposed to, the better its chances of long-term survival. The greater the exposure, the greater the chance of serious illness and death.

What falls into this category? *A LOT of stuff, unfortunately.*
In the "naturally-occurring" department we have toxic heavy metals like mercury and aluminum (which are used as preservatives and adjuvants in many canine vaccines), uranium and lead, as well as the "true" toxins (such as the post-synaptic neurotoxin *a-Cobratoxin* unique to cobras) produced by various snakes, insects, and plants and the icky little microorganisms called *endotoxins*.

In the "man-made" department we have ionic radiation (most commonly from x-rays) and somewhere in the neighborhood of around 60,000 man-made chemicals, most of which are toxic at some level of exposure.
These range from ethylene glycol, the killer ingredient in antifreeze, to BPA found in plastics, to synthetic neurotoxins like those found in flea and heartworm preventatives. In fact, according to the EPA, of the 3,000 high-volume production chemicals (meaning over a million pounds of each is produced in or imported to the US each year) *over 40% of them have never even been TESTED for toxicity.*

Environmental disorders manifest in many ways, the most well-known of which are cancers.
So this one is the exception to the rule— although the heritability is pretty much zilch, hybrid vigor cannot help much here, either. The only real defense is to avoid unnecessary exposure to toxins insofar as possible in the first place, which is the owner's responsibility.

Nutritional disorders.

Nutritional disorders arise when the dog's diet is deficient in one or more essential amino acids, vitamins, or minerals. In general, people probably obsess a lot more about possible nutritional deficiencies than they really need to, given that close to 50% of America's dogs now suffer from obesity.

Because dogs fed a homemade diet are generally given a vitamin/mineral supplement and all commercial dog food is formulated to contain the minimum daily requirement of nutrients, nutritional deficiencies in American dogs are now pretty rare, with the possible exception of Vitamin D, which can be "cooked off" in processing if the manufacturing plant is not careful about temperature.

(Companies which do not maintain their own research facilities and have no in-house population of dogs on which to test their product are especially vulnerable here, because the *only* way to determine if a dog food contains the necessary levels of bioavailable nutrients when it comes out of the bag is to periodically run periodic blood levels on dogs actually eating it.)

The good news is that dogs, like people, can manufacture all the Vitamin D they need if they're simply exposed to sunlight. The bad news is that dogs, like their owners, are spending a lot more time indoors than Mother Nature had ever imagined they would, but this is clearly something the owner can control.

With the exception of actual genetic diseases like Cobalamin Malabsorption Syndrome (where a mutated gene prevents absorption of a common nutrient) most nutritional disorders rank pretty low in the heritability department, and so it's probably not surprising that the ability to utilize nutrients is increased with hybridization—what are called *feed conversion rates* are increased in hybrid offspring.

This means hybrids both grow faster and pack on fat easier than purebreds eating the same amount and type of food. This is a real advantage if you're raising beef cattle, but when it comes to dogs...*not so much.*

Since lean dogs live longer and are significantly less susceptible to orthopedic problems, the average hybrid owner really needs to worry more about overfeeding and excess nutrition resulting in too-fast growth and weight gain than to worry about nutritional deficiencies.

Because of this, Aussiedoodle puppies destined to be medium-to-large-sized dogs should be fed a diet specifically designed for larger breeds, whether commercial or homemade.

Immune System Disorders.

This group, which comprises the last category, are probably the most complex of the bunch, but they all share the same common cause—*dysregulation of the immune system*. To quote the National Cancer Institute, from whence most of this information originated: "When the immune system malfunctions, it can release a veritable torrent of diseases and disorders." This torrent can be broken down into three major categories, according to the nice folks at the NCI:

Allergies:

An "allergy" is an inappropriate or exaggerated immune response to common substances that are not generally harmful. The most common allergies in dogs are flea bite dermatitis (caused by an exaggerated reaction to flea saliva) and atopia, which is caused by a reaction to environmental allergens. Together these account for about 90% of itching and skin problems seen in dogs.
Atopic dermatitis in dogs is actually the canine version of hay fever, and is often triggered by the same things.
In both species, IgE antibodies (whose original function is protection against parasites) coat *mast cells*, where they consequently sit waiting for contact with the parasite proteins for which they are sensitized. If encountered, the mast cell releases histamines which will attempt to destroy the invader. (This is why dogs with healthy immune systems are rarely bothered much by fleas, by the way.)

In allergic animals, the whole system is oversensitive and histamines are released inappropriately in response to innocuous substances such as pollen, mold, and dust mites. *In dogs, however, rather than being concentrated in the linings of the respiratory system, these mast cells are concentrated in the skin, with the greatest number found in the face and feet.* This is why dogs respond to allergens by scratching, rubbing their faces on furniture and chewing on their feet, rather than wheezing and sneezing like people.

It's worth noting (again!) that food allergies, which is usually the *first* thing owners suspect when a dog is itchy, actually account for only 10% of allergies in dogs. And about 80% of dogs with food allergies also have *atopy,* which accounts for the high failure rate in treating food allergies by diet manipulation alone.
As with autoimmune disease, susceptibility to allergies, which tend to run in both human and canine families, is linked to genes that control immune function. What causes the oversensitivity in some genetically susceptible individuals and not others ? Environmental triggers.

It is now pretty well understood that *over-vaccinating a puppy* can over-stimulate the immune system, and the AVMA does not recommend it for that reason.

Autoimmune Disorders

These disorders are the result of the immune system's inability to distinguish between antigens produced by foreign pathogens and healthy tissue. Unable to determine the difference between "self" and "non-self", the immune system begins to attack its own tissue, resulting in what we call autoimmune disease. **Autoimmune disorders are the fastest-growing group of diseases in dogs, especially among purebreds.**

All autoimmune diseases recognized to date in dogs and humans have one thing in common—they all are associated with genes that regulate the immune response. In dogs, these genes are gathered in a distinct region on canine chromosome 12. An identical region exists in all species of mammals and birds and is known as the major Histocompatibility Complex (MHC).

The MHC of the dog has been designated the "dog leukocyte antigen' (DLA) complex. The DLA complex is divided into four regions, containing Class I,II, III, and IV genes.

A strong association between autoimmune disorders and the DLA class II genes has been shown for a number of canine disorders to date, including diabetes, hypothyroidism, Addison's disease, autoimmune arthritis, immune-mediated hemolytic anemia, chronic granulomatous meningoencephalitis and most recently chronic canine inflammatory liver disease.

Particular DLA haplotypes have been shown to have significantly increased *susceptibility* to these autoimmune diseases, especially when they have inherited the haplotype in a "double dose".

The main function of the DLA genes is self/non-self recognition. The immune system must be able to identify every foreign protein that invades the body, whether it is on a bacteria, virus, fungi parasite, etc, as being "non-self", and to recognize every protein that is part of itself and *not* react to it.

As genetic variability is lost in the DLA, not only does the immune system lose the ability to mount an appropriate response, but the ability to differentiate between what is "self" and what is "non-self" becomes more and more tenuous.

Although there are well over 140 different haplotypes spread across the canine world, most breeds have now been reduced to only a very few, many of which are unique to each particular breed.

F1 hybrids are likely to inherit an entirely different haplotype from each parent, and are therefore less susceptible to the autoimmune diseases that plague their parent breeds.

Cancer

In the final analysis, cancer really represents a catastrophic breakdown of the immune system. As cells constantly reproduce, errors naturally occur, and it is the job of specific cells of the immune system to constantly seek and destroy these aberrant cells by recognizing the antigens they produce as "non-self" invaders.

When this surveillance system fails, tumors form and cancer results.

It has long been recognized that genetic susceptibility to cancer may be due in part to inherited variation on MHC genes. In fact, in recent years, several specific HLA gene alleles have been associated with either susceptibility to, or protection from, various types of cancers in humans, including breast cancer.

The fact that different breeds of dogs are predisposed to different cancers pretty much reinforces the theory that cancers have a genetic component. By some estimates, purebreds have a cancer incidence rate nearly twice that of mixed breeds — fully 60% of Golden Retrievers now die of cancer, for example, mostly hemangiosarcomas and lymphosarcomas. This indicates that genetic diversity is probably advantageous here as well.

Since even cancer susceptibility appears polygenic rather than caused by single gene mutations, a dog whose genes are a blend of two breeds is simply less likely to inherit all the genes (including those in the DLA complex) necessary for susceptibility to a cancer that may plague one of its parent breeds.

But the key word here is *susceptibility*. Cancer, like all disorders of the immune system, clearly has a genetic component, but the heritability is nowhere near 100% on any of them, even where a specific DLA haplotype has been identified that clearly increases risk.

Like allergies and autoimmune disorders, cancer is primarily a disease of the developed world, and that indicates some fairly strong environmental factors at work, which act as "triggers". For example, it is known that rabies vaccination can trigger a particularly lethal form of sarcoma at the injection site in both cats and dog, although we don't know which ones are susceptible until the cancer develops.

In other words, with diseases involving the immune system, genetics loads the gun....
but environment pulls the trigger.

By virtue of its genetic diversity, the immune system of a hybrid dog should be in pretty good shape genetically, but even the best immune system can be overwhelmed by environmental factors *that are totally within the owner's control*. Keeping your Aussiedoodle healthy is not only the job of your vet....IT'S YOURS.

Why Choosing the Right Vet is Critical

The time to find a vet is *before* you bring your puppy home, and since this will be your puppy's Primary Care Provider, you want to put some thought and energy into finding the best one you can, not just the one who is closest or recommended by a dog-owning friend. You'll need to check out websites, make some phone calls and ask some questions.

As with breeders, all vets are *not* created equal —common sense should tell us that *somebody* graduated dead-last in class back at vet school, and also that the lucky recipient of that dubious distinction is unlikely to have a plaque displayed in his office commemorating it.

Likewise, some vets continue to keep up with current research in their field while others appear to have never cracked a book or read a scientific journal since the day they left vet school. You need to shop around to find one from the first category. How can you tell who's who?

The easiest way to tell if a veterinary practice is up-to-date is by simply asking about their vaccination protocols.

For many years, vaccinations were administered annually whether the dog needed them or not, and no one thought much about it. (Odds are your previous dogs were vaccinated annually, and a lot of "expert" advice on the internet still recommends this.)

All this changed back in 2003, when the American Animal Hospital Association, the American Veterinary Medical Association, and most veterinary teaching hospitals changed their vaccination protocols based on new research. All now recommend only "core" vaccines for all dogs, with others added only where necessary, based on a dog's individual risk. And none recommend annual vaccination.

However, it is absolutely amazing how many vets in clinical practice around the country seemed to have missed the memo ten years ago. You do NOT want to take your puppy to one of those guys, because we now know this sort of vaccination regime can compromise his long-term health and well-being.

Although necessary to protect a puppy against infectious disease, vaccines can also be one of the triggers for autoimmune disorders.

So let's talk about vaccination here, because unless you're well-informed yourself, it's going to be pretty hard to figure out if a prospective vet is!

ALL the statements in boldface below were copied *verbatim* from the **American Veterinary Medical Association's 2011 Vaccine Policy Statement**, just so you know…you might want to be wary of any vet who finds them totally unfamiliar.

Revaccination of patients with sufficient immunity does not necessarily add to their disease protection and may increase the potential risk of post-vaccination adverse events."

Exactly what are these adverse events?
"Possible adverse events include, but are not necessarily limited to, failure to immunize, anaphylaxis, immuno-suppression, autoimmune disorders, transient infections, long-term infected carrier states, and local development of tumors."

And when it comes to triggering autoimmune disorders, over-vaccination is clearly one trigger you do not *need* to pull. Here's why:
"Unnecessary stimulation of the immune system does not necessarily result in enhanced disease resistance, and may increase the potential risk of post-vaccination adverse events."

But how do you and your vet figure out if your dog actually needs another vaccination in order to be protected? Here's the AVMA again, with the answer:
"Due to the emergence of newer and improved antibody tests, serological assays are being used to determine immune status and establish vaccination protocols for animal patients."

These serological antibody assays are commonly called "titer tests" (that's pronounced like "tighter" just so you don't embarrass yourself) and they use a simple blood sample. The cost of in-house titer testing currently runs between $30 and $50 in most parts of the country, and is worth every penny.

So *"Do you routinely run titers in your practice?"* is also a good question to ask.

What about "booster shots"?

Aside from rabies, the "core" vaccines your dog needs are now all *modified live or recombinant vaccines* and according to all scientific evidence do *not* need to be boosted in order to be effective. *Killed vaccines*, which do require a "booster", have not been used in decades for these diseases.

According to the 2011 AAHA Guidelines (which any vet should have read) *a single dose* of a modified live vaccine administered to a dog over 14 weeks of age will both "prime" the immune system *and* provide immunity for several years.

Being immune is a lot like being pregnant—it's an either/or sort of thing. You cannot make an already immune dog *more* immune by "boosting" it— the dog either has immunity against a disease or he does not. And a dog with an adequate antibody titer is considered immune. (Actually, because of what's called "cell memory", a lot of dogs who display an inadequate titer have demonstrated immunity when challenged, but most vets and owners prefer to err on the side of caution here.)

The ONLY reason puppies get a series of puppy shots is because of possible interference from maternally derived antibodies, *not because the vaccines themselves need "boosting".*

Here's what happens: Puppies display "passive immunity" for those diseases to which their mothers were exposed—either naturally or through vaccination. These maternally derived antibodies, passed primarily through colostrum in the first 48 hours of life, can last anywhere from 5 to 16 weeks, depending on the puppy. Puppies under 5 weeks are usually completely protected.

However, for each puppy, there is about a week when there are still sufficient maternal antibodies to destroy the attenuated antigens in the vaccine, but not enough to fight off the disease itself if the puppy is exposed. This period is called the "window of vulnerability".

At 6 weeks, only 37% of puppies are protected by a vaccination given at that time—the other 63% still carry enough maternal antibodies to prevent the vaccine from working.

Some of those puppies may have high enough maternal antibody levels to protect them if they are exposed to the disease itself over the next couple of weeks, while others may not.

Because the vet does not know which puppies are protected, a second vaccination is generally given to all puppies only because it is frankly cheaper than running titers on all of them.

Now, if you read the stuff from the AVMA carefully, you don't need more than three functioning brain cells to figure out that the poor guys in the 37% who *were* protected by the first vaccine are the ones at risk for adverse effects from over-stimulation of the immune system when they get the second round.

This is why many breeders and vets now believe that where the risk of parvo and distemper is not high, the first shot not be given until 8-9 weeks, when around 80% of puppies will be protected by it. By 12 weeks, over 95% of the puppies in a litter will have outgrown their maternal immunity to the point where they will be protected by vaccination. (In fact, research in the UK indicates that the new "high-titer" vaccines *now used both there and in the US* provide protection for nearly all puppies by 10 weeks.)
By 16 weeks, maternal immunity is no longer a factor, and every puppy who can seroconvert will do so and be protected by a single vaccination given at that time, even if it's the first one he's had.

So it should be pretty clear that if a puppy misses one of the shots in the series for some reason, there is no earthly reason to give him "extra" shots to get to some magic number *as long as the last one given produced a titer or was administered at 16 weeks or later.*

Once the puppy goes to his new home, the owner can elect to have titers run BEFORE any subsequent shots are automatically administered.

Because this is hands-down the SAFEST approach for the puppy from both a "short-term protection" and a "long-term immune function" standpoint, all vets should offer this option, although few actually do.

To be on the safe side, titers should be run 5-7 days after the last vaccination. If the puppy does *not* have a positive titer, it means he was one of the puppies with a high level of maternal antibodies at the time the vaccination was given and the shot "didn't take." In that case, the vaccines can be re-administered to protect him.

On the other hand, if he *does* have a positive titer, the 8-week shot "took" and there is no logical reason to increase his risk of adverse reaction by giving him vaccines he does not need. (Remember, immunity is a lot like pregnancy— there is no such thing as "more immune"!!)

And if your puppy has a positive titer at 10 or 12 weeks, you can take him out and about for socialization without worrying about waiting until he's "completed his puppy shots" at 16 weeks.

How cool is THAT?

And that way his vaccination protocol is designed *for his individual immune response,* rather than representing a "one-size-fits-all" approach that can lead to autoimmune problems down the road. The vet you choose should be on board with that philosophy.

Aside from unnecessary revaccination, the other danger to a puppy's immune system and overall future health is from the sheer NUMBER of different vaccines given, especially if they are given all at the same time, or in a combination (*polyvalent*) vaccine.

Here's the AVMA's advice on the subject:
" Vaccines, including polyvalent products, should be selected to include only those antigens appropriate for the specific risk of the patient, thereby eliminating unnecessary immune system stimulation and thus lowering potential risks of adverse events.
Veterinarians should be aware of the risk of "endotoxin stacking" with the use of multiple Gram-negative vaccines."

What does this mean? The more vaccines given at one time, the greater the risk of over-stimulating and thus damaging the immune system. This includes a single shot that contains multiple antigens – the above-mentioned "polyvalent products".

Endotoxins are intracellular toxins found in gram-negative bacteria, and are found in all vaccines (although they are generally present in highest numbers in vaccines that protect against bacterial diseases like leptospirosis).

When released, endotoxins produce a powerful inflammatory response in the system, and "endotoxin stacking" by combining vaccines makes it worse. Common symptoms of what is essentially toxic shock can include both fever and lethargy, which are all too common in puppies after vaccination.

In a recent large study on adverse vaccine reactions in dogs published in the JAVMA, the two greatest risk factors were found to be **the size of the dog** and **the number of vaccines given at one time**. In fact....

Research showed *each additional vaccine* given to a dog weighing less than 22 pounds increased the risk of adverse reaction by 27%!!!!

The size part makes perfect sense because *all dogs get the same vaccines*, no matter what their size or age. That's right— your 15 pound Aussiedoodle puppy will receive *exactly the same vaccine* as an adult Newfoundland weighing 150 pounds! It's amazing how many people logically assume there are different vaccines for different sized dogs, but unfortunately, that is just not the case.

This means that proportionally, a puppy's immature little system has to deal with 10 times the amount of antigen (that's the viral or bacteria component) as well as 10 times the *endotoxins, adjuvants, carriers and preservatives* as a large adult dog. These include a fair number of toxic substances including (but certainly not limited to) aluminum, formaldehyde, and mercury. And obviously, the more vaccines a puppy is given at one time, the more of these toxic substances he is exposed to at one time.

And the worst part of this is that many of these vaccines protect against diseases for which the dog is at little or no risk in the first place.

Plain old common sense should tell us that an animal would never experience this sort of "all-at-once" exposure in nature, and no immune system is designed to handle it. Sort of like flying in the cargo hold of a 727, the possibility of vaccination as it is now too often practiced just never occurred to Mother Nature when she was designing the canine immune system.

Not to put too fine a point on it, but if the vet you are considering using as your puppy's primary health provider doesn't know any of this, he needs to take a brush-up course in Immunology 101 *and you need to find a different vet.*

The days when being a responsible dog owner meant taking your dog in to the vet for his "yearly shots" without even knowing what on earth the dog was being vaccinated against or whether he even needed another vaccination at all are OVER. *Keeping your puppy healthy means you have to do your homework.*

No state, county or city in the US actually requires vaccination for anything other than rabies. *It's amazing how many people do not know this.* Now, most training classes, boarding kennels, day care facilities and even groomers require more than that, but it's not the "law". So let's see what he needs to be both protected from life-threatening diseases *and* welcome in most canine establishments.

Understanding "Puppy Shots"

The most important thing to understand is that all so-called "puppy shots" are not the same.
Depending on the vet, if you do not specify, a "puppy shot" may be a DP, a DHP, a DHPP, a DA2PPVL, a DA2PPV+CV, or the mother of all combos— the dazzling DA2PPVL+CV, which many vaccine experts wish would simply vanish from this earth.

And those are just from *Merck's* personal Vaccine Buffet. If you throw in the various offerings of Pfizer and Merial (which is really the animal products line of pharmaceutical giant Sanofi), you are pretty much guaranteed to be lost in the Alphabet Soup of canine vaccines forever.

The whole thing is further complicated by the fact that in the last few years there have been a rash of mergers in the pharmaceutical world— for example, Intervet became part of Shering Plough, which then merged with industry giant Merck, and all animal vaccines formerly made by those three companies (including the Galaxy and Proguard vaccines) are being relabeled under the Nobivac brand.
Fort Dodge was bought out by pharmaceutical giant Weyeth, which recently merged with Pfizer, which markets the Vanguard line of animal vaccines, but then Pfizer announced in 2011 that it planned to sell off its Animal Health division completely, so who knows where they will end up.

What all this means is you can't just assume your new dog is getting the same vaccinations your last dog got, or that your vet is using the same vaccines he used to use. And If this is starting to remind you forcibly of the Wonderful World of Dog Food, you're not alone….

So let's try to sort this mess out so you'll know what your puppy needs and what he really doesn't need so you'll know what to ask for…and remember, YOU can specify which vaccines you want your dog to get.

The Four "Core" Vaccines

Back in 2003, after years of study, the Association of Animal Hospitals came up with a new vaccination protocol for veterinarians. At that time they decided to recommend only FOUR vaccines for all dogs, which they designated "core vaccines". Certain other vaccines could be given only as necessary if a dog is at particular risk, while some are not recommended at all. (Some combination vaccines routinely given to puppies actually include these "non-core" and "not recommended" vaccines, which is why you need to read this part carefully.) Presumably all vets got this memo.

All 4 core vaccines can be covered in two "shots" – the DHP and the Rabies shot.

Although the core vaccines can be given separately, three of them are usually combined in the puppy shots, while rabies vaccine is always administered as a single shot. Here's the breakdown of the DHP and what's in it:

Distemper (that's the "D")

First described by Edward Jenner (the smallpox guy) back in the 18th century, distemper is an old disease. Primarily affecting puppies under 6 months of age, canine distemper is rarely seen in the US today outside of shelter populations, and many vets in practice today have never seen a single case. But prior to the 1960s, when widespread vaccination of dogs really took off, it killed roughly *half the puppies* born in the US in any given year.

Distemper begins with an upper respiratory infection (often characterized by a thick greenish discharge from the nose and eyes) before progressing to the nervous system, where it can cause seizures and even death. Because it is caused by a virus, the only treatment for distemper is supportive. And it's a pretty horrific disease—without supportive treatment, close to 90% of puppies who contract it will die. Even *with* supportive treatment, a puppy's odds of survival are not all that hot, and those who do survive often have lifelong neurological and ocular damage.

The reason all dogs still need to be vaccinated for what is now a pretty rare disease is because both wild animals (in 1994, a third of the lions in the Serengeti died from canine distemper) and shelter populations provide a constant "reservoir" for the virus. The virus is spread primarily through direct contact and is not particularly hardy in the environment. For this reason, puppies from shelters and commercial breeding operations (i.e. purchased through pet stores and online brokers) are at higher risk than puppies from small private breeders. But dogs adopted or purchased from these places can shed the virus for weeks if they've been exposed, putting all unvaccinated dogs who come in contact with them at risk.

The distemper virus, which is a close cousin of the human measles virus, has been shown to deplete the body's store of Vitamin A – in fact, the symptoms of distemper closely resemble the symptoms of serious Vitamin A deficiency. In one study, ferrets who were Vitamin A replete were shown to be completely resistant to challenge with the distemper virus. For this reason, a teaspoonful of old-fashioned cod liver oil a couple days before a dog is scheduled for a distemper vaccine to boost his Vitamin A levels might lessen the chance of reaction and certainly can't hurt.

Canine Infectious Hepatitis (that's the "H")

This is another disease that's rare in the US since widespread vaccination began in the 1960s—in fact, it's so rare *there hasn't been a single case of it* recorded in dogs in this country in the last 20 years at least and probably longer. (Why it was included as a Core Vaccine is frankly a total mystery.)

Caused by the CAV-1 (Canine Adenovirus- type 1) virus, infectious hepatitis primarily attacks the liver, kidneys, spleen and eyes- symptoms can range anywhere from relatively mild with spontaneous recovery to death within hours, with mortality most likely in puppies. The CAV1 virus is highly contagious and is spread primarily through ingestion of urine, feces and saliva of infected dogs. The virus is considered hardy and can survive in the environment for 6 months or more.

Somewhat oddly, modern vaccines do not actually contain the CAV-1 antigen, as early vaccines using it produced pretty severe side effects like corneal opacity (blue eye), which is also one of the symptoms of the disease. However, it was discovered that vaccination against CAV-2 (a similar virus but which only causes a mild self-limiting respiratory infection) also protected dogs against the more serious CAV1, and that antigen is now used instead.

So, if your dog is given a "3-way", he's actually protected against both canine infectious hepatitis (CAV1) and the milder CAV2, which means the DHP "3-way" actually protects against 4 diseases. Since the risk for puppies in the US contracting canine hepatitis is low to non-existent and the risk of adverse reaction is statistically higher than the risk of contracting the disease (especially if the puppy weighs under 22 pounds at the time of vaccination), the CAV2 antigen is usually the one that is left out of the initial puppy shots by many holistic vets and breeders, who opt for the DP combination instead.

Parvovirus (that's the "P")

"Parvo" is a word that strikes terror in the hearts of breeders everywhere, and with good reason. The parvovirus attacks the rapidly dividing cells in the digestive tract, which is where the virus does the most damage, causing vomiting and bloody diarrhea. Untreated, 80% of affected puppies will die usually of dehydration. With the best supportive treatment, maybe 75% will survive, but it's going to cost a breeder untold thousands of dollars to try and save a litter, and a quarter of them probably won't make it no matter what they do. *Fear of parvo is the reason so many breeders limit visitors when they have a litter.*

The virus first appeared in dogs back in the 1970s, and prior to development of a vaccine, thousands of dogs of all ages across the US died a pretty horrific death. Today, because of widespread vaccination and because the virus is ubiquitous in the environment, parvo is primarily a disease of puppies between 6 weeks and 6 months of age.

The *bad news* about parvo is that unlike distemper, the virus is extremely hardy in the environment, spread through the feces of infected dogs and picked up by human shoes. Once in the soil, it can live for up to 9 months outdoors, and actually longer if the ground freezes during that time.

The *good news* is parvo is actually pretty easy to kill indoors. A simple solution of water and chlorine bleach at a ratio of 30:1 will effectively kill it. (And anyone who bred dogs back in the 1970s probably still remembers that 30:1 translates to a quarter of a cup of bleach to a gallon of water.)

The truth is, out of the whole bunch, parvo is really the virus a puppy in the US is most likely to come in contact with. Unlike distemper, it is not confined to shelters, pet shops and puppy mills. Because it is so ubiquitous in the soil, unprotected puppies are at risk anytime they leave their own fenced yard.

Until you know for sure that your puppy is protected by running a titer, his feet really shouldn't touch the ground off your property, *even in the vet's office.* Bring him in his crate and keep him in it except when he's on a newly disinfected examining table, because the last dog who walked through the waiting room may have tracked it in on his paws. That dog may be vaccinated and therefore immune, but your puppy may not be. Remember, parvo is not an airborne virus – it is spread through feces, and clings to surfaces that it comes in contact with, like paws and shoes.

Now, since the 3-way DHP combination vaccine will take care of all the recommended core vaccines except rabies, one would logically think all vets would administer it. They don't.

For some unfathomable reason, many clinics in the US routinely use the CHPP combination instead, which includes parainfluenza, a non-core vaccine that protects against a second mild self-limiting respiratory infection. This would be fine except that each added vaccine increases the risk of adverse reaction in a dog under 22 pounds by 27%! (And most Aussiedoodle puppies are under 22 pounds when they are getting vaccinated.)

So, assuming your vet does not even carry the DP (which most do not), be sure and ask for the 3-way DHP instead of the 4-way DHPP.

Rabies

The last of the 4 "Core Vaccines", this one is always given as a single shot and is never a component of a combination vaccine. Because rabies poses a public health risk to humans, it is the only canine vaccination required by law in all 50 states.

However, because it is a killed vaccine and has a higher level of adjuvants and endotoxins than an MLV, it is also the cause of a LOT of serious vaccine reactions in dogs, so what we want to do is vaccinate our dogs to protect both them and us and to comply with state laws, but not over-vaccinate or vaccinate earlier than needed for protection and thereby increase the risk of adverse reactions.

Unfortunately, most people have little or no knowledge about the rabies virus, the disease it causes, actual risk to their dog or the laws in their state, and so there is an appalling tendency to over-vaccinate for rabies. Understanding both the disease and the relative risks of contracting it will help you make better decisions for your Dood.

Rabies is a particularly nasty viral disease first described back in 2000 BC. It can technically infect any warm-blooded vertebrate, although it is common in some (like canines) and virtually unheard of in others (like rodents).

Rabies is *zoonotic* and is passed from animals to other animals or humans through saliva (or rarely through actual tissue in the case of organ transplants), but *cannot* be transmitted through feces, urine, or blood. The virus is not hardy in the environment and becomes noninfectious when it dries out or is exposed to sunlight, usually within minutes or at most a few hours. (Simply petting or handling a rabid animal does not automatically constitute exposure, at least according to the CDC...who knew?)

Once it enters a new host, usually through a bite, the virus travels through the peripheral nerves (which can take weeks or even several months depending on where the bite occurred) until it reaches the central nervous system, at which point it causes acute encephalitis and is almost always 100% fatal, usually within days of symptoms appearing. In humans who've been exposed, the rabies vaccine can be successfully administered as a prophylactic prior to the appearance of symptoms, usually in a series of 5 shots. Unvaccinated dogs who have been exposed are generally euthanized.

How prevalent is it? Rabies kills around 55,000 people a year, mostly contracted from dog bites, with the overwhelming majority of rabies cases occurring in Africa and Asia. A hundred years ago, the US averaged about 100 human deaths from rabies every year, and nearly all were the result of dog bites. Once widespread vaccination, that changed radically, and in 2007 the CDC declared the US to be officially free of canine rabies, a "vaccine success story" by any measure. But in spite of that, there were 59 cases of rabies in dogs and 2 rabies cases in humans reported to the CDC in the Continental US in 2010. *This is because there are several other strains of rabies besides the canine one.*

Carried by wild animals, these strains can be transmitted to both animals and humans, and until we figure out how to eradicate those strains, dogs will continue to need rabies shots. (It's worth noting that there are almost *five times* more cases of rabies reported in (free-roaming) cats than in dogs every year, the only species for which incidence is actually rising. So what are the risks of your Doodle puppy contracting a "wild animal" strain of rabies before he's had his first rabies shot? It all depends upon where you live.

The following map (which changes little from year to year) shows the incidence of confirmed rabies in dogs in the US in 2010....all 59 of them. Each dot represents one case.

In humans, virtually *all cases* of rabies contracted in the US are caused by bites from infected bats, and rabid bats have been identified in most states, making rabies pretty much of an equal opportunity disease for humans from a geographical standpoint. *(It's also good to know that your odds of contracting rabies from a bat in the US are somewhere in the neighborhood of one in 155 million- you actually have a better chance of winning the lottery. Or being elected President.)*

Dogs, on the other hand, are unlikely to contract rabies from bat bites— in fact, there are exactly ZERO "bat-to-dog" rabies cases recorded by the CDC over the years. Go figure.

Instead, both dogs and cats are nearly always infected by bites from rabid skunks, raccoons and foxes, with skunks leading raccoons by a margin of two to one and foxes barely in the money.

And for unknown reasons, the incidence of rabies in raccoons is limited almost entirely to states along the Eastern seaboard and Texas, while the incidence in skunks is greatest in the Eastern states from Maine to Georgia and in a vertical band through the Midwest extending from Minnesota down to Texas, with a few scattered on the Pacific coast. Not surprisingly, if you look at the map, you'll notice the incidence of rabies in dogs and cats occurs primarily in those areas as well.

Contrary to popular belief, squirrels, chipmunks, rabbits, rats and mice are NOT carriers of rabies in the US, and pose no rabies risk to an unvaccinated puppy. (Good to know that we've been worrying unnecessarily about backyard squirrels and chipmunks all these years, huh?)

Now, that pretty much confines his risk to areas where these skunks, raccoons and foxes are found (in other words, *outdoors*) and then only in those parts of the country where they carry the rabies virus.

A dog cannot "catch" rabies from casual contact.

The only way a puppy *could* conceivably contract rabies is if he were allowed out unsupervised (in other words off-leash) in a state where rabid animals are found and happens to get bitten by a rabid one in the "furious" late stage of the disease, so it makes sense to avoid letting your puppy run loose in parks, landfills and around dumpsters prior to vaccination if you live in one of those states.

But you'd have to be a total *dunce* to do that anyway for a wealth of other reasons...I mean, just *think* about it— statistically, a loose puppy is about a million times more likely to get hit by a car than he is to contract rabies from being bitten by a rabid skunk or raccoon that just happened by *at that very moment.*

And even if you *are* a total dunce, the statistics are still weighted heavily in a dog's favor— remember, there are over 75 million dogs in America, and between 50-70 total cases of rabies in dogs per year.

Given all this, it's pretty obvious there is no reason your puppy needs to get his first rabies shot on the same day as his other puppy shots at 12 or 14 weeks, because his risk of contracting rabies is so low. *It is simply not necessary and will seriously increase his chances of an immediate or delayed vaccine reaction, so don't let anyone talk you into it.*

What About the Law?

Ah….*the Law*. Now that you understand the actual risks or lack thereof, you can probably wait the recommended 3-4 weeks needed to give his immune system time to recover after his last puppy vaccines before getting him his first rabies shot and still not run afoul of most state and municipal rabies laws.

And extensive research has failed to turn up anyone who's ever gone to jail (or even been fined) for waiting until their puppy was 6 months old before having him vaccinated for rabies. He just can't get a dog license until he has proof of rabies vaccination.

In most states the first vaccine is a "one-year vaccine", so a second will need to be given a year after the first in order to comply with most licensing laws, although according to the CDC, a dog is considered immune to rabies 28 days after a single rabies vaccine. (That's a year after the first, not when the dog turns a year old , by the way.)

And thanks to a lot of lobbying by concerned vets and owners, all subsequent rabies vaccinations are now good for three years in every single state. This is an improvement over the old "annual rabies vaccine" laws, but it's still probably overkill—most immunologists and vaccine experts agree that a rabies vaccination provides immunity for at least 5 and probably 7 years.

(In fact, there is an ongoing research study at the University of Wisconsin designed to prove exactly that, so that state rabies laws can be changed. For more information on it, Google the Rabies Challenge Fund. And feel free to donate while you're on the website, because as one might imagine, the entire study is being funded by private donations rather than by the pharmaceutical companies that manufacture and sell rabies vaccines.)

To reiterate:
- **The risk of your puppy contracting rabies from a wild animal is statistically very, very low.**
- **NO state requires annual rabies vaccination any more, so do not allow your vet to do so..**
- **And NEVER allow the rabies shot to be given within 3-4 weeks of any other vaccination.**

It's just not worth the risk to your dog.

Other suggestions from vaccine experts
for decreasing the chance of a rabies vaccine reaction include:

- *Using a "clean" (i.e. containing the least number of adjuvants) vaccine*
- *Giving the homeopathic remedy lyssin 30c (anyone can purchase this online) the day before and within 2 hours after vaccination may lessen the risk of reaction.*
- *Always delaying vaccination on a dog who is, or has recently been, ill, especially with GI problems.*
- *Delaying vaccination when the dog is under stress or has recently changed homes.*
- *Adding probiotics to the dog's diet for a week or two before and after vaccination*

Many vets erroneously assume the only adverse reactions to rabies vaccine are immediate acute reactions (anaphylaxis), but delayed reactions to rabies vaccines (vaccinosis) may occur up to 45 days later, and so no one associates them with the recent vaccine given, especially seizures, which are often misdiagnosed as "idiopathic epilepsy".

Delayed reactions to rabies vaccine may include:

- *Behavior changes such as aggression and separation anxiety*
- *Obsessive behavior, self-mutilation, tail-chewing, shredding bedding*
- *Pica- eating wood, stones, earth, stool*
- *Destructive behavior, shredding bedding*
- *Seizures, epilepsy*
- *Fibrosarcomas (cancer) at injection site*
- *Autoimmune disease (like immune-mediated hemolytic anemia)*
- *Chronic gastrointestinal problems*

If any of these problems appear after a rabies vaccine, your best bet is to locate a holistic or homeopathic vet who can prescribe specific remedies that can actually help a lot. (Most "conventional" vets are frankly not much use when dealing with vaccinosis, especially if they administered the vaccines...) Or as a last resort, contact Dr Jean Dodds at Hemopet for advice.

In fact, many holistic vets suggest that any previously unseen behaviors or health problems occurring within a month or two of rabies vaccination should probably be viewed with suspicion.

If your Dood reacts adversely to the rabies vaccine in spite of all efforts to be careful, it's good to know that in the following states at least, he can get a Medical Rabies Waiver from his vet. This is *critical* because if a dog has reacted adversely to rabies vaccine once, odds are the next time will be worse.

States with Medical Rabies Waivers as of 2012:

Alabama, California, Colorado, Connecticut, Florida, Illinois, Maine, Massachusetts, Missouri, Oregon, New Hampshire, New Jersey, New York, Vermont, Virginia, Wisconsin

If your state does *not* currently have a Medical Rabies Waiver Form, or if your county or municipality still requires annual rabies vaccination, visit the **Rabies Challenge Fund** website to see how you can help change these dangerously outdated laws.

Non-Core Vaccines

The AAHA Guidelines consider some vaccines to be "non-core vaccines", or optional, based on the individual dog's lifestyle, environment and risk of exposure. These include parainfluenza, bordatella, Leptospirosis, Lyme disease, and a rattlesnake vaccine. Because, like the rabies shot, all these vaccines are made with *killed* rather than *modified live* antigens and therefore require adjuvants, the risk of adverse reaction is by definition higher.

So before you let your puppy automatically be given one or even several of these, let's see who really needs them.

Kennel Cough (Parainfluenza and Bordatella)

Along with the CAV2 virus already used in core vaccines to protect against its Hepatitis cousin, the parainfluenza virus and bordatella bronchiseptica bacterium are primarily responsible for *Canine Infectious Tracheobronchitis*, more commonly known as "kennel cough".

Although not a life-threatening or even particularly serious disease (it's usually self-limiting even without treatment) kennel cough is highly contagious, so training classes, groomers, doggy daycare, boarding kennels all generally require proof of vaccination.

Even though the vaccines available are not long-lasting or effective against all the strains out there (lots of dogs who are current on the kennel cough vaccinations still end up with kennel cough), your dog is likely to need proof of vaccination against kennel cough to be welcome in most doggy venues.

The intranasal versions (which are literally squirted up the dog's nose) are the least reactive, and the most popular is probably Intra-Trac3, which includes CAV2, parainfluenza and bordatella.

Of course, if your puppy was vaccinated with the popular "4-way" DHPP vaccine instead of the 3-way DHP, he's already covered for CAV2 and parainfluenza (which is the second P) and in the interest of not over-vaccinating you should request that bordatella be administered as a single intranasal vaccine.

Lyme Disease

As anyone who's had it can attest, Lyme disease in humans is a serious and often debilitating chronic disease. Because of that, a lot of people automatically assume it's the same for dogs and that their puppy needs to be vaccinated against Lyme, especially if he lives in an endemic state. However, the most current data available indicates this may not be the case at all.

Also caused by the spirochete *borrelia bergdorferi* and transmitted primarily through the saliva of infected ticks, the symptoms of Lyme disease in dogs differ from those in people, and are for the most part far less devastating.
In addition, symptoms usually occur much later (according to Cornell's Baker Institute up to 2-5 months after a bite by an infected tick) and the classic Lyme rash is almost never seen.

Symptoms in dogs most commonly include low grade fever, lethargy, loss of appetite and shifting lameness. These usually resolve within 48 hours after treatment with oral doxycycline, which should be continued for a full 4 weeks due to the slow replication rate of *borrelia bergdorferi*.

Puppies should be treated with amoxicillin to avoid damage to the enamel on developing teeth, and probiotics should always be given after the course of antibiotics to restore normal gut flora.

But more importantly, based on nationwide test results,
it is now estimated that over 95% of dogs infected with the Lyme spirochete
never develop any clinical symptoms at all.

At this point, no one really knows why this is the case, but in humans, research has shown that chronic Lyme is associated with—big surprise!—a particular allele in one of the Class II HLA genes, so it's not much of a stretch to postulate that resistance to Lyme is associated with the Class II DLA genes in dogs…in other words, there's likely a genetic predisposition to susceptibility to this particular bug, and not surprisingly, some breeds appear to be particularly susceptible. In some purebreds, Lyme can cause serious kidney disease.

Most experts recommend asymptomatic dogs with a positive Lyme titer have a blood panel drawn and an auscultation to preclude the possibility of sub clinical cardiac or kidney involvement, and because of the "lag time" between exposure and the development of symptoms, some vets feel that it is prudent to treat Lyme-positive dogs with doxycycline simply to err on the side of caution.

And much like rabies, Lyme risk is entirely geographical.

In 2010, 95% of the reported cases of Lyme came from 12 states, with another 4% coming from California. All other states combined accounted for the other 1%.

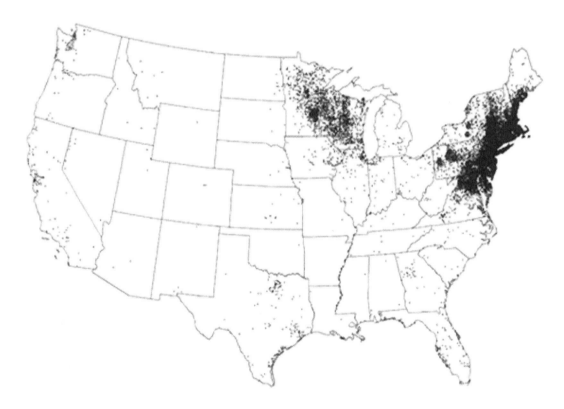

And even in Lyme endemic states like those in the Northeast, around 90% of healthy dogs have positive Lyme antibody tests. That's why those maps that show incidence of tick-borne diseases are so scary—they are not showing actual disease *incidence* so much as *exposure*. (And it's good t remember that those maps are brought to you by the manufacturers of Lyme vaccines and the companies that sell the snap-test kits….all of whom have a financial interest in selling more of their products.)

So why not vaccinate your puppy against Lyme "just to be on the safe side", in case he's one of the 5% who will develop symptoms after exposure? *Because it may not be the "safe" side at all.*

Serious questions have been raised about the safety of the Lyme Vaccine.

Testing on Lyme-vaccinated dogs with chronic inflammatory autoimmune arthritis (which does not typically occur in dogs naturally infected with Lyme) and other autoimmune diseases has revealed the presence of *vaccine-strain*, rather than wild-strain, Lyme. This raises the alarming possibility that *the vaccine itself is causing the problems*. (Not coincidentally, the human Lyme vaccine was pulled from the market when similar reports started coming in.)

At this point in time, the safest universally-recommended defense against Lyme is simply the prompt removal of ticks. After a tick attaches and begins to feed, spirochetes residing in the midgut of the tick begin to migrate into the salivary glands and from there into the host, which can take up to 12 hours. Because of that, there is actually little chance of infection during the first few hours of tick feeding, although it rises exponentially after that. So as long as you remove ticks promptly, the odds of a dog becoming infected with Lyme are pretty low.

And if you're *still* worried, you can always give your Dood a single capsule of doxycycline, which is an old drug and long-proven safe for adult dogs. Why?

A large randomized double-blind placebo-controlled human study conducted in an endemic area of New York determined that a single 200 mg dose of doxycycline administered within 72 hours after a tick bite could prevent the development of Lyme disease. Efficacy was determined to be around 87%, which is coincidentally about the same as most Lyme vaccines, but without the risk of adverse vaccine reaction. How cool is that?

It's also worth knowing that currently, the University Of Wisconsin School Of Veterinary Medicine, (located in a Lyme-endemic state) neither recommends nor administers Lyme vaccinations.

Lepto

Another non-core vaccine, this is one that a lot of vets try to scare clients into buying based on a "Lepto outbreak" in their area. *This is unfortunate*, because like the rabies vaccine, the lepto vaccine is one of the most likely to cause life-threatening adverse reactions (anaphylaxis) in dogs.

Unlike rabies, however, the lepto vaccine is neither required by law nor even necessary for *any* dog, no matter what the local risk at any given point in time.
Really.

Called Rat-Catcher's Yellows in earlier times, Leptospirosis is an old disease that's been around for a long time. It is caused by infection with the water-borne spirochete *leptospirosa*. Over 200 different strains (or *serovars*) of lepto have been identified to date, at least eight of which are known to cause Leptospirosis in dogs. The most current vaccines protect against FOUR of them.

On top of that, because it is a killed vaccine, two doses must be administered within weeks of each other to elicit an immune response (which effectively doubles the chance of reaction), and the most recent evidence suggests protection may only last 6-8 months. Combine that with the risk of adverse reaction, and the whole "lepto vaccination" picture is not particularly impressive.

So what is the real risk of your dog contracting Leptospirosis?
Probably pretty low.

A survey of the Veterinary Medical Database between 1983 and 1998 turned up a total of 340 reported cases. Even assuming that represents some serious under-reporting, putting those numbers into the framework of a canine population of maybe 50 million dogs during that 15 year period, it's not exactly what you'd call an epidemic.

Although Lepto is zoonotic, direct transfer from people to dogs or dogs to people (or even dog-to-dog) is pretty much nonexistent in the US. Instead, because the lepto spirochete is aquatic (it can survive up to 2-3 weeks in fresh (not salt) water, damp soil or mud) it is primarily transmitted through drinking or inhaling water containing the urine of an infected animal.

For this reason, lepto outbreaks tend to be clustered in small geographic areas, and are most likely to occur after flooding and overwhelmingly during September, October and November. Hunting and herding dogs, who are much more likely to drink out of stagnant ponds and such, are at highest risk.

So how serious is Lepto if the dog actually contracts it?
Like Lyme, it varies greatly from dog to dog.

Some infected dogs may be totally asymptomatic, while others become pretty violently ill within days, with high fever, and/or vomiting, excessive thirst and reduced dark-colored urine, generalized pain and often jaundice, because if not treated promptly, Lepto can attack and damage the liver and kidneys and cause death. On the other hand, if diagnosed and treated promptly with common garden-variety antibiotics (usually a combination of amoxicillin and doxycycline) response is good and mortality in healthy adult dogs is low.

There is no data on the actual incidence of asymptomatic dogs testing positive for Lepto in the US as there is with Lyme, but a large human study in Nicaragua in 1999 revealed that over 70% of those testing positive for Lepto were totally asymptomatic; canine studies in Germany revealed a similar pattern in dogs. Once again, resistance to the disease may well be a function of the individual immune system.

So, assuming you decide not to routinely vaccinate your dog against Lepto, what do you do if your vet tells you there has been an outbreak in your area—are you stuck with vaccinating? *Luckily, the answer is no.*

At least three separate human trials
have shown that 200 mg of our old friend doxycycline administered once a week
will prevent Leptospirosis with over 95% efficacy.

And unlike the vaccine, which is only effective against 4 of the 240 strains, *doxycycline will protect against all of them*, and will also prevent shedding of the organism in the urine, which is a definite plus with a zoonotic pathogen. Given the fact that most vaccines—including rabies!—only have to produce an efficacy rate of 80% or better for FDA approval, doxycycline's 95% is pretty impressive.

In fact, the CDC recommends that Americans traveling to parts of the world where Leptospirosis is endemic begin a regimen of one 200 mg dose of doxycycline weekly, starting 1-2 days before arriving and continuing for the duration.

However, be apprised that most vets are not aware of the use of doxycycline as a prophylactic for Leptospirosis, and may simply think you're nuts.

To avoid this possibility, you may want to download and print the information from the CDC and maybe the original NEJM publication yourself and bring it along to support your case—given the high possibility of adverse reaction to the vaccine, it's probably well-worth the effort. (Your vet may still think you're nuts, but at least you'll have some hard evidence-based medicine in your corner.)

To make that easier, links to the research on using doxycycline as a prophylactic for Lepto as well as the CDC's advice can be found in the Resources section at the end of this book.

Coronavirus, Giardia, Canine Influenza and Rattlesnake Vaccines

In the interest of not wasting anyone's time this section will be mercifully brief—the first one is another "vaccine in search of a disease" and any vet who actually recommends Corona vaccine ought to be viewed with suspicion.

The second two are not recommended by anybody except the pharmaceutical companies that manufacture and sell them. In other words, they all pretty much failed the AAHA's benefit/risk test, and there's no reason to risk overstressing any poor dog's immune system for this bunch.

The need for the last one, on the other hand, is entirely based on where you live and the number of rattlers your Dood is honestly likely to encounter, because a rattlesnake bite can kill a dog. Hunting dogs and Search and Rescue dogs working in rattlesnake country where the possibility of getting to a vet in a big hurry is problematic both fall into the "probably want to consider this one" category.

Because a lot of dogs do have an adverse reaction to it though, even when it's really needed the rattlesnake vaccine should always be administered by itself and never within 3-4 weeks of any other vaccines to lessen the risk.

OK, now that we've pretty much beaten the whole vaccine issue to death, let's move right on to the *other* area where you really need to educate yourself, because as with vaccination, the choices you make in this one from puppyhood on can also have a long-term influence on your Aussiedoodle's lifelong health and longevity. And that would be…

Parasites...Internal and External

Ok, let's face it, nobody likes parasites. We don't even like to *think* about parasites. And luckily, now that we have all these monthly pills and "topicals" we can easily protect our dogs with, we really don't have to think about them at all. *Think again.*

There's a growing body of evidence that all this stuff we've been merrily popping down our dogs' throats and squishing between their shoulder blades every month may, like over-vaccination, also be contributing to a lot of the health issues we're now seeing in dogs—everything from food allergies to autoimmune diseases to seizures. In fact, it is now pretty widely accepted than early exposure to these helminths are necessary to normal development of the IgE antibodies in the immune system, and a total lack of exposure contributes to development of allergies. (This is called the Old Friends Hypothesis.)

For Aussiedoodles, the whole problem becomes a LOT more complicated, because of the possibility of the presence of the MDR1 mutation, which can cause a toxic buildup of various drugs and insecticides in the brain, and is just about guaranteed to cause seizures...or worse.

To begin with, way too many owners (and their vets!) erroneously view monthly heartworm (and systemic flea and tick products) as "preventative medicine" and routinely give them on a monthly basis year-round with little or no further engagement of the thought process.

This is unfortunately incorrect on several levels. **None of these products actually *prevent* fleas, ticks, heartworm or anything else from entering your environment or attacking your dog, nor are they really *medicines*, although the manufacturers certainly market them that way.**

(As their manufacturers are quick to point out, a couple of the avermectins also used as antiparasitics in humans are in fact approved as "drugs" by the FDA, but when *those exact same chemicals* are sprayed on cotton fields to kill bugs, they mysteriously become "insecticides" and are regulated as such by EPA...go figure.)

Technically, these products are heartworm and flea *treatments,* not preventatives, and marketing them as "meds" really borders on the unethical. **They are really just plain old *insecticides* which kill parasites that happen to be on (or in) the dog at that moment.**

Some of the flea and tick products also contain a *hormone disrupter* that prevents parasites from reproducing or maturing normally, but again, they don't *prevent* the flea or tick or worm from attacking your dog, and in clinical trials, they made close to 15% of the dogs in the study really itchy.

The most popular of these insecticides are a group of *macrolycyclic lactones* derived from the bacterium *Streptomyces avernitilis* known as *avermectins,* and developed back in 1975 by scientists at Merck Laboratories from soil found on a golf course in Japan.

This group includes **ivermectin** (*Merial's Heartgard*), **selemectin** (*Pfizer's Revolution),* and **moxidectin** (*Bayer's Advantage, Fort Dodge's ProHeart*) as well as **milbemycin** (*Novartis's Interceptor and Sentinel)* .

And ALL of these will produce toxicity in dogs with the MDR1 mutation.
(Even the one in Interceptor, which was originally believed to be safe.)

Like most insecticides, they are all *neurotoxins*. In fact, that's how they all kill bugs—- they cause massive damage to their little bug nervous systems, resulting in seizures, coma and death.

What we count on is the fact that these neurotoxins do not readily cross the blood-brain barrier in *mammals.* But the key word here is "readily", which no one ever seems to notice.

According to their own manufacturers, "exposure at high levels" will produce all the classic symptoms of neurotoxicity (tremors, ataxia, seizures and coma) even in animals *not* carrying the MDR1 mutation, which would indicate that they *are* indeed capable of permeating the mammalian blood-brain barrier, wouldn't it? And since researcher know that dogs with the MDR1 mutation *cannot clear these chemicals from their brains,* it's pretty obvious they're ending up there.

And unbelievably, the effects of chronic low-level exposure to avermectins
has never been clinically studied in dogs *at all.*

The longest clinical trial appears to be a 24 month study on ivermectin (the active ingredient in Heartguard) performed decades ago…and that was *on rats.* No study has ever looked at the safety of monthly year-round use over a dog's lifetime. Ever.

And since these insecticides all end up in the liver sooner or later, it's probably NOT a coincidence that chronic liver problems and seizures started becoming a lot more common back in the 1980s, when dogs were suddenly exposed to these insecticides every month year-round for their entire lives. (The incidence of seizures in Australian Shepherds is inexplicably rising, and may well be linked to these chemicals.—even if they initially clear the brain, they can toxify the liver and result in seizures.)

So how do you safely protect your Aussiedoodle from heartworm?

Obviously, the first thing every Aussiedoodle owner should do is have their dog tested for the MDR1 mutation, so they know what level of sensitivity they're dealing with.

The researchers at Washington State, who seem to know more about this than anybody else, claim the avermectins will not cause neurological toxicity (or at least *obvious* toxicity, since I was unable to find any actual clinical testing on this) in dogs with the MDR1 mutation at the dose used to prevent heartworm infection, while the higher doses used to treat other parasites (like mites) will.

However, there also appear to have been ZERO studies to date on the possible adverse effects of chronic low-level exposure in MDR1 dogs treated with avermectins on a year-round monthly basis, which is more than a little worrisome, since that is the regimen now recommended by most vets.

Before automatically agreeing to monthly year-round treatment, it's good to know a little something about heartworms, and heartworm infestation, in dogs.

Unfortunately, most of the available information on this topic (including the brochures in your vet's office) comes from the American Heartworm Society, which is problematic.
A little casual research reveals that this organization, and its website, are in reality a marketing tool aimed at buyers and resellers of heartworm meds, and its sponsors are a *Who's Who* of drug companies. Fort Dodge (Wyeth), Merial and Pfizer are "Platinum Sponsors." Bayer merits Silver. Novartis, Schering-Plough, Virbac and Eli Lilly get Bronze. IDEXX, which is making a fortune selling heartworm tests, is also a sponsor. *Most of these companies have sales reps that regularly call on vets and show them how to sell you heartworm meds.*

Make no mistake about it, so-called "Heartworm Prevention" is Big Business, worth billions a year, and scaring pet owners is very profitable. Because of this, most information provided on heartworm by the drug companies "glosses over" some very important facts, *including what is actually required for transmission to your dog.*

So let's look first at the "natural" cycle of the heartworm, without the use of any insecticides:

- **To start the cycle, a *particular species* of female mosquito must bite a dog infected with circulating L1, which is the first larval stage in the life cycle of the heartworm, and ingest these L1 larvae.**

- The mosquito must then carry these larvae while they mature from the L1 stage to L2 and then L3, which takes 2-4 weeks and requires sustained day and night temperatures above 64 degrees. If the temperature drops below that at any point, the cycle is broken and the mosquito cannot infect another dog. *(The manufacturers all know this— in fact, they funded the research at U.Penn. that revealed it!)*

- Assuming the larvae (and the mosquito!) survive that long, the mosquito must then bite your dog, injecting the L3 larvae she picked up from the infected dog into the skin. If the dog has optimal immune function, the IgE antibodies on the mast cells will attack and kill all or at least most of them. (IgE antibodies were designed to deal with parasites, remember?)

- Those that make it through mature under the skin, where they will mature in 5-7 months into threadlike adults 2-3 inches long, eventually migrating to the arteries of the lungs. (In spite of their name, most heartworms are not in fact wrapped around the heart as shown in those photographs of severe infestations in the vet's office) If both male and female worms are present, they can reproduce. The larvae produced, called microfilaria, will circulate in the bloodstream, *but cannot mature into adults within the host dog.* They must complete part of their life cycle in a female mosquito.

- The adult worms will live around 2-3 years in the dog and then die of old age. Because of this, most heartworm infections are in fact self-limiting, and unless there are a whole lot of them or the dog's immune system is compromised, no symptoms will be seen in an otherwise healthy dog. (Most dogs who test positive for adult heartworms on an IDEXX test are completely asymptomatic.)

This is actually an elegant example of the symbiotic nature of the parasite/host relationship as designed by Mother Nature. Think about it...whether the designated host is a tree or an animal, there is absolutely no benefit to the parasite killing it, as that would also ensure its own demise. (As far as we know, there are no Kamikaze parasites.)

The "intermediary host" that many parasites employ— in this case the mosquito— helps keep the odds from tipping in favor of the parasite, as does the IgE "surveillance system" of a healthy host. The whole thing is a system of checks and balances, sort of like the three branches of the US Government we all learned about back in 8th grade Civics class.

In a well-functioning ecosystem, heavy parasite infestations, like infectious diseases, are generally limited to weak and old animals with compromised immune systems and serve a natural and necessary (if somewhat brutal) Darwinian function….which probably explains why parasites, like viruses, are still sharing the planet with us.

However, once the environment becomes toxic, the whole system of checks and balances breaks down.

In a toxic environment, the immune systems on what would normally be healthy young animals often take the biggest hit. And without an immune system that's firing on all its cylinders, the dog is unable to keep parasites under control, and severe infestations result.

Given the 60,000 made-made and mostly untested chemicals we've unleashed on the environment in the past century, this pretty much describes the situation in which most of us now live, which is why autoimmune disorders and chronic disease are rampant….and it's why very few owners (and fewer vets!) feel comfortable trusting in the natural balances designed by Mother Nature when it comes to infectious diseases and parasites.

So what we need to do is tip the odds back in favor of the host a little here, without adding to his toxic load any more than is necessary. And if the real goal of "heartworm prevention" is prevention of an *infestation of adult heartworms*, which can cause serious problems, let's look at what is actually known:

- **Most adult heartworms actually reside in the pulmonary arterial system (lung arteries) for the most part, where the primary effect on the health of the animal is damage to the lung vessels and tissues caused by inflammation. They only occasionally migrate to the heart.**

- **According to the University of Pennsylvania, (*which unlike most vets is not in the lucrative business of selling these neurotoxins*), "if you live in the Northeast part of the USA you only need to give heartworm preventative from June 1 through November 1, since maturation of the heartworm larvae requires average daily temperature above 64° F for any one-month period. There is therefore NO need to give heartworm chemoprophylaxis year-round, unless administration between June 1 and Nov 1 is occasionally missed." (You can easily adjust these dates to your own area of the country.)**

- **And as far as that "occasional missing" part is concerned, lapses of up to four months between doses of ivermectin-based products still provides 95% protection from adult worms. This is called the "reach-back effect" and is well-documented scientifically.**

- **"Reach back" is important because none of these insecticides kill 100% of the L3 larvae even if administered monthly—it's probably more like 97 or 98%. And 97% effective does NOT mean 100% effective on 97% of dogs, it means the insecticide kills 97% of the larvae exposed to it. Big difference.**

It should be pretty obvious at this point that the only possible reason for giving dogs so-called "heartworm meds" every month year round is a desire to bolster the coffers of the pharmaceutical giants who manufacture and sell them, and last time I looked, they didn't need much help in that department.

Vets, who buy this stuff wholesale from the pharmaceutical companies and sell it retail to pet owners are also making a boatload of money on it, which is the only possible reason for them to recommend dogs stay on it year-round, since the science just doesn't back it up as a practice.

Heartworm testing is now recommended for dogs on year-round and seasonal heartworm programs, but since Immiticide (the arsenic-based treatment for heartworm infection) is currently only available for dogs with Stage 3 and 4 infection, one might wonder why. (Immiticide has a VERY low safety level, which may be why it's no longer automatically used on symptomatic dogs.)

Weekly ivermectin will also kill adult heartworm, although more slowly, and many vets are recommending that for asymptomatic dogs, although it is NOT recommended for dogs with the MDR1 mutation...those guys are basically stuck with waiting for the heartworms to die of old age.

Other Internal Parasites

Since the avermectins are such effective broad-spectrum anti-helmitics, roundworms and hookworms are simply not as common as they used to be, even in puppies, and many owners will never encounter them. **Pyrantel pamoate** (Nemex) is still regularly used on young puppies, and it's been around a long time and has a pretty good safety record.

On the other hand, the one thing that the avermectins can't touch are tapeworms. Since the tapeworm requires the flea to complete its life cycle, any time you have even *a single flea*, a dog can end up with a tapeworm. The tapeworm will not show up in a fecal float like helminths— the ONLY way to diagnose it is to see tapeworm segments stuck to the dog's fur around his anal area or in his stool— they look like flattish grains of rice.

The insecticide of choice here is ***praziquantel.*** Until fairly recently, you had to buy it from your vet (Bayer's Droncit) and it cost a whopping $10 per tablet, but the patent must have run out or something, because you can now buy a generic version on Amazon for as little as a dollar per tablet. Praziquantel is praziquantel and there's really no sense paying ten times more than you need to.

External Parasites.... AKA .... Flea and Tick Prevention

Unlike helminths, there is no evidence at present that fleas and ticks serve any purpose other than to drive us crazy. Both are *ectoparasites*, which means they have a hard external skeleton.

Both have been around longer than man and his canine buddy and both will undoubtedly be around long after we're gone, because they are both unbelievably tough and highly adaptable.

The real frustration has always been trying to find something that will poison fleas and ticks *without* poisoning us and our dogs.

For the last several years, once-a-month topical insecticides looked like the answer, but that premise is starting to be questioned—and by the EPA itself, no less, a government agency usually frustratingly slow to react when it comes to potential dangers from pesticides.

Given that, the fact that topical insecticides (this includes ALL of them rather than a particular brand) are currently under investigation by the EPA should be enough to give one pause.
This investigation began after EPA received some 44,000 (that's forty-four thousand) reports of adverse effects to topical insecticides in 2008 alone.

And since let's face it, since hardly any of us even knew that adverse reactions to stuff like Frontline is supposed to be reported to *the Environmental Protection Agency* in the first place (or how to go about doing that), those numbers probably just represent the tip of a much bigger iceberg.

According to results of their preliminary investigation, the three systems most often affected were the skin, the intestinal tract and the central nervous system, with symptoms ranging from itching, chronic skin problems, vomiting and diarrhea all the way to seizures, coma and death.

Until they discover exactly what it is about these topical formulas that is causing these problems, owners who want to minimize risk to their dog's health might want to err on the side of caution and consider some safer alternatives.

One of the best pieces of advice from EPA (and which honestly wouldn't occur to most owners) is to bathe the dog IMMEDIATELY if he seems to be showing any adverse (or even odd) symptoms at all after his monthly treatment, using mild shampoo and lots of water. In other words, the sooner you get that stuff off the dog, the better. Doing so may actually save his life.

And in the "your tax dollar at work" department, here is some more advice from our friends at the EPA, copied verbatim from their website:

Discuss with your veterinarian whether topical flea treatments are even necessary for your dog. *(Note: If your dog doesn't actually HAVE fleas on him, the logical answer here is probably no. Killing fleas you don't have is a little like treating for malaria if you live in Duluth.)*

Vacuuming on a daily basis to remove eggs, larvae and adults is the best method for initial control of a flea infestation. It is important to vacuum the following areas: carpets, cushioned furniture, cracks and crevices on floors, along baseboards and the basement. *(Recent studies have shown that a plain old vacuum cleaner will remove around 95% of fleas in **all life stages** from the indoor environment, which is about as effective as most of the toxic insecticides currently available. Needless to say, these studies have not received a lot of press from the multi-billion-dollar Flea Industry...)*

Steam cleaning carpets may also help as the *hot steam and soap can kill fleas in all stages of the life cycle.* Pay particular attention to areas where pets sleep. *(Like vacuuming, steam cleaning is every bit as effective as the hormone-disrupting Insect Growth Regulators found in many flea products and a lot less creepy.)*

Wash all pet bedding and family bedding on which pets lie in hot, soapy water every two to three weeks. *(That's pretty self-explanatory.)*

Flea combs are very effective tools in the suppression of adult fleas. They allow hair to pass through the tines but not the fleas, removing fleas as well as flea feces and dried blood. Focus combing on those parts of the pet where the most fleas congregate, usually the neck or tail area. When fleas are caught, deposit them in hot soapy water to kill them. *(If a flea comb reveals no fleas or little black granules of dried blood called "flea dirt", odds are you have no fleas in your indoor or outdoor environment, and no need to expose your dog to unnecessary neurotoxins.)*

What the EPA clearly understands that most owners do not is that fleas and ticks are an *environmental* problem. What the monthly "preventatives" actually do is turn your dog into a four-footed toxic vacuum cleaner, gathering up any fleas or ticks that happen to jump onto him for a meal and either killing them outright or rendering them incapable of reproduction via toxins delivered through the animal's skin or bloodstream.

Unfortunately, this method by definition requires that the dog's skin or bloodstream be constantly infused with neurotoxic insecticides, some of which are harmful not only to the dog but to humans and the environment, and one of which has recently been linked to Hive Collapse, which is decimating the honeybee population in the US.

Natural Flea and Tick Repellants

Of course, the best way to prevent flea infestation in your home is to keep fleas the dog may encounter outdoors from jumping on him in the first place. That way they won't end up in the house. (The same is true of ticks, by the way.) What you need is a non-toxic flea and tick *repellant*.

The other advantage here is that you can spray down your dog when he leaves his own yard, which will help to keep your own yard flea and tick-free.

Essential Oils and Octopomine

And as it happens, Mother Nature has thoughtfully provided us with a fair number of them. They are found in many essential oils.

What these plant-based substances all do is interfere with the *octopomine neuroreceptors* of pheromone-driven insects and arthropods. Octopomine is sort of the insect version of adrenaline, and blocking the receptors for it causes quick death by CNS collapse. Insects are hard-wired to avoid these substances, all of which are aromatic. This is why they act as *repellants* as well as *insecticides*, and thus protect the plant from insect damage. It's an elegant example of Nature at her most brilliant. And….

Unlike most insecticides, octopomine is not toxic to people or dogs because mammals, fish and birds *don't have octopomine receptors.*

Clever.

Most of these substances have been used effectively for literally thousands of years without poisoning the planet, and really only fell out of favor in the last 30 years or so, when the big chemical and pharmaceutical companies decided they could do better.

Of course, as the toxicity of these made-made insecticides becomes more and more apparent, this is may well be another example of where "better is the enemy of good".

Along with others that may not smell as good (like neem oil and citronella, which a lot of people don't care for), the following more pleasantly aromatic essential oils have also been laboratory-tested and have been found to be both safe and effective in both repelling and killing both fleas and ticks:

- Cedar
- Lemongrass
- Peppermint
- Cinnamon
- Clove

All are FDA approved as human food additives, and are considered safe by the EPA when used as directed. (In other words, keep them out of the eyes and don't use them full strength on the skin)

Cedar oil, which has been used effectively for at least 3 thousand years as an insect repellant, is probably the overall winner here, as it's better than most at repelling ticks as well as fleas, although some owners claim peppermint oil is also effective on ticks. If you live in an area where ticks are a problem, that's worth knowing.

Non-toxic sprays and shampoos containing these essential oils are readily available commercially—you can find a wealth of them on Amazon if you search for "all-natural flea sprays" once you get there.

Most list their ingredients and you can sort of guess what they'll smell like based on that.
Barklogic, which gets good reviews, is primarily lemongrass and has a lemony aroma.
Vet's Best, another brand with good reviews, is peppermint and clove-y.
PetNaturals spray is a lemongrass/cinnamon combination that also gets high reviews.
Natural Chemistry's whole line of shampoos and sprays well and smell flat-out yummy.

There are lots more to choose from— just read the reviews and choose one that fits your needs. Remember that buying a product online that *doesn't actually list its ingredients* can be a little dicey, though — neem oil, for example, is a very safe and effective natural insecticide but smells a lot like burnt peanut butter.
Most of these companies make both a shampoo and a spray. If you are going to go this "non-toxic" route, you will need both.
A lot of dog owners swear by the whole line of **Cedarcide** products, which can be sprayed outside as well.

Making Your Own Flea and Tick Repellants

Of course, you can also make your own natural flea and tick repellant spray by simply adding a couple tablespoons of essential cedar oil to a spray bottle of water, and then adding a teaspoon or so of any of the other bug-repellant essential oils you happen to like....truth is, it's hardly rocket science and it's a lot cheaper that way if you're a "do-it-yourself" type. Here's a pretty easy "recipe":

Natural Flea and Tick Repellant

2 Tablespoons Cedar oil

1 Teaspoon Cinnamon oil

1 Teaspoon Clove oil

2 Teaspoons Vanilla extract

1 drop Dawn dish soap (keeps spray nozzle from clogging)

12 oz filtered or distilled water

Mix together in a plastic spray bottle and shake well before each use.

Spray head (cover eyes with your hand first), feet and legs and underside well. Lightly spray top of dog and work it into the fur with your hands, or brush through the damp coat, which is even better.

This spray can also be used on dog beds, furniture, baseboards and anywhere else you want to use it, checking upholstery fabric in an inconspicuous spot first to be sure it doesn't stain.

Remember, you want to spray the dog mostly where fleas and ticks are going to jump on hitch a ride And adding a couple tablespoonfuls of cedar oil (along with a teaspoon or two of any other essential oils you feel like adding) to a bottle any shampoo will turn it into a safe and effective flea shampoo, although it's best to start with an unscented shampoo so you don't end up with something over-whelming.

And always spray it on the inside of your arm before spraying it on your dog to make sure it's not irri-tating—if it is, pour some out, add more water and try again. And always keep it away from the eyes and mouth.

Now, unlike the once-a-month stuff, these sprays do have to be applied every day or two during the flea season, and you might want to spray your dog down again right before taking him for a walk in tick-heavy areas, but they really will repel fleas and ticks if used religiously, and they won't cause seizures or other weird side effects.

Besides insecticides that you actually put on or in your dog, the other major possibility for toxic exposure that the intelligent dog owner may want to consider is:

Lawn Chemicals

We all want a healthy, green lawn for our families to enjoy. But many people do not know that using synthetic lawn chemicals in your yard may increase your dog's risk of developing certain types of cancer.

A landmark 2004 study from Purdue University involving Scottish Terriers showed that dogs exposed to chemically treated lawns, specifically those treated with a chemical called **2,4-D** had a risk of transitional cell carcinoma (bladder cancer) 400% to 700% higher than that of dogs not exposed to these toxins.

An earlier study published in The Journal of the National Cancer Institute, a link was found between 2, 4-D and malignant lymphoma in dogs and non-Hodgkin's lymphoma in people, while a third study showed 2,4-D in the urine of dogs exposed to treated lawns.

This is probably not all that surprising when you consider that 2,4-D was one of the two primary components of *Agent Orange*, the jungle defoliant widely used during the Vietnam war and associated with a horrific number of immune problems, cancers, reproductive issues and birth defects in humans and animals exposed to it. Why it is approved for use on America's lawns is a total mystery.

Although most lawn care companies will try to convince you that their products are "safe for children and pets", there are a few things to consider before treating your lawn. First, they're only obligated to provide information on ***"Active Ingredients"*** in their products. This list leaves out the many ***"Inert Ingredients"*** also found in the products, many of which are known carcinogens or have documented health risks associated with them. One chemical that is often (amazingly) considered an inert ingredient is **2, 4-D** , the focus of the Purdue cancer study.

Dogs are at greater risk of exposure and potential side effects from lawn care chemicals because dogs do not generally wear clothes so chemicals get on fur and are more easily absorbed into the skin. Nor do dogs wear shoes -- lawn chemicals are absorbed through the paw pads, can be tracked into your home, and may be ingested when dogs lick their paws, as they often do. They also have a higher ratio of skin surface in relation to their body size, which gives them a proportionally larger surface area which can absorb toxins.

And dogs don't just walk on the grass— they roll in it, lay in it, sniff around in it and dig in it -- all opportunities to inhale, ingest and absorb more toxins than the average human would.

And last but certainly not least, in addition to walking on and playing in grass, Lord knows it's not uncommon for dogs to EAT grass while out in the yard, either intentionally or as part of all of the sticks and other things that they chew on while outside. ***Chemically treated grass was never meant to be eaten.*** Even if you don't treat your own lawn, it's good to remember when taking him for a walk that your neighbors might treat theirs. If you think your Dood may have been exposed to "toxic grass", hose off his feet (especially the pads on the underside) after you get home. That way he won't end up tracking the toxins onto his bed or ingesting it if he licks his paws.

In summary....

OK, now you know that with the exception of classical genetic disorders over which you have no control, a whole LOT of how healthy your Aussiedoodle ends up is really up to you, and the decisions YOU make for him from puppyhood on.
Remember, *less toxins equal better overall health*. Choosing a more "holistic" vet who is up to date on immunology and who understands the dangers of over-vaccination and overuse of insecticides and antibiotics will make things a lot easier, because you won't have to argue with someone who's basically trying to sell you what are often *totally unnecessary* toxins.

That said, in spite of all efforts, your Dood may find himself in need of emergency treatment at some point in his life, because of an accident or the ingestion of something not intended for ingestion. In these cases time is often of the essence.

Post the phone numbers for your vet, the nearest emergency clinic
and the poison control center on the WALL rather than in your cell phone
so everyone in the house has access to it.

CHAPTER EIGHT:

Aussiedoodle Coat Care and Grooming
(or...why people own shorthaired dogs)

No matter what you may have read on the internet, the Aussiedoodle is a pretty *high-maintenance* breed, and this should be clearly understood before you commit to adding one to your household.

Breeders who "gloss over" the substantial grooming requirements of a breed in an effort to sell puppies do potential owners and the breed itself a disservice, and actually contribute to the numbers of dogs finding themselves in need of a new home.

Much of the well-meaning information about coat care for ALL the Poodle hybrids available on the internet is pretty useless.

The main reason for this is because very few of these breeders started out showing and breeding Poodles, which have a very different coat (and very different coat-care needs) than most other breeds. Not surprisingly, a lot of these unique coat qualities are passed on to the Poodle hybrids, including the Aussiedoodle, which is one of the reasons people get them.

But because the very *thought* of Poodle hybrids sends experienced and knowledgeable Poodle breeders into fits of apoplexy, they are pretty disinclined to share their wealth of knowledge with the hybrid community at large, which is especially bad news for the breeders and owners of Doodles and Poos.

Here's an example;
Maintenance of the Poodle coat requires very specific combs and brushes to prevent matting, and virtually all Poodle breeders tend to swear by the same ones. But because they do not *share* this information, most Doodle breeders just recommend the ever-popular slicker brush, and most owners consequently use one to brush their Doodles. *This is the worst possible brush for this coat.*
And because Doodle breeders rarely stress the importance of early table-training as Poodle breeders do, most Doodles are not table-trained at all when they get to the groomer's for their first appointment.

This inevitably causes the following all-too-common scenario:

The owner drops an adorable but shaggy Doodle off at the groomers in the morning, with explicit instructions for a bath, a brush-out and a trim, as well as instructions "not to shave him or on any account make him look like a Poodle", a possibility the owner has already been warned about by Doodle breeders and owners everywhere, and which is often construed as an insult by the groomer.

When the owner comes back to pick him up in the afternoon, she's presented with an exorbitant bill by an extremely grumpy groomer, who tersely explains that the dog was "matted to the skin", along with a shaved-down dog who looks like a cross between a naked Poodle and Mamie Eisenhower with a mustache.

The disgruntled owner, who swears the dog wasn't matted, adds her voice to the legion Doodle owners badmouthing professional groomers.

Meanwhile the groomer, who's lost money by spending way too much time on a matted dog who's "not even table-trained", adds her voice to the legion of professional groomers badmouthing both Doodles *and* their owners, who they think are stupid people who "spent way too much money on a mutt".
(It's helpful to know that many professional groomers are purebred Poodle owners and breeders, and

many dislike Poodle hybrids on principle...so it's always good to ask how they feel about grooming Doodles before hiring the services of any groomer.)

This animosity between owners and groomers has gotten so bad that an alarming number of groomers will no longer take any new Doodle clients. At any price.
And the real pity here is that this whole scenario could be easily prevented if Doodle breeders would do what all reputable purebred breeders of what we call "coated breeds" have done for years:

- Teach new owners exactly what it takes to keep the breed's coat conditioned and groomed.
- Provide a list of tools and products that work well on that specific breed.
- Explain the necessity of a thorough comb-out *at least once a week*.
- Explain the necessity for a grooming table and post.

Then professional groomers could do a great job in half the time even if the dog was only brought in once a *year* and everybody would be happy.

Since that's probably not going to happen any time in the foreseeable future, however, let's do the next best thing and honestly explain what's required to keep an Aussiedoodle looking good, and exactly what the owner needs to do and what tools are required, whether they want to keep him short, long, or anywhere in between. The same principles apply whether they plan to employ the services of a professional or want to learn how to groom their dog at home.

Since most owners are probably going to use a professional groomer, let's start there, because the basics are actually the same for both groups.

Avoid Disaster....Know the "Look" You Want

First off, if you are planning to have your Aussiedoodle groomed professionally, you have to decide exactly what you want the end result to look like so you can clearly communicate that. Groomers really DO want to please their clients (it's better for business and the tips are more generous), but they are *not* mind-readers, and most do not keep a resident psychic on staff.

Bring a photo to the first appointment....with a caveat.

Many websites suggest bringing a photo of the look you want along when you drop the dog off, and this is actually pretty good advice, except for one problem—*nine out of ten Doodle owners will bring a photo of a dog that (to the groomer's experienced eye) is pretty clearly several weeks out from its last grooming appointment.*

Faced with these photos, many groomers have concluded that (unlike the rest of their clients, whom they perceive as sane) what all these crazy Doodle owners really want are dogs who leave their grooming shops looking, well… *totally ungroomed*…which they simply cannot get their heads around.

I mean, *think* about it for a minute—odds are pro groomers *became* groomers in the first place because they personally *like* the looks of sculpted, plush, sort of "frou-frou" dogs. Remember… these are people who actually think little bright-colored satin bows stuck onto various parts of a dog's head with teeny-weeny rubber bands are *cute,* and photos of shaggy dogs romping on the beach just don't do anything for them.

So for Heaven's sake find a photo of a *freshly-groomed* dog that illustrates the length and overall pattern you want. (Hint: these photos usually involve a dog actually standing on a grooming table.) Also make sure it's a dog with the same sort of coat that yours has—what works for a slightly wavy dog will be impossible to achieve with a curly one and vice-versa.

Unfortunately, unlike the Bichon or the Bedlington or the Dandie Dinmont, there is no immediately recognizable "official" trim pattern for the Aussiedoodle (or any other Doodle for that matter) to be found in the classic grooming texts, which seriously complicates things. This is mostly because they have no history of being exhibited at dog shows, which is where the various trims that different breeds sport evolved over the years.

That said, the one thing that *all* owners seem to agree on is that they do not want their Doodle to "look like a Poodle", so let's examine that, because it clearly means different things to different people.

What Makes a Doodle Look Like a Poodle?

In the US, all the different Poodle trims involve varying amounts of plush body coat in various (and seemingly random) places, but all of them require a closely clipped muzzle and feet, with a "pompadour" on the top of the head ranging anywhere from a short rounded dome shape in the Sporting Trim favored by most pet owners to topknots of truly astonishing heights in the Puppy, English Saddle and Continental Clips required in the show ring.

All are finished with a sculpted pompon on the tail.

Although a well-groomed Poodle is a work of art (the best groomers are really topiary sculptors whose chosen medium is hair), collectively this is not a look most owners seem to desire in an Aussiedoodle, and shaving the muzzle pretty much destroys the breed's characteristic expression.

On the other hand, if what is meant by a "Poodle look" involves more overall body shape rather than just the head, tail and feet, we have a different problem, because if both are clipped to the same length stem to stern with a 10 blade, it's going to be pretty hard to tell a clipped-down Aussiedoodle from a clipped-down Poodle with a higher ear set and a blocky muzzle. *That's just a fact of life.*

Because many of the physical traits of a Poodle tend to be controlled by dominant genes, the average Poodle hybrid is built way more like a Poodle than its other parent breed. Clipped short all over, both are revealed as square, leggy, lean breeds propped well up in front with a fair amount of tuck-up and rear angulation and the pretty typical lean heads seen on most pointing breeds.

If you do happen to like it, the clipped-down no-frills "sporting" look is far and away the easiest to maintain and probably best for people with allergies, because dogs in this clip can be bathed frequently with very little prep or finish work required. If your Aussiedoodle happens to be a merle, it's still going to stop traffic in this cut. (In fact, if this is the look you want for your dog, you can skip a lot of this chapter….!)
Virtually any groomer can take down a dog with a 10 blade, or you can buy a decent set of electric clippers and learn to do it yourself in no time flat, as there is not a great deal of artistry required—it's the canine version of the military buzz cut.

However, this utilitarian trim is not every Aussiedoodle owner's cup of tea, and has reduced more than a few to tears when a dog comes out of the groomer's sporting it.

The "official" trim that actually comes the closest to what most Doodle owners seem to want is probably the pet trim for the Soft Coated Wheaten Terrier, with the only real difference in the trimming of the top of the head, the ears and the tail.

To see what this looks like, just Google "pet wheaten images" and you'll find lots of examples. The F1 Aussiedoodle and the Wheaten have very similar coats, and the overall body proportions and angles very similar as well, which is why this works. The main anatomical differences are in tail set —even the head proportions and ear set are pretty similar.

The basic pet Wheaten trim can vary in length, depending upon the owner's wishes, but in all cases it involves a shorter "jacket" on the body (either clippered with a 4 blade or ideally scissored) blended into slightly longer hair on the underbody and the legs, which are scissored in a column straight down to the toes, without shaving the feet.

Any professional groomer should know how to do this trim—just be sure and tell them to scissor the head into a "Benji" trim rather than a standard Wheaten show trim, and to leave a plume on the tail. Unless the groomer is completely inept, requesting a modified Wheaten trim will pretty much guarantee that your Dood does not end up being mistaken for a clipped-down blonde Poodle.

Plush vs. Shaggy

Of course, what *some* owners really mean when they say they "don't want their Doodle to look like a Poodle" is simply that they don't want them to look overly "coiffed", because it is the shaggy, casually tousled appearance that attracted them to Doodles in the first place.

In reality, this is a difficult look for the majority of groomers to achieve, and virtually *impossible* to achieve with just a clipper, which is what most groomers use. Even with a snap-on comb attachment that leaves the hair up to an inch long, all the hair will be the same length and the finish will be "plush" rather than shaggy.

No matter what pattern is used, the *only* way to achieve a shaggy rather than a smooth plush finish is by using a peculiar breed of scissors called a "chunker". In essence a one-sided thinning shears with very coarse teeth, they are also called a "texturing shears". Popular for some years with hairdressers, these are relatively new to the dog grooming world.
Although just starting to catch on, groomers who know about them love them, as do their clients, because they truly are capable of producing a more natural, shaggy-dog look while still taking off needed inches of hair. If that's really the look you want, request that the groomer use a chunker. If they don't know what you're talking about, find one who does, because the results will be worth it.

How often does an Aussiedoodle REALLY need to be taken to the groomer ... and what will it cost?

If you want to keep your Aussiedoodle in a fairly short trim (maybe between one to three inches), most groomers agree he will ideally need to be trimmed every 4-6 weeks or so, although many owners can stretch it out to 8 weeks if they are religious about brushing. The Poodle coat spends more time in the anagen, or growth, phase than most breeds— this translates to a really fast-growing coat, and most Doodles appear to have inherited that trait, especially the multi-generational ones.

If you do not want to brush your own dog at all but don't want to keep him really short, most groomers agree he should be taken to the groomer's *weekly*, because that's the bare minimum of how often the average one needs to be brushed out in order to avoid matting.

Currently, the cost for having a medium-to large Doodle groomed runs between $50 and $100 per visit, depending on where you live. (Some groomers will give a discount to owners who bring their dogs in frequently, because it takes them significantly less time to groom these dogs, and groomers' fees are really based on the hours involved.) Spreading out the time between groomings rarely saves money in the long run, because the groomer will have to charge more if the coat has been neglected.

But any way you slice it, keeping your dog pretty short will quickly add up to hundreds of dollars a year and untold thousands of dollars over his lifetime if you plan to have him professionally groomed, so you need to factor that in before deciding to add one to your family.

Grooming Your Dood at Home

Can you do it yourself? Yes, absolutely. Anyone can learn to bathe and brush a dog. And if you have maybe two hours once every 4 to 6 weeks to put into the project, you can invest in two decent pairs of shears (one of which is the aforementioned chunkers) and learn to scissor your dog yourself to whatever length you prefer, which frankly is NOT rocket science.

Although your first efforts may produce less than stellar results, the soft wavy Aussiedoodle coat is both forgiving of scissoring errors and grows back with astonishing swiftness, so you'll have lots of opportunity to practice your technique. (A do-it-yourself trimming guide follows the sections on brushing and bathing because whether you have your dog trimmed professionally or do it yourself, that is the order that needs to be followed.) And all of the equipment needed to do the job will cost less than a single year's grooming bills.

The "Full Coat" Option

OR you can opt keep him in full length coat, in which case you can be prepared to literally stop traffic wherever you go. Although it also requires regular and thorough line brushing, which will take longer than brushing out a shorter coat (you can do it while you're watching TV), you will save thousands of dollars in grooming costs over the years. A dog in full coat will only need periodic "hygienic" scissoring of his feet, around his eyes and beneath his tail, which almost anyone can master.

If you have a particularly curly F1b or F2b dog, a full-length coat will tend to stand away from the body like a giant dandelion puff and probably isn't a great idea, but most F1 Doods that look pretty curly cut down would only display a slight wave if kept in full coat, because the weight pulls out the wave in dogs just as it does in people.

And although no one ever believes this, a longhaired dog of any breed who's *never* had his coat trimmed will actually tangle and mat way less than one who has, because the hair is allowed to maintain its natural growth pattern of different lengths, which is lost forever as soon as it is trimmed to all one length.

Whether you decide to have your dog trimmed by a professional, or plan to do it yourself, and no matter what length you wish to keep him at, the average Doodle still needs frequent and thorough comb-outs *at least once a week,* and some of them (mostly F1bs) frankly need to be done daily, especially during the adolescent period when the coat is transitioning from puppy coat to adult coat. The frequency varies from dog to dog, but in general, softer coats with more curl will tangle and mat faster than straighter coarser ones, which can usually be managed with a thorough going-through once a week.

If mats never have a chance to develop, the process will be painless and relaxing and both you and your Dood will come to enjoy the grooming sessions. (A short daily grooming session will actually help to develop a strong bond between the groomer and the "groomee", and will make all other aspects of training easier.)

On the other hand, if you put it off, the combing out of snarls and mats will turn it into a long and painful chore for both of you, and *nobody* will enjoy it.

Using "the Right Stuff"

Whether or not you'll actually keep your dog mat-free depends to a large degree on how easy or difficult the job is. And that depends entirely upon having the right equipment. With "the right stuff", a thorough daily comb-out should not take more than 10 minutes tops for a well-trained Doodle puppy and maybe twice that long for a large adult. And if you really truly do it once a day starting from the day he arrives at your home, your dog will be well-trained in short order!

The equipment and the grooming techniques that follow are probably different than what you may have used previously, or even different than what most pet groomers use. That's because they are the tools and techniques dog-show people use to groom *their* dogs…you know, the ones you see floating around the ring at Westminster with flowing silky coats. (Trust me, those coats have *never* seen a slicker brush, and they've never been brushed out standing on the floor.)

For years, the only place you could buy this stuff was from one of the big general supply booths at a dog show, but now, pretty much everything else can be purchased online from Amazon and www.BBird.biz in one fell swoop. So without further ado, here it is….

The Quintessential Grooming Supply List for Doodles

- **A grooming table and post.** *There is no way to overstate this: the grooming table is the single most important piece of equipment needed here. Besides saving your back and preventing your dog from up and leaving right in the middle of the grooming session, every professional groomer on the planet uses a grooming table, and they unanimously complain about the fact that Doodles are never table-trained, which makes grooming take a whole lot longer...and for which you, dear reader, will pay dearly in hard cash. You can buy one on Amazon with a grooming post and loop for under a hundred dollars.*

- **A PSI wood-handled poodle comb.** *If this were the ONLY grooming tool you owned, your Doodle would be mat-free for life. Regular use of this comb from the roots to the ends will ensure a "fleece" of matted coat doesn't form at the skin, which is almost sure to happen with a slicker brush.*

- **A Chris Christensen 16mm T-brush.** *Even though a poodle comb really will suffice, most people will feel the need to brush their Dood anyway. This brush is far and away the best one for the job. Well-made in Germany with smooth polished pins that won't damage the coat or scratch the skin like cheaper ones will, it has a smooth t-shaped wooden handle and an ergonomic shape that's far easier on the wrist than a traditional pin brush. It comes in two sizes—the large one works for most dogs, while the smaller "mini" is a better choice for their smaller cousins and puppies.*

- **A plastic spray bottle.** *As every dog-show groomer knows, brushing a dry coat is totally verboten if you want to avoid coat damage. Since damaged coats mat far more easily than coats that are not, it's well-worth the small effort involved in lightly misting the dog's coat each and every time you take a brush or comb to it— once you do get into the habit of doing this, brushing a dry dog will seem as wrong as driving off without fastening your seat belt! As far as what to mist the coat with, plain water with a teaspoon of unscented conditioner added will work just fine. Adding a couple tablespoonfuls of cedar oil will also repel fleas and ticks, so you can kill two birds with one stone here.*

- Detangler. *A silicone-based detangler applied to mat and allowed to dry before detangling will make the job easier. Chris Christensen's Ice on Ice spray works well., as does Silk Drops , which is made for people.*

- A guillotine-style nail clipper and a nail file or emery board. *On a dog the size of a Aussie-doodle, the guillotine will work far better than the scissors-type with a so-called 'safety guard'. They can be purchased at any pet store or from Amazon. If used correctly (instructions are included later on) they are not scary at all, in spite of their ghastly name. A sturdy nail file or emery board will smooth the nail after clipping and avoid inadvertent scratches from an exuberant dog. It's a good idea to buy a little container of Qwik-Stop at the same time, which will stop any bleeding immediately if you accidentally do cut a nail a little too short.*

- A box of cornstarch and a plastic parmesan cheese shaker. *You can buy a box of cornstarch at any grocery store and the cheese shaker is another dollar store item. (You can also use cornstarch baby powder if you don't mind the scent, in which case you won't need the shaker.)*

- Coconut oil and a bag of cotton balls. *These will be used for cleaning the ears, which should be done every week or so. Coconut oil has great natural anti-viral, anti-bacterial and anti-fungal properties, and will actually help prevent ear infections.*

- A good 7 or 8 inch straight hairdresser's shears or a good pair of chunkers. *If your Dood is curly, this is the scissors you want. Pro-line makes a good pair for around a hundred dollars, and if you don't use them for anything else or trim a sand-covered dog with them, they'll keep a good edge for a long time.   For straighter and wavy coats, the chunker will allow you to achieve the "natural" look Dood owners like, and is by definition very forgiving of errors as you perfect your scissoring skills. The Pro-line 7-inch chunker is a good choice. Its $139 dollar price tag might seem steep, but not when you consider you'll spend at least that amount in three grooming appointments. Don't even TRY to trim your dog with a cheap pair of scissors – a good pair will last for decades and you simply won't be able to do a good job if you try to save money here. You'll end up with a ragged-looking dog and a bad case of carpal tunnel syndrome.*

- A 5 or 6 inch straight shears with ball tips. *Breaking the rule here, this one doesn't really have to be all that good, because you're not cutting much with it, so if you need to save money, this is* *the place to do it. Don't go much under $15 or $20 though, or they'll get dull in a couple sessions and you'll be sorry. Even if you plan to have your Dood trimmed professionally, you'll need this one for hygienic trimming around the eyes, butt and feet between times.*

- *A bag of special "grooming treats", reserved for grooming only. What's most important is that it's a treat he only gets when he's completed a grooming session, so he'll make the association and actually look forward to being groomed. It works—dogs who always get a treat after nails trimming will cheerfully offer up their paws rather than fight you.*

And except for the grooming table, which folds up when not in use, all this stuff will fit in a basket that can sit on a shelf in the laundry room.

Notice that the "slicker brush" recommended on so many websites is NOT on this list.
This is not an oversight.

In fact, if you already own a slicker, *throw it out right now.* First off, it is REALLY painful….seriously, try brushing your *own* hair with one and I guarantee you that you'll feel guilty that you ever subjected your poor dog to it! No wonder so many of America's dogs "hate being brushed" and won't hold still for it—if that's all they've ever been brushed with, you can hardly blame them. You'd run and hide, too—in fact, did you ever wonder why if it's so great they don't make a brush like this for people?

Unless you want to cause serious skin abrasion, there is absolutely no way a slicker, with that stupid bend in its nasty wire bristles, can get all the way to the root of the hair, which is why so many dogs come into the groomer's brushed on the outside and literally felted at the skin. This requires that they be sheared down like a Suffolk, because that's the only way the groomer can get under the felt, and *nobody ends up happy.*

As if *that* isn't bad enough, the slicker roughs up the cuticle on the hair shaft, which damages the hair and actually *causes* mats. Next to the retractable leash, the ubiquitous slicker brush is the worst thing to ever happen to dog ownership. Allowing a brush that looks like it was designed for scrubbing a barbeque grill anywhere near a dog just makes no sense at all.

It's probably not a coincidence that internet grooming instructions that involve the use of a slicker are invariably written by people who also misspell the word "mat", which ought to tell you something…it's not a "matt", folks.

The other item intentionally missing from the list is a mat-splitter.

Another perfectly awful invention inflicted on the unsuspecting pet-owner, it's far better to learn to untangle a mat using a detangler spray, your fingers and cornstarch. If a mat cannot be teased apart (and almost any mat can be), it's really better to just use a scissors blade as explained further on. Like slickers, mat-splitters and so-called "mat rakes" are hard on the coat and painful for the dog, and will also cause him to hate being groomed.

Line Brushing

Ok, now that you have all the right equipment, it's time to learn to *line brush*. Before you can do it, though, you need to train your puppy (or adult Dood if you're starting late) to lie on his side on the grooming table while being brushed, because that will allow you to easily get to the parts that are most likely to mat. It's really the ONLY way to line brush, no matter what size the dog.

Table-Training 101

1. *Set up your table* with have your supplies close at hand.

2. *Lift your puppy onto the table* with his head to your left and his tail to your right.

3. *Now lie him on his side.* The way you do this is to wrap your left hand around his right foreleg about halfway up (this is the leg farthest from you!) and your right hand around his right hind leg and pull gently towards you while saying "Rufus, side" (unless of course his name isn't Rufus, in which case you'll want to use his own name so as not to confuse him) in a firm and cheery voice. Voila! In one fell swoop your dog will end up lying flat on his right side with his feet facing you. He'll also be pretty surprised if he's never done it before, so you'll want to praise him like mad for learning this new trick. If he's big enough, he'll soon be hopping up there and lying down on his own like a seasoned show dog as soon as you give him the command. (Puppies and Minidoodles need to be lifted up but should lie on their side on command.)

4. *Now, as soon as he's on his side and before he has a chance to scramble back up, take your left arm and lay it firmly across his body.* Put your elbow at his point of shoulder, your forearm across his ribcage and your palm flat on the point of hip.

5. *With the brush in your right hand, GENTLY brush over his feet, legs and body.* Pick up each leg and brush lightly between them. (The goal here is not to thoroughly brush him so much as to

get him used to being brushed while he's lying on his side.) Be sure and tell him what a good boy he is while you're doing it, because you want the whole experience to be positive. If he starts to get up, a quick tug on both of the right legs will put him neatly back on his side without having to wrestle with him. Repeat the "side" command while you're pulling and praise him when he's back on his side.

6. **When you've gone over his left side with the brush, do the same with the other side.** *The easiest way to do this is to allow him to stand, turn him all the way around so his head is facing in the other direction and repeat step 3, this time with your left hand around his left hind leg and your right hand around his right foreleg as you give the "side" command, remembering to praise him lavishly when he's on his side once more. (This time when you lay your arm across him your elbow will be on his hip and your palm will be on his shoulder.)*

7. **Once the second side is done, stand the puppy up and slide his head into the grooming loop.** *Tell him to "stand" and "stay". Quickly brush his head and ears and brush the body coat down. Pick up his feet one by one, examine them and put them back down. Finish off with his special grooming treat, praise him lavishly, tell him he's gorgeous, and lift him down.*

The whole process shouldn't take more than a couple minutes, and even an 8 week old puppy can learn this in a couple lessons. Once he's big enough (and brushing isn't a painful experience for him!), he'll be hopping up there and lying down on his side on his own like a seasoned show dog as soon as you give him the command. (Puppies and small Minidoodles will need to be lifted up.)

In fact, the "side" command can be used any time you want your dog to lie on his side – in case this hasn't occurred to you, it's the first step if you want to teach a dog to roll over.
"Stand" is another fairly easy command- it basically means don't go anywhere and don't sit down. Even the most dim-witted show dog learns this one with very little effort, so it should be no problem for your genius Dood. In both cases, it's good to practice these commands in lots of different places both indoors and out, lest the dog think they are only required on a table.
It goes without saying that even if your dog has the "stay" command down pat, no dog should EVER be left unattended on a grooming table, especially if he is attached to the grooming post— groomers don't call that loop that slides over his head a grooming "noose" for nothing!

Now, once your puppy understands the "side" command and will stay there on his own, you can actually begin line brushing.

Line Brushing Step by-Step

1. *With the dog on his side, begin by misting lightly all over.* Now brush all the hair in the opposite direction of its natural growth—in other words....up.

2. *Start with the hind foot.* Mist the whole leg lightly, then take your Poodle comb and comb a small section back down, being sure to comb all the way from the root to the end. As soon as that layer's combed through, part off another layer maybe two inches above the first one with the last tooth on your comb (or a knitting needle if the coat is full-length) and then comb that one down, adding it to the bottom layer. Keep adding layers until the rear leg is combed through all the way to the spine.

3. *Lift the leg slightly and comb out the inside of the opposite leg.* Keep your left arm across his body with firm but gentle pressure, Any time he starts to right himself, a slight tug on the offside leg will neatly put him back on his side without a wrestling match. (This quick movement will become second nature in short order.) Comb through the tail while you're back there.

4. *Move next to the ribcage area.* Start by combing out the first layer on the tummy from elbow to the already-combed-out hindquarters, adding layers as you go until you've combed everything to the spine. (If your Dood is really big, you may want to do the upper part by rotating him end-for-end while he's lying on his side until his feet are on the other side of the table ;this can save a lot of wear and tear on your back .)

5. *Move on to the front foot.* Using the same technique, add layers until you've combed down everything from foot to the spine, including the whole shoulder area.

6. *Lift the leg you just brushed and comb through the inside of the opposite leg, and then comb through the chest area between the front legs.* Make sure you have carefully combed out the area inside the elbow— that's a prime area for mats to form because the coat there rubs against itself with every step the dog takes. That hair can actually be trimmed short if you want.

7. *Turn the puppy around so his head is facing in the other direction, lie him down on his left side, and repeat the whole process.*

8. *Put your puppy on a sit-stay and slide the grooming loop over his head.* Adjust the slide so he can't back out of it. Now comb through his ears, neck, head and muzzle. (This is also when you'll want to clean ears, brush teeth and trim nails, all of which should be done weekly.)

9. *Stand him up (giving him the "stand" command), mist the coat lightly all over and brush the entire coat down with the pin brush.*

10. *Praise lavishly.* Give him his grooming treat, and lift him off the table. Take him outside to relieve himself, and then spend at least the next 5 minutes doing fun stuff with him.

If you actually follow the directions above on a daily basis, you will never need the following instructions, because your Dood will go through life mat-free. But since life often gets in the way of our best intentions, here's what to do if your comb actually hits a snag—*detangle* it.

What we call "mats" are really nothing more than tangled-up hair, some of which is probably attached to the dog's skin and some of which is not. Here's how to untangle it:

Detangling a Mat Step-by-Step

1. *Don't pull. Stop combing immediately.* Spray the area lightly with detangler and let it dry while you brush somewhere else.

2. *Take your shaker and sprinkle a little cornstarch or baby powder on the tangled area and work it in well with your fingers.* This will help untangle the mat by smoothing the roughed-up hair cuticles or something. (Never mind why—it just works.)

3. *Using only the thumb and index fingers of each hand, tease the mat apart bit by bit, always pulling sideways, until it looks more like a dust bunny than a mat.* Rub in more cornstarch as needed. (For some reason, this sideways pulling is not painful for the dog at all.)

4. *Pinch the area firmly at the roots. Now take your comb and use only the very last tooth to split the mat into small sections if needed.* You can also saw through it, using the blade of your opened scissors, sawing gently out from the root to the end. Remember to keep the scissors open and saw rather than cut (don't use your chunkers here.)

5. *Comb through the area with short strokes in stages, starting with the ends and working your way toward the root.* Finish by brushing through it with the pin brush if needed.

NOTE: This method will painlessly remove most "garden variety" mats—you can untangle a mat the size of your fist using this method if you have the time and inclination without causing pain or losing any hair that's still attached to the dog.

However, it WILL NOT work when the dog is matted in a "fleece" all over about a half-inch from the skin, so don't even try. That condition is almost always caused by improper brushing (usually from using a slicker brush) and the only painless cure for it is an electric clipper and a ten blade. If it happens, it's not the end of the world…your Dood will just look like a big shaved rat with long legs for a few weeks, and you'll know enough so that it won't ever happen again.

Bathing Your Aussiedoodle

Many websites state that Doodles "don't need frequent bathing". *I guess that depends on what you want your dog to smell like.*

Besides the doggy odor, dirty dogs mat faster than clean ones, and will carry more of the *Can f* proteins that cause allergic reactions, so if you got the dog for his hypoallergenic qualities, failing to bathe him frequently will be entirely counterproductive.

Most Doods need to be bathed twice a month, although once a month may suffice. This can be done in the bathtub or shower with a handheld spray attachment or outside with the hose if it's hot enough. (Although most Doods like cold water well enough to swim in it, an outside hot/cold faucet will be appreciated at bath time.

Besides a source of water and a drain, here's what you're gonna need to do the job right

- **Shampoo and cream rinse.** *If one of the reasons you got an Aussiedoodle in the first place was because of allergies in the family, it's pretty dumb to cover him in shampoo and conditioner that's loaded with chemicals and artificial scents that provoke allergies. There are now lots of brands to choose from if allergies are a problem. Pawganics makes a line of non-toxic hypoallergenic unscented dog shampoos and conditioners that are available on Amazon. If you want to turn it into a non-toxic flea shampoo, simply add two tablespoons of cedar oil to the shampoo and shake well. If allergies are not an issue, the Chris Christensen line of products are hard to beat, and beloved by show people everywhere. You can buy them online from their website, chrissystems.com. (Along with their shampoos and conditioners, their Ice on Ice Detangler is a total winner.*

- **An Absorber synthetic drying chamois or two and/or a couple of old bath towels.** *Once you've used an Absorber to dry your dog, you'll never go back to regular towels. Way better than chamois cloths, they are more like big (like 27 x 17 inch) extraordinarily thin sponges and are the best idea to come out of Japan since the compact car. Actually made for drying cars, they will take a ton of water off a dog and can be squeezed out and used over and over until the dog is nearly dry. If you buy two, you'll think of lots of cool things to do with the second one. You may not even need the bath towels, although you can use one to finish him off if it makes you feel better. The Absorber can be purchased on –where else?–Amazon for under twelve bucks.*

- **A Hair dryer on a stand** *Unless you live somewhere very hot and dry, air-drying your dog year-round is probably not practical, and waiting "until the weather warms up" to give him a bath isn't a great idea if you happen to live somewhere like Duluth, when that could be awhile. What everybody eventually figures out is that it takes three hands to dry even a well-trained dog, so you need a dryer on a stand. A table-top stand dryer is useless for the average Aussiedoodle, because there's not enough room on the table for both the dryer and the dog, and it'll only dry his feet and halfway up his legs in its little stand, so you have to pick it up to get the high parts, which sort of defeats the purpose. You need a FLOOR-stand dryer. The Rolls Royce here is the Oster Hi-Velocity Stand Dryer. Rock-solid, it will last forever and adjusts to every position needed to dry every conceivable part of a dog of any size with little effort. It's as good as a dryer can get. It also retails for around six hundred dollars. If that's more than you want to pay for a doggy hair dryer, all is not lost. For $12.95 you can buy a Jobar Hair Dryer Stand from Amazon to which you can attach your very own hand-held hair dryer made for people. You'll save mucho dinero and still have both hands free.*

OK, now that you have the right stuff, it's time to bathe. Although this seems like it should be pretty straightforward, the truth is 99% of people actually do it *wrong,* and cause the coat to mat.
This is why even when he's been brushed out beforehand, you'll often encounter snarls when blow-drying that seemingly *appeared out of nowhere.* They didn't…you created them your veryownself by incorrectly bathing! Here's how to do it right, start to finish, in Eight Easy Steps:

Doodle bathing 101

1. *Wet the dog thoroughly and pour the shampoo down the spine from head to tail.* Respray the shampooed part lightly and comb the shampoo through the dripping coat with your fingers only in the direction that the hair grows. Do NOT mash the hair around every which way to spread the shampoo – that's what causes matting, because the cuticles of each hair are softened and open at this point and will snag on each other when you do all that mashing around.

2. *Add more shampoo to the legs,* applying some at the top of each leg and combing it down the leg with your fingers from top to bottom, again without smooshing the hair up and down like you're scrubbing socks on a washboard.

3. *Do basically the same thing on the head, ears and neck,* finger-combing the shampoo through in the direction the hair naturally falls, and then shampoo the tail, adding the shampoo along the top and finger-combing it down through the feathering.

4. *Rinse thoroughly and apply the conditioner* using the exact same technique.

5. *Squeegee off the excess water with your hands and then use your Absorber to remove as much water as possible,* again wiping firmly in the direction the coat grows rather than "against the grain" or around in circles. As soon as the absorber is pretty wet, wring it out and go over the dog again as many times as needed. Run it down each leg from top to bottom several times, wringing it out as needed. You can do this while he's still in the tub or shower, which will keep everything (including you) a lot drier.

6. *Once you have him at least halfway dry, cover him with the dry towel and blot, don't rub.* If you're going to let him air-dry, run the Poodle comb through and set him free. Otherwise go to Step 7.

7. *Spread the other towel on the grooming table and lift your Dood onto it, sliding the grooming loop over his head.* Turn on the dryer to low and use your pin brush to fluff the coat as you dry it in sections, rather than all over. A lot of it can be done while he's sitting, or even lying down. Give him the "stand" command to finish the underside.

8. *Reward with his special "grooming treat" and take him outside to play for a couple of minutes.* Be sure and tell him how gorgeous he is!

Trimming for Your Own Dog

One of the main advantages of trimming your Dood yourself is that you can scissor the coat to whatever length you want as often as you want, instead of the dog spending a third of his life much *shorter* than you like and another third much *longer* than you like! You can take an inch or so off whenever needed in an hour or less, which will keep him pretty much looking the same all the time.

These instructions are for scissoring only. It's best to learn to scissor first, and then, once you're comfortable, reasonably proficient and committed to grooming your dog yourself, invest in a good clipper IF you decide you need to do a faster job, or want to keep your Dood in a really short sporting clip. (The reason professional pet groomers mostly use an electric clipper is because it's faster, and for a pro groomer, time is money. It's *not* because it does a better job than a scissors, which is what the perfection-oriented show groomers use.)

And if you decide to buy a clipper to try it, a fifty-dollar "home pet clipper set" is just not going to do it— you'll be lucky to get through halfway down the back before it heats up and bogs down. You'll need a decent professional-quality 2-speed clipper like the Oster Golden A-5 or the Andis AGC, and then you'll need a couple of extra blades (like a 4 F and a 7F) and maybe a set of steel combs because the 10-blade that comes with them will only leave 1/16 of an inch of hair, so by the time you're done you'll have well over $200 in the project.

Contrary to popular belief, unless to plan to keep him in a buzz cut, learning to use a clipper is actually *harder* than learning to scissor, because you can make really big holes in the coat in a heartbeat if the dog moves at the wrong time, and clipper burns (the mark of the inept) are downright painful for the dog. Besides, scissoring is much quieter and way more fun!

Now, until pretty recently, unless he was pretty curly, scissoring a Dood took a fair amount of skill and practice if you didn't want him to look like it had been trimmed by a first-grader. That changed with the scissors known as a "chunker". By definition, this scissors will leave a feathered edge that looks natural (unlike the "plush" look an electric clipper produces) and it's very forgiving of mistakes. It is the PERFECT scissors for the slightly wavy coat typical of the F1 Aussiedoodle. (Curly dogs really do not need a chunker, although it works fine on them too.)

Using a Scissors...the Right Way

Before you start cutting on your dog, it's best to take a minute to practice with your scissors because nine out of ten people hold a scissors wrong, and unless you are a professional hairdresser, odds are pretty good you're one of 'em.

Here's how to use a grooming scissors correctly, assuming you're going to cut with your right hand:

- *Slide your right thumb in the hole that does NOT have a finger rest attached to it.*

- *Put your RING finger through the other hole, resting your pinkie on the finger rest.*

- *Turn your wrist so that the blade controlled by your thumb is on the bottom.*

- *Now move your thumb (and only your thumb!) to open and close the lower blade ALL THE WAY, while keeping the top blade still.*

Holding the scissors correctly will keep you from dipping into the coat and making choppy little cuts with the last two inches of the blade (which is what happens when you use your thumb and index finger the way your kindergarten teacher taught you) instead of making long smooth cuts with the whole blade. Practice doing this until the motion becomes both comfortable and second nature.

If you're using a chunker, there's actually a video by grooming maven Barbara Bird demonstrating the use of a chunker on a dog that's well-worth watching before you start—just go to YouTube, type in "GroomClassroom" and scroll down until you get to the video titled "Cool Tools for Pet Grooming". A picture is truly worth a thousand words here.

(Barbara's grooming blog also has lots of wonderful information and photos on it, including stuff on grooming Doodles.)

Until you and your dog are more experienced, it's good to have an extra person (a spouse or a large child works well) to help hold him, otherwise you'll just have to use your grooming post and the "stand" command, which you WILL have practiced beforehand if you're smart.

Note: If you're left-handed, follow these instructions as written, replacing "right" with "left" and "left" with "right", which you're probably used to by now. Don't even bother to look for left-handed chunkers.

Scissoring a Doodle, Step-by-Step

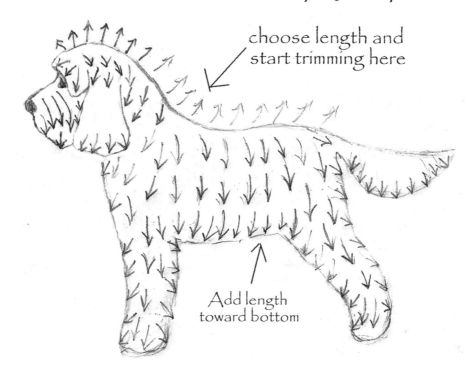

choose length and
start trimming here

Add length
toward bottom

With the dog standing on the table with his head to your left, lift the hair along the spine just behind the shoulders with your Poodle comb, which you should be holding in your left hand. Decide how long you want the hair to be, and with the scissors in your right hand, start cutting from the shoulders toward the tail at that length, keeping the scissors parallel to the spine and remembering to use the whole blade. (Instead of the single cut you'll make with a plain shears, you will need to make two or three rapid cuts with the chunker, moving the scissors very slightly each time to create a natural feathered finish to the hair.) Lift each area with the comb before you start cutting. Trim until you've got a swath about four to six inches wide cut down the back all the way to the base of the tail that's the length you want. Now "fluff and comb" through the whole area in the direction the coat grows to remove any cut hair that didn't fall off and touch up where needed.

With the scissors pointing down, start moving down the side of the rump closest to you, remembering to fluff the hair with the comb before each cut. Trim this hair to approximately the same length as the back. Make sure the tips of your scissors are not dipping in to the coat, and that you are cutting with the entire length of the blade.

Still working with the scissors vertically, move down the leg, trimming all the way around and making a straight column to the foot, leaving this hair slightly longer than the "jacket". Blend the coat at the elbow to get a smooth transition between the jacket and the leg. (This is easier than it sounds.)

Brush the hair around the foot straight down and pick up the foot, wrapping your hand around it. With your straight scissors, trim off all the hair that sticks out below the foot, and trim any excess hair between the pads. (You can use your little ball-tipped scissors to do the pads if you're afraid of slicing a pad.) When you put the foot back down, you should have a nice round circle with maybe a tuft or two sticking out. Starting with the blade of your straight shears nearly flat on the table, tip it up about 45 degrees and trim neatly around the foot. The resulting angle will make the dog appear "well up on his toes".

Next move to the ribcage, and work your way down that area (again keeping your scissors pointed down), fluffing as you go. To maintain the Aussiedoodle outline, you want to leave it a little longer starting about halfway down the ribcage. Now working with your scissors parallel to the table, trim the underside, blending it into the sides and leaving enough length behind the ribcage to avoid a "poodley" or "greyhound" look. (In other words, you don't want to carve a lot of tuck-up under the loin.)

Move to the shoulder and trim the front leg pretty much as described in section 3. Lift the front foot and trim the same way as you did the back one.

Working from the head down, trim the neck, throat and chest, taking the throat and neck area down to the length of the back and leaving the hair slightly longer as you move to the chest. (Remember, you can always shorten an area afterwards, but you can't put hair back on!) Lift the ear and trim the entire area under it, blending into the neck- keeping the hair under the ear short will allow for airflow and will reduce the incidence of ear infections.

Now stand back and check out what you've done so far. Make sure the line of the back is level, and neaten up the outline.
Turn the dog around, and repeat the process on the other side.
Now check your work from the front and the rear, to make sure both sides match, trimming as needed down the shoulders, hips and sides of the legs to get there.

Trimming the tail

Once the body is done, stand the dog up and brush through the tail. Now scoop all the tail feathering into your hand, slide your hand all the way out to the tip and hold the tail out straight behind him. Trim off everything in your hand that extends beyond the end of the tail about an inch from the tip. Now comb the feathering down and trim it into an elongated triangle from base to tip at whatever length you prefer. (This sort of assumes your Aussiedoodle has a natural tail. ...if it's short, just trim the hair on what tail is there neatly.)
Use your ball-tipped scissors to trim around the anal and genital areas for hygienic purposes, including the first inch or so on the underside of the tail. Itself. (This ideally needs to be done every couple of weeks even if you are having your dog professionally trimmed.)

Trimming the head

First decide what length you want here, and keep a photo handy- tape one to the wall (a photo taken from the angle of the one on the next page is most helpful) so you can look at it as you work. You'll get better results if trim the whole head at once rather than one side at a time, so you want the dog facing you dead-on for this part. He can be sitting down for this.

- *Lift the hair on the top skull with your comb and trim it to the desired length,* starting at the center of the head between the eyes and working front to back, trimming in an arch that follows the line of the skull rather than straight across. Now lift the hair between the trimmed area and the ear to your left with your comb. Turning your scissors so the tip is pointing to the ear, blend this hair into the top of the ear, again working in a curve rather than straight across.

- *Next, brush the hair on the muzzle and beard, brushing toward the nose.* Using your chunkers so that you get a natural finish, trim it to the desired length, trimming in a half-circle on each side rather than chopping it straight across. Some owners prefer to shorten the hair more around the jaw behind the muzzle, while others prefer a fuller face—there's no rule here, so go with your personal preference...you can always start fuller and remove more later if you like.

- *Now, using your ball-tipped scissors with the tip up rather than down, trim the hair between the eyes into an inverted V shape.* (It helps to cover the dog's eye with your left hand as you're doing this on each side, as it will keep him from jerking back.)

- *Trim the bangs to the desired length,* always working in a half-circle shorter in the center and longer toward the ears to avoid the Mamie Eisenhower look.

- *Trim the ears to the desired length* with the chunkers, making a rounded curve rather than a straight -across cut.

OK, you're done! Remember to give your Dood his special grooming treat, praise him lavishly for being such a great dog, compliment him on his good looks and take him out to play fetch for a couple of minutes.

It's also good to remember that, depending on your own temperament and the patience of your four-footed buddy, this trimming does not have to be done in one marathon session (although it really shouldn't take more than an hour tops once you've done it a couple times) but can be broken up into several sessions.

As with regular grooming, the important thing is to keep it from becoming a drag for the dog. And the best way to accomplish this is to *talk* to him while you're snipping way or combing…unlike everyone else in your life, *here's a friend who never tires of the sound of your voice.* He thinks you're brilliant, witty and the smartest person on the planet and your voice is music to his ears. Tell him about your job, or your love life, or practice chatting to him in a foreign language—at least he won't laugh at your accent! If you can carry a tune, you can sing the entire score of The Sound of Music while you're grooming. Come to think about it, you can do that even if you *can't* carry a tune…odds are good he's never heard Julie Andrews anyway, so he'll have nothing to compare it to.

"Grooming" Involves More Than Hair

In addition to an attractive tangle-free coat, a well-groomed dog also has clean ears, clean teeth and short nails. These are all things that you can and should tend to between regular haircuts, to avoid problems down the road.

Dental Care for Doods

A mere decade or two ago, anyone who suggested actually *brushing a dog's teeth* would have been widely considered certifiable. Today it's an integral part of responsible 21st century dog ownership.

Vets now suggest periodic professional cleanings at least once or twice a year (at $250-$500 a pop, depending on where you live), and there are now a wealth of doggy toothbrushes, special doggy toothpastes and doggy mouthwashes on the market, all of which you are supposed to use daily to prevent *periodontal disease*, which vets claim are associated with a host of other life-threatening diseases in dogs.

Is this just a new way for vets to make more money, or is it truly necessary for a dog's health and well-being? After all, dogs went for thousands of years without dental care and survived just fine. Unlike people, dogs don't even get *cavities*. And as older dog owners know well, not too long ago most dogs died of old age with all their teeth intact; simply gnawing on bones kept those teeth shiny and white. *Not so much any more.*

Veterinary data reveals that periodontal disease is now the most common disease found in dogs, and affects an astonishing 80% of dogs over the age of three.

OK, it appears this dental thing is pretty clearly not hype. So what's going on?

A wealth of new evidence now suggests that periodontal disease in both man and beast is an *autoimmune disorder.*

Basically, what happens is the same old bacteria that have always adhered to the teeth and formed plaque are now causing an inappropriate response by the immune system (sound eerily familiar?), which then overproduces cytokines like TNF-alpha and interleukin 1beta, probably not coincidentally the same pair also involved in allergies. Ordinarily important for healing, in excess these cytokines produce inflammation and ultimately destroy the *periodontium*, the tissues that support the teeth. It's that same inability of the immune system to distinguish between self and non-self that is the hallmark of all autoimmune diseases.

This also explains the association between periodontal disease and heart and other organ problems that have been noted. It's not so much that periodontal disease causes heart and liver problems, but that all of them are caused by the same underlying inflammatory processes.

Armed with this new knowledge, it should be pretty obvious that the BEST way to avoid periodontal disease is *to protect your Dood's immune system in the first place* through careful choices in food, vaccination and anti-parasitic regimens, rather than trying to use band-aid solutions to treat the symptoms of an autoimmune disease after the immune system is overstressed by environmental factors

That said, brushing your dog's teeth is not a bad idea, and if you want to do it, by all means have a go—just make sure and use toothpaste made especially for dogs, because fluoride is toxic and dogs can't spit. The main problem with doggy tooth brushing is that most dogs hate it and most owners don't really *do* it— they mostly just buy the toothpaste and toothbrush from the vet and then feel *guilty* about it. A little casual research reveals that truth be told, the doggy toothbrush is right up there with the AbBlaster in the "Least Likely to be Used After Purchase" department.

If that describes you, all is not lost…luckily there are several products out there that will pretty effectively remove plaque and tartar that you can just spray in your dog's mouth a couple times a week.

One that a fair number of vets (who probably know damn well that their clients are not really going to brush their dogs' teeth every day no matter what they say) carry in their office is made by *Petzlife*; it comes in both a gel you can rub on the dog's teeth and a spray, which is hands-down the easiest. If your vet doesn't carry it, Amazon does. Actually buying this and using it a few times a week may well preclude the need for professional cleaning under general anesthesia, which both your dog and your pocketbook will appreciate, even if your vet does not!

Maintaining Healthy Ears

Your Dood's ears should be ideally be cleaned whenever he gets a bath. This is easily done with a cotton ball or two dipped in coconut oil. Coconut oil (which you can buy almost anywhere) is great stuff, and should be part of any holistic dog owner's dog kit. It's non-irritating and yet has strong anti-fungal, anti-bacterial and anti-viral properties.

The inside of a dog's ear is a little like the gut— there needs to be a balance of flora in there for optimum ear health. When that balance is upset (most often by strong antibacterial products) yeast overgrowth occurs, and you can end up with a secondary yeast infection. If he's shaking his head and scratching at his ears a lot, or if you detect a "yeasty" odor in his ears, he'll probably have to be treated for an ear infection. (If the vet puts him on a course of oral antibiotics, be sure and give him probiotics or Greek yogurt for a week or two after treatment to rebalance intestinal flora.)

Because of their Poodle ancestry, some Aussiedoodles carry a lot of hair in the ear canal, which blocks airflow and consequently provides an ideal environment for infections. Groomers routinely pull this excess hair from the ears using a hemostat, which some vets agree with and others think is a really bad idea because it can cause inflammation.

This is one of those places where you probably need to ask for your own vet's opinion, because he is, after all, your dog's primary health provider. (However, do not be surprised if the various vets in a single practice hold differing opinions. here) It's good to keep in mind that like so much else, susceptibility to ear infections are a reflection of a dog's immune function at any particular point in time, and stressors like vaccination will often trigger them.

Trimming Nails

For some reason, this is one aspect of dog ownership that causes more anxiety on the owner's part than it needs to. Dog's being the intuitive creatures they are, this owner anxiety is transferred directly to the dog, and nail-trimming then becomes a Major Event, when it really should be no more traumatic for the dog to have his nails trimmed than it is for the owner, who rarely screams and carries on like she's being murdered during a manicure.

Because of this, most pet dogs are forced to endure nails that are too long, which is not good for them at all. *Here's the rule of nail trimming: if you can hear the nails click when the dog walks across the floor, they are too long.*
When this happens, your dog is going to have to adjust his entire skeleton to compensate, because he needs to put his weight on the *pads* of his feet, not the nails, and it will eventually cause him to break down at the pasterns, and can actually cause spinal and joint problems.
This is especially important in the Aussiedoodle, who naturally "stands well up on his toes" like a Poodle, and is not built with a lot of natural bend in the pastern.

Keeping your dog's nails off the floor is easy to do if you take a little bit off once a week, and if you cut them at the correct angle, which 99% of people do not do. In fact, most diagrams you'll find on the internet are incorrect! Cutting correctly will actually cause the quick to recede.

The diagram on the opposite page shows the *correct* angle to cut a dog's nails. If you hold the nail trimmer in the correct position and cut the nails vertically as shown, you can get them back where they should be in a couple of weeks without cutting into the quick. On the other hand, if you cut at a 45 degree angle, as most people do, your chances of bleeding the nails go way up, and you still won't be able to get his nails off the floor. (If you do cut into the quick, a dab of Qwik Stop will stop any minimal bleeding that results in short order, and odds are your dogs won't even notice.)

So here's the technique:

- *With your dog's head in the grooming loop, lift each foot in turn without much ado and quickly snip off the end of each nail at the angle shown.*
- *Follow with a couple of quick swipes of the file to smooth out the rough edges and you're done.*
- *Reward him with one of his special "grooming treats".*

If you start trimming nails regularly when he's little and approach it with an air of cheerful confidence, it just won't be a big deal for the dog. Or you.

Properly trimmed nail

The long and the short of Aussiedoodle grooming:
As you've probably figured out, keeping your Aussiedoodle well-groomed is not rocket science, and is well within the average owner's capabilities. But it DOES require a commitment to investing a fair amount of time and effort on at least a weekly basis, even if you plan to use a professional groomer for the "haircut" part. If you are frankly unable or unwilling to make that commitment, this is probably not the right breed for you.

CHAPTER NINE:

Beyond the Basics

(or...cool stuff to do with Aussiedoodles)

Because Aussiedoodles are intelligent dogs who actually *enjoy* training, there are lots of other things you can do with your Dood once he has mastered basic obedience.

Dogs were developed over thousands of years to work and thrive on it – because of their hard-wiring, dogs without a job are more prone to anxiety and health and behavioral issues than dogs with one. In other words, chronic unemployment is no healthier for a dog than it is for a person. This is especially true for breeds descended from working dogs. So get your Dood off the dole and put him to work!

The Entertainment Industry.... AKA Stupid Dog Tricks

Everybody loves dog tricks...including dogs! Dogs are natural performers, and learning tricks is a huge confidence-builder for them, especially if you start when they're puppies. Any dog who has mastered the sit/stay and a decent indoor recall can learn a plethora of tricks.

Although people have been teaching dogs tricks on their own for eons, a good place to start if you want help is with the book *Dog Tricks*, by Captain Haggerty and Carol Lea Benjamin.
Any dog who works his way through these eighty-eight tricks, some very useful and some just silly,

can go on to do *anything* in the world of dogs, since all these tricks involve a lot of the basics used in "real" work. Plus every trick your dog successfully masters will make the next one easier, because of a phenomenon known to behavioralists as *chaining*.

It's probably worth noting that Chapter Two in this book (which was written back in 1978) involves teaching the "retrieve" command using a collar twist, which is controversial in today's "positive-only" world of pet dog training, although many serious professionals still use it for working dogs.

Since Aussiedoodles are generally pretty good natural retrievers, you can easily teach him the "take it" command, which is necessary, without using a collar at all by simply tossing the desired object a very short distance and working your way *back* to dropping and then placing it directly in front of him instead of the other way around. (Forced retrieving is really only necessary for working dogs who don't naturally put things in their mouths, and odds are pretty good you don't have one of those anyway.)

Teaching him "out" to release an item on command is also critical, and the instructions given for doing that are pretty time-honored. But for heaven's sake don't try to teach "take it" or "out" with food treats, especially on a breed as naturally willing to work for praise as the Aussiedoodle.

Agility, Obedience and Rally

Once entirely the province of purebreds, the AKC opened competition in their three Companion events to mixed-breeds under their new Canine Partners Program in 2010, much to everyone's surprise.
This decision effectively allowed Doodles to enter and compete for titles as long as their breed is listed as "All-American" rather than as an "Aussiedoodle" or "Goldendoodle" or whatever. (Hey, it's a start...and as we all know, once Lady Sybil married the Irish chauffeur, things were never quite the same at Downton Abbey.)

In addition to the Companion events, dogs listed with the Canine Partners program are eligible for AKC's new Therapy Dog title.

Undoubtedly one of the better financial decisions they've made in several lifetimes, over 20,000 entries by mixed breeds were recorded around the country in the first year alone, so you don't have to worry about feeling like the Lone Ranger if you decide to enter this Longtime Bastion of Purebredness.

UKC is also accepting mixed breeds in Companion Events under their LP program, and also allows them to compete in dock-diving and weight-pulling events.

And not surprisingly for such an agile, intelligent and intelligent breed, there are a lot of Aussiedoodles out there doing really well in Agility, Rally and Obedience, earning lots of titles, and between the two organizations there are trials in nearly every part of the country on any given weekend.

Virtually every city in the US has Agility and Obedience training clubs where you can learn the basics even if you don't want to compete for titles. (AKC-affiliated clubs are listed on their website. Go to their homepage at www.akc.org , click on Clubs and Delegates, then click on Club Search.) Most Obedience and Agility Clubs, even if AKC-affiliated, have long accepted non-AKC registered dogs in training classes as long as you pay the fees.

OK, so my dog is maybe cut out for this stuff... but what about ME?

Unlike AKC's Conformation shows, which operate on the competitive principle that "the last dog standing" is the winner (much like beauty pageants for any species), all of these sports are non-competitive. Each dog "qualifies" by achieving the required score rather than by beating the other dogs, and a predetermined number of qualifying scores need to be accrued at each title level. You can enter as many trials as you need to in order to get your green (qualifying) ribbons.

In general, **Rally** trials are the easiest and least formal, and it's a good place for beginners, kids... and people with bad backs and dickey knees. Your dog should know how to heel and sit while on a leash. Basically, you and your dog follow whatever directions you find on the signs set around in a seemingly random and ever-changing pattern in a fenced-in course. And you can chat merrily away with your dog on the course, which is sort of frowned on in Obedience trials.

Obedience trials are more formal and precision-oriented (with half-point infractions for things like crooked sits) in their set routines, and the sport appeals to some human and canine temperaments far more than others. Speed is not of the essence here, except maybe for the dog's recall, so you don't have to be particularly athletic to compete, although you'll occasionally need to bend over and/or trot a bit.

Agility trials are about speed as well as agility, as runs are timed. This sport does require both the handler and dog to be in pretty good shape, as the handler runs sort of beside the dog, although not through the tunnels and weave poles or over the jumps, thank Heavens. Basic obedience is required for this one, because the dogs are by necessity working off leash.

More information on all of these programs for mixed breeds can be found at both AKC's website at www.akc.org and UKC's at www.ukcdogs.com , including dates and locations for trials near you.. Be sure and tell 'em I sentcha!

Dock Jumping

If your Dood likes water and retrieving out of it, this may be the PERFECT sport for him, and at least a couple Aussiedoodles are out there competing already!

 One of the newest and fastest-growing dog sports, dock jumping as a competitive sport "officially" began in 1997 when Purina added it to their Incredible Dog Challenge Program, and most people have seen dock diving on TV.

Several organizations quickly emerged in the last few years to sponsor events and competitions, the best-known of which are probably Ultimate Air Dogs, which is affiliated with Purina and the UKC, and Dock Dogs, which is independent. Both groups have maps on their websites showing event locations.

Both organizations welcome newcomers to the sport and allow practice time for novice dogs in the pool between competitions. The whole sport is fun and casual and all breeds are welcome...the only requirement is that your dog be a strong swimmer, although life jackets are allowed.

Canine Freestyle

If Dock Diving is a sport that generally appeals to men (and a majority of its participants are males between the ages of 24 and 54) Canine Freestyle is a sport almost entirely dominated by women. More specifically, *women who like to dance.*

Canine Freestyle, often called "dancing with your dog", began in the 1990s and spread rapidly, with many local Obedience Clubs now offering classes. With choreographed routines performed in often flashy costumes to music, it probably resembles pairs figure skating more than anything else on the planet, except that it's done on the floor rather than ice and one of the pair is a dog.

Although any dog can learn freestyle, an agile dog with a love of performing will be easiest to work with, and the Aussiedoodle is genetically well-suited for it—along with the almost ubiquitous Border collie, both his parent breeds are popular freestyle dogs.

You can find a class near you by simply googling "canine freestyle" along with the name of your nearest midsize city or your state. The Canine Freestyle Federation also maintains a list of classes available around the country on its website, which can be accessed at www.canine-freestyle.org.

If, on the other hand, this is something you maybe want to fool around with first in the privacy of your own home, the absolute best place to start is Sandra Davis's website at www.caninefreestyle.com. Sandra Davis quite literally wrote the book on canine freestyle, which is available for purchase here, as are several instructional DVDs.

If you'd like to see how good Freestyle can get (and you've somehow missed them on TV) you can go to YouTube and search for one of Sandra and the amazing Pepper's many videotaped performances.

(As a side note, Ms Davis, who was one of the early pioneers of Agility in the 1980s before introducing a huge chunk of the dog world to Freestyle, is now pioneering a fascinating new sport she's calling **K-9 Dressage**. If you have a background in dressage and your interest is piqued, you can find out more about that also on her website.)

It's probably not surprising that in addition to their dancing skills, Canine Freestylers are often certified as Therapy Dog teams, and enjoy "taking their show on the road" to nursing homes and other health care facilities. And of course Therapy is another activity where Aussiedoodles shine, so let's move to that one n

Animal-Assisted Therapy

Therapy dogs do not perform specific tasks for people with disabilities, but rather visit facilities like hospitals, special needs centers, schools and nursing homes with their owners. The Aussiedoodle's low -shedding hypoallergenic coats makes him especially welcome.

Although they certainly don't need to be able to dance, therapy dogs DO need to have exemplary temperaments and good social skills as well as basic obedience.

And after a few visits with their Therapy vests on, Therapy Dogs quickly grasp the importance of the job they've been asked to do, and clearly look forward to it. An amazing number even know when it's "Therapy day" as soon as they wake up that morning—is it because dogs have an internal calendar, or are they reading the handler's mind? No one knows, and it really doesn't matter, but it's certainly cool.

Therapy work is one of the most singularly rewarding things you can do with your Dood, and there is a shortage of certified Therapy Dogs in many areas, as health care facilities have begun to realize their immense therapeutic value. Beyond merely brightening the days of those confined to a medical facility, the regularly scheduled presence of a Therapy Dog can initiate very real healing, for reasons we simply do not yet understand.

There are three large national organizations that partner with local groups to train, test and register dog/handler teams across the US. You can visit their respective websites to learn exactly what required to prepare for therapy work and to find a group near you.

- **Therapy Dogs Inc:** Founded in 1990, they boast 12,000 handler/dog teams in the US and Canada. They can be found on the web at www.therapydogs.com

- **Therapy Dogs International:** The oldest and largest, TDI was founded in 1976 and has 24,000 handler dog teams registered. Their web address is www.tdi-dog.org.

- **Pet Partners:** Founded back in 1977 and long known as Delta Society, their name was changed in 2012 to better reflect the work done by their 10,000 registered dog/handler teams across the country. They can still be found at their www.deltasociety.org web address, however.

Service Dogs

When most people think of service dogs, the first thing that comes to mind is the classic Guide Dog working in harness to guide his blind partner through a maze of city streets, or perhaps the Assistance Dog performing a variety of complex tasks like opening refrigerator doors and pushing elevator buttons for the wheelchair-bound.

These dogs are traditionally donated by breeders to training facilities as puppies. They are often raised by volunteers until old enough for formal training, and then placed with selected disabled owners as adults once their training is completed. This whole process takes the better part of two years, and is obviously not something we can (or even wish to) do with the family Doodle, although there are several organizations that have trained Aussiedoodles donated by breeders very successfully.

But the world of Service Dogs has expanded greatly in recent years, and dogs now perform a variety of tasks for people with a wide range of physical and mental disabilities that can greatly enhance their ability to lead normal lives.

And the natural alertness to his environment and attentiveness to his owner hard-wired into his DNA makes even the smallest Aussiedoodle really well-suited for a lot of these newer forms of service, since several of them specifically involve *alerting the owner* to either external situations (in the case of hearing dogs or peanut alert dogs) or extremely subtle unidentified changes in the owner that signal the onset of a potentially life-threatening problem (in the cases of diabetic and seizure alerting).

Some of these new jobs in the "Canine Service Industry" include:

- Medical Alert Dogs (most often Diabetic Alert Dogs)
- Seizure Response/Alert Dogs
- Autism Assistance Dogs
- Allergen Alert Dogs (also called "peanut dogs")
- Hearing Dogs

Obviously, there are some very cool jobs here! And although many are unaware of it, all of these dogs are granted the same public access rights as the better-known Guide and Assistant Dogs under the Americans with Disabilities Act of 1990, whether trained professionally *or owner-trained*. If you are interested in learning more about any of these newer kinds of Service Dogs just Google their name – there's lots of information on the internet

There is also a lot of *misinformation* floating around about Service Dogs and the law, so let's address that here first, just so you don't end up confused by conflicting information you may encounter from the usual internet "experts" The following information is from the US Dept of Justice and is current at the time of writing.

- *The definition of "disability" for purposes of public accommodation under the ADA is broader than that of agencies like SSA.* It essentially covers anyone with "a physical or mental impairment that limits one or more major life activities". (Since "breathing" is actually on that list of activities, potentially life-threatening food allergies are covered, just in case you were wondering about Allergen Alert Dogs.)
- *By Federal law, Service Dogs do NOT require any "certification" by any organization, nor do they need to pass any tests.* In order to be protected under the ADA along with their owners, they just need to be "individually trained to do work or perform tasks for the benefit of an individual with a physical, sensory, psychiatric, intellectual or other mental disability", at least according to the US Dept of Justice, which has the last word, bearing in mind that "the work or tasks performed by the service animal must be directly related to the handler's disability."

- *Service Dogs are not pets.* Because Service Dogs are not considered pets by the DOJ, municipal, county and state "no pets allowed" laws do not apply to them.

- *"Psychological Support dogs or Emotional Support Dogs are NOT considered Service Dogs and are not covered by the ADA.* Providing comfort or emotional support, while certainly useful, is insufficient—the dog has to be trained to perform specific tasks.

- *Contrary to popular belief, do you need "a letter from your doctor" in order to have a Service Dog.* In fact, the ADA prohibits anyone from requesting one.

- *Service dogs are not required to wear identifying vests or ID in order to be allowed public access.* However, since most people are not mind readers, it's a very good idea and will usually make access automatic.

- *Service Dogs in Training are not automatically guaranteed access under the ADA, although many state statutes grant them the same rights as trained Service Dogs.* In states that do allow access (California and Florida are two states that do) the dog must be accompanied by his trainer

It is, however, illegal to *pretend* your dog is a Service Dog, or to identify him as one with a vest or a tag, just to get him on a bus or allow him to ride in the cabin of the plane for free, even if you have a letter from your doctor claiming the dog provides needed emotional support. *Doing so is against the law in most states, and will result in heavy fines and possible jail time, so don't even THINK about it.*

The most up-to-date and accurate information on federal laws concerning Service Dogs is available at: www.ada.gov/service_animals_2010.
If you use a Service dog, it's worth printing it out and carrying it with you for reference if needed.

So, all that said…if you or your child have diabetes, or if you have a child with a severe peanut allergy (or *any* life-threatening food allergy for that matter) or autism or any other disability and you enjoy training, there are lots of resources available to help you train your own dog to be a Service dog, which will probably please him no end, since dogs *like* to have a job.

And if the truth be told, with the exception of seizure alerting, which some dogs just seem to be born with, it's really not all that difficult to train dogs for a variety of service tasks…for example, the average dog can be trained to do reliable scent detection with passive or active signaling in 8-12 weeks, maybe working with him an hour a day, by anyone with fair-to-middling training skills and a minimum of equipment. There are at least as many ways of training an alert dog as there are trainers, and no real evidence that one works better than the other, so just find a method you and your dog are comfortable with.

OK, so…if much of this training within the province of the average owner, why are so many people out there scrimping and fund-raising to afford the exorbitant price of trained Service dogs for their children? Are they being scammed?

Usually not. Although there are a few horror stories out there from people who paid thousands of dollars for trained Service Dogs from fly-by-nighters that turned out to be totally *un*trained, common sense dictates one should definitely do serious homework prior to shelling out big bucks on anything.

But the *real* reason trained Service Dogs are worth anywhere from $10,000 to $25,000 is not because trainers are carpet-bagging, or because the dogs are somehow special—in fact, Hearing Dogs have traditionally come from shelters.
It's simply because the costs of *raising the dog from puppyhood* – including early socialization, food, grooming, routine vet costs, health screening, and the basic obedience required before he begins task-specific training—are all factored into the cost, and many of the people doing that have to pay the mortgage, even if they have not-for-profit tax status.

If the trainer doesn't fund-raise to offset the costs (which legitimate charities like the Guide Dog organizations have traditionally done over the years) that cost will have to be borne by the new owner. Some Service Dog organizations do use the Guide Dog model, of course—*Tender Loving Canines* in San Diego is an exemplary example of a group that solicits donations and uses volunteer labor to provide PTSD and Autism Service dogs at no cost-- but others do not.

But you already *have* the dog, and you've already invested all that time and money and done the basic obedience work yourself, so you can move right to the fun stuff…and finding things is truly one of the great joys in a dog's life. To him, it's just another Stupid Dog Trick. Think about it—dogs unerringly detect drugs, bombs, peanut or dairy products or low blood sugar levels not because they intrinsically understand that these are "bad" things, but because they think it's FUN and he wants to please you.

If training your dog for a service job for yourself or another family member sounds like something you would like to try, a good place to start is of course the internet.

There are wonderful YouTube videos put together by pros showing the basics of scent detection training and lots of other tasks…just go to You Tube and search for "detection dog training". There's a website at www.owner-trained-service-dogs.com that's a good place to start. Or you can work with a local search and rescue group or an experienced trainer of detection dogs, because the basics are the same.

Bear in mind while researching that there are at least as many methods of training a Service dog as there are trainers, and no real empirical evidence that one works better than the other (although law enforcement dogs are never food-trained for a wealth of reasons), so just find a method you and your dog are comfortable with. Do beware of trainers who claim their method is the only one that will produce a reliable dog, though, because odds are they haven't been at it very long.

And a lot of this work can actually be started when they're still puppies. Learning the basics of searching is well within the capabilities of puppies 3- 4 months old, and once they've grasped the concept, they can be trained to search and signal for anything. *Including people.* And that, of course, is what search and rescue is all about.

Search and Rescue

Everybody loves a hero, and the highest-profile heroes in the canine world are inarguably Search and Rescue Dogs. From the events of 9/11 to Hurricane Katrina to the horrific earthquakes in Haiti and Japan, these dogs and their handlers have saved innumerable lives, as well as providing closure for the families of those for whom rescue was impossible. These dogs have been certified by FEMA as Disaster Search Dogs, and there are over 250 such teams in the US today. Trained to be *non-scent discriminatory*, they will alert on any scent of a given type (such as human scent) rather than an individual, and they are also certified as HRD (cadavar) dogs.

Maintaining a much lower profile but no less incredible, hundreds more teams are out in the field on any given day rescuing children and adults lost in wilderness areas, as well as recovering autistic children and mentally disabled adults in suburban and urban neighborhoods. These dogs must demonstrate proficiency in *scent discrimination,* which means they search for a particular missing person based on a scent article, usually using a combination of air scenting and tracking/trailing, based upon the situation and/or terrain.

Of all the jobs that dogs can do, this one requires the highest level of fitness, talent and training on the part of dog as well as the highest level of fitness, training and commitment on the part of the handler.

(It also requires a fairly good-sized dog, and is probably best suited to Aussiedoodles on the bigger end of the size scale.)

Training of an SAR team typically takes several years, because in addition to the dog's training, the human half of the team needs to be proficient in orienteering and wilderness survival and certified to the required level of emergency medical training. Most of this training and the travel required to achieve it, is at the owner's expense. Once certified, these teams provide search and rescue support for local, county and state law enforcement, and are on call 24 hours a day, 7 days a week, 365 days a year, so the human half of the team needs a flexible work schedule.

And when they're not actually working, or doing public awareness and education on wilderness safety for schools and civic groups, these teams *practice*, because keeping skill levels sharp is critical to performance in emergency situations, and it is generally accepted that in order to be performance-ready a team must work at least once a week, usually for 4-8 hours. (SAR work requires an uncommonly high level of endurance, in case you haven't figured that out.) Needless to say, this isn't for everybody.

If it *does* appeal to you, however, there is certainly opportunity to get involved. Remember, the largest proportion of Search and Rescue Dogs teams are unpaid volunteers organized into fairly small units around the country. They tend to be by definition inclusive rather than exclusive, and there's no gender bias as long as you're fit and tough and have a dog that can cut the mustard.

Because there is no national directory, the best way to find a local SAR unit is to simply Google "search and rescue dogs" along with the name of your state or county, which should turn up a website or two. These units are all non-profit groups comprised of civilian volunteers who do not charge for their services to the state, county and municipal law enforcement agencies that they work with.

So........... there you go.

That should cover almost everything you need to know about Aussiedoodles.

And what's most important to remember in all this?

Easy. More than just a sized-down version of his bigger cousins, the unique characteristics brought to the mix by his herding ancestors make the charming Aussiedoodle

A Very Different Doodle Indeed.

~ INDEX ~

~RESOURCES~
Gene testing

MDR1 mutation:
Washington State University **(www.vetmed.wsu.edu)** Lots of information on the MDR1 gene mutation as well as instructions on how to order a test for your dog. (cost is currently $70)

Hereditary Cataracts:
Animal Genetics Inc **(www.animalgentics.us)** Information on Hereditary Cataracts in Australian Shepherds—gene test kit for owners and breeders is available from them. (current price $45)

Color and coat genes:
Vetgen, Ann Arbor, MI **(www.vetgen.org)** offers testing for both the curly and furnishings genes and tests for sable and ee red. Information on ordering test kits is available on their website.
VGL, Davis, CA **(www.vgl.ucd.edu)** offers testing for coat variations and color genes, including piebald. Information on ordering test kits is available on their website as well.

IDEXX is currently the only lab testing for the merle gene. Test must be ordered through a vet with an IDEXX account. Code # for merle test is 3341.

Cobalamin Malabsorption Syndrome
An informative article on this can be downloaded at **www.ashgi.org/articles/metabol_b12.htm,** printed out and taken to your vet if your puppy experiences symptoms of this disease. Vets who suspect possible CMS should contact U Penn at **www.research.vet.upenn.edu** to order a gene test, which is diagnostic.

DLA Diversity
Test determines the level of heterozygosity at the MHC II locus to measure hybrid vigor in multigen breedings. Currently only available from Genoscoper **(www.genoscoper.com)**

BAER testing

A wealth of information on Congenital Deafness, including various published research papers and a list of BAER testing sites can be found at the website of LSU's Dr George Strain, who is unquestionably the world's leading authority on the topic: **(http://www.lsu.edu/deafness/deaf)**

CERF information

A list of Board-certified canine ophthalmologists who can perform CERF exams can be found at
http://member.acvo.org/location_search_public
Many of these specialists also conduct clinics open to the public, often sponsored by various Dog Clubs. (Registration is usually required in advance.) The cost of screening at these clinics is usually significantly reduced. A list of clinics around the country can be found at:
www.vmdb.org/upcomingCERFclinics.html
www.cavalierhealth.org/health_clinics.htm
http://www.offa.org/clinics.html
Some of these clinics also offer BAER testing at significantly reduced rates also.

Color Genetics Information

A lot of the "color genetics" websites on the internet are woefully out of date, or just plain inaccurate. Those interested in learning more about the subject will find the most accurate and up-to-date information on the following websites:

This one, which is the work of Dr. Sheila Schmutz at the University of Saskatchewan, is pretty all-inclusive and covers all known colors and patterns to date:
http://homepage.usask.ca/~schmutz/dogcolors.html

This one, which is maintained by Dr. Leigh Ann Clark, head of the Clark Lab at Clemson University, deals primarily with the merle and harlequin genes, both of which were identified by Dr Clark.
www.clemsoncaninegenetics.com/genetictesting.htm

Updates

The world of dogs is a constantly changing one, especially in the areas of canine genetics and cool stuff dog owners may need but haven't heard about yet. When I find something interesting or useful, I try to post in on my website, so it's worth checking in there occasionally:
www.dianeklumb.com

Made in the USA
San Bernardino, CA
22 December 2013